Holt, Rinehart and Winston
Advance Review and Examination Copy

This advance copy is solely for review purposes, and
not for sale. Orders cannot be delivered before
January 1, 1989, when this publication is offered for
general sale.

EDUCATIONAL CURRICULUM
LABORATORY

SUNDROPS

BOOK OVERVIEW

TITLE	DECODING/VOCABULARY		COMPREHENSION/THINKING	
Review Unit pages 1–10 (T10–T41)	M	**Concept vocabulary:** direction words		
	M	**Concept vocabulary:** position words		
	M	**Concept vocabulary:** left-to-right progression		
	M	**Visual discrimination:** letters		
	M	**Visual discrimination:** capital and small letters		
	M	**Auditory discrimination:** beginning sounds		
Mice pages 11–18 (T42–T71)	I, T	**Sound/symbol correspondence:** consonant /m/*m* (initial, final)	I	**Critical thinking:** prior knowledge
			I, T	**Literal:** sequence
Ants pages 19–26 (T72–T101)	I, T	**Sound/symbol correspondence:** vowel /a/*a* (initial, medial)	I	**Critical thinking:** prior knowledge
	R, T	**Sound/symbol correspondence:** consonant /m/*m*, vowel /a/*a* (initial)	I, T	**Literal:** cause and effect
The Sun pages 27–36 (T102–T136)	I, T	**Sound/symbol correspondence:** consonant /s/*s* (initial, final)	I	**Critical thinking:** prior knowledge
	R, T	**Sound/symbol correspondence:** consonants /s/*s*, /m/*m*; vowel /a/*a* (initial)	I, T	**Inferential:** main idea
	I	**Vocabulary:** word building		
	I, T	**Vocabulary:** word meaning		
	I	**Vocabulary:** words in context		
Mid-Book Review pages 37–40 (T137–T141)	R, T	**Sound/symbol correspondence:** consonants /m/*m*, /s/*s*; vowel /a/*a* (initial)	R, T	**Literal:** sequence
	R, T	**Sound/symbol correspondence:** consonants /m/*m*, /s/*s* (final)		
	R, T	**Sound/symbol correspondence:** vowel /a/*a* (medial)		
	R, T	**Vocabulary:** word meaning		

Key: **I** Introduced in this lesson
R Reinforced from an earlier lesson in this level
M Maintained from previous levels
T Tested in this level

STUDY SKILLS	LANGUAGE	LANGUAGE APPLICATIONS
	I **Listening:** poetry **I** **Speaking:** telling stories from pictures	**Listening:** poetry; fiction
I **Organizing information:** classification	**I** **Listening:** story comprehension **I** **Listening:** rhyming words **R** **Listening:** poetry **I** **Speaking:** retelling stories **I** **Writing:** language-experience stories	**Listening:** fiction; poetry; rhymes; information
	R **Listening:** story comprehension **R** **Speaking:** retelling stories **R** **Speaking:** telling stories from pictures	**Listening:** fiction; poetry; information **Writing:** poetry
I **Graphic aids:** illustrations	**I** **Listening:** specific information **R** **Speaking:** telling stories from pictures **I** **Conventions of language:** end punctuation (period) **R** **Writing:** language-experience stories	**Listening:** poetry; fiction; tongue twisters; information **Speaking:** telling about observations **Singing:** songs

TITLE	DECODING/VOCABULARY		COMPREHENSION/THINKING	
Dogs pages 41–50 (T142–T177)	I, T	**Sound/symbol correspondence:** consonant /d/d (initial, final)	I	**Critical thinking:** prior knowledge
	R, T	**Sound/symbol correspondence:** consonants /d/d, /s/s; vowel /a/a (initial)	R, T	**Literal:** sequence
	I	**Vocabulary:** word building	R, T	**Literal:** cause and effect
	I, T	**Vocabulary:** word meaning		
	I	**Vocabulary:** words in context		
Turtles pages 51–60 (T178–T213)	I, T	**Sound/symbol correspondence:** consonant /t/t (initial, final)	I	**Critical thinking:** prior knowledge
	R, T	**Sound/symbol correspondence:** consonants /m/m, /s/s, /d/d (initial)	R, T	**Inferential:** main idea
	I	**Vocabulary:** word building	R, T	**Literal:** sequence
	I, T	**Vocabulary:** word meaning		
	I	**Vocabulary:** words in context		
Seeds pages 61–70 (T214–T248)	I, T	**Sound/symbol correspondence:** vowel /ē/ea, ee	R	**Critical thinking:** prior knowledge
	R, T	**Sound/symbol correspondence:** vowel /a/a (initial, medial)	R, T	**Literal:** sequence
	I	**Vocabulary:** word building	R, T	**Literal:** cause and effect
	I, T	**Vocabulary:** word meaning		
	I	**Vocabulary:** words in context		
	I	**Word structure:** inflectional ending -s		
End-of-Book Review pages 71–74 (T249–T253)	R, T	**Sound/symbol correspondence:** consonants /d/d, /t/t (initial)	R, T	**Inferential:** main idea
	R, T	**Sound/symbol correspondence:** consonants /d/d, /t/t (final)		
	R, T	**Sound/symbol correspondence:** vowel /ē/ee, ea		
	R, T	**Vocabulary:** word meaning		

STUDY SKILLS	LANGUAGE	LANGUAGE APPLICATIONS
R **Organizing information:** classification	R **Listening:** story comprehension R **Speaking:** retelling stories I **Conventions of language:** end punctuation (question mark)	**Speaking:** telling about a picture **Listening:** fiction; poetry; information
R **Graphic aids:** illustrations	R **Listening:** specific information R **Writing:** language-experience stories	**Listening:** fiction; tongue twisters; poetry; information **Speaking:** retelling stories
	R **Listening:** story comprehension R **Speaking:** retelling stories R **Conventions of language:** end punctuation (period, question mark) R **Conventions of language:** end punctuation (quotation mark)	**Speaking:** role playing; telling about a picture; using complete sentences; telling about observations **Listening:** fiction; poetry; information

BOOK INTRODUCTION

Introducing *Sundrops*
(T6–T9)

Materials

Sundrops, Level 1
Big Book
Teacher's Idea Book

Special Populations

See the *Teacher's Idea Book* for additional suggestions to help pupils with limited English proficiency.

Using the Title Page

Display the *Big Book* for *Sundrops.* Explain that this book is just like the book that pupils will have. Since this book is so large, it is called the *Big Book.* Point to the title of the book.

SAY **This word is the name, or the title, of the book. The title of this book is *Sundrops.* Say the title with me: *Sundrops.* We can see raindrops when the weather is rainy. Can we see sundrops when the weather is sunny?** (no) **What do you think you might do if you could see and catch some sundrops?** (Possible answers include: put them in a jar; save them until dark.)

Distribute individual copies of *Sundrops* and allow pupils to look through the books. Then ask them to point to the title on the front of the book and to say the name of the book. (*Sundrops*)

Explain that it is sometimes fun to make-believe and that you hope pupils will have fun using their new books to help them learn to read.

READING TODAY AND TOMORROW
SUNDROPS
LEVEL I

READING TODAY AND TOMORROW
SUNDROPS
LEVEL I

Isabel Beck, Senior Author

Bonnie Armbruster   Taffy Raphael

Margaret McKeown   Lenore Ringler

Donna Ogle

HOLT, RINEHART AND WINSTON, INC.
Austin   New York   Chicago   San Diego   Toronto   Montreal

Printed in the United States of America
ISBN 0-15-718000-X
78901 000 7654321

Acknowledgments

For permission to reprint copyrighted material, grateful acknowledgment is made to the following sources:

Doubleday & Company, Inc.: Illustrations from *Angus and the Ducks* by Marjorie Flack. Copyright © 1930 by Doubleday & Company, Inc.

E.P. Dutton, a division of New American Library: Illustrations from pp. 17 and 19 in *Henry's Awful Mistake* by Robert Quackenbush. Copyright © 1980 by Robert Quackenbush.

Greenwillow Books, a division of William Morrow & Company, Inc.: "Play" and accompanying illustration from *Country Pie* by Frank Asch. Copyright © 1979 by Frank Asch.

Harcourt Brace Jovanovich, Inc.: Illustrations from pp. 7, 10, 13, 15, 21, and 26 in *Sun Up, Sun Down* by Gail Gibbons. Copyright © 1983 by Gail Gibbons.

Macmillan Publishing Company: Untitled poem (Titled: "Ant") from *Inside Turtle's Shell and Other Poems of the Field* by Joanne Ryder. Text copyright © 1985 by Joanne Ryder.

Random House, Inc.: Illustrations from *Moon Mouse* by Adelaide Holl, illustrated by Cyndy Szekeres Prozzo. Illustrations copyright © 1969 by Cyndy Szekeres Prozzo.

Charles Scribner's Sons: Illustrations from *Turtle Pond* by Berniece Freschet, illustrated by Donald Carrick. Illustrations copyright © 1971 by Donald Carrick.

Mabel Watts: "Maytime Magic" by Mabel Watts from *Humpty Dumpty* Magazine, 1954.

Design: Kirchoff/Wohlberg, Inc.

Illustrators

Liz Callen (3, 4-8, 13-14, 16, 21, 23-24, 29, 31, 39, 43-46, 53, 55-56, 63-64, 67, 72-73); Tom O'Sullivan (3 top left, 20, 33-35, 40, 47-49, 57-59, 65-66, 68-69, 74); Dorothy Stott (2, 9-10, 28, 42, 52, 61-62); Jane Yamada (12, 15, 17-18, 22, 25-26, 30, 32, 36-38, 50, 54, 60, 70-71).

Cover Art: Lois Ehlert

Using the Table of Contents

Open the *Big Book* to the Table of Contents. Explain that this page tells the page number of each activity that the pupils will do. Ask pupils to open their books to the Table of Contents at the front of the book. Have them put their fingers on the page number of the first activity in the book. (*1*) Then ask them to find the last page number in the book. (*76*) If necessary, identify the number 76 for them.

As you page through the *Big Book,* explain to pupils that some pages in *Sundrops* have pictures that tell stories while other pages have activities that will involve printing and drawing. Call attention to the alphabet on the last two pages of the book and explain that letters are joined to form words. Tell pupils that they will learn to print letters and read many words as they use *Sundrops.*

LEVEL 1

Contents

REVIEW UNIT

pages 1–10
(T10–T41)

Note: The activities in this unit are designed to review some of the basic reading readiness skills taught in Level K, including alphabet recognition. Although mastery of the alphabet is not necessary for success with the lessons in this level, a quick review will help you identify individual needs.

Skill Strands

READINESS CONCEPTS

M   **Concept vocabulary:** direction words
M   **Concept vocabulary:** position words
M   **Concept vocabulary:** left-to-right progression
M   **Visual discrimination:** letters
M   **Visual discrimination:** capital and small letters
M   **Auditory discrimination:** beginning sounds

LANGUAGE

I   **Listening:** poetry
I   **Speaking:** telling stories from pictures

Materials

Sundrops, Level 1: pages 1–10
Big Book: pages 1, 2, 9
Practice Masters: pages 1–9
Resource Box: Letter Cards b, f, g, n
Pocket Chart
Teacher's Idea Book

Language Applications

EXTENDING SELECTION CONCEPTS
Listening: poetry
Listening: fiction

Special Populations

See *Teacher's Idea Book* for additional suggestions to help pupils with limited English proficiency.

Key to Symbols
I   Introduced in this lesson
R   Reinforced from an earlier lesson in this level
M   Maintained from previous levels
T   Tested in this level

T10   *Sundrops,* Level 1

Idea Center

BIG BOOK

If you do not have a *Big Book,* display a Level 1 pupil's book. A *Big Book* is suggested in the lesson plans for this level to allow for shared reading experiences. The teacher also uses the *Big Book* to model what pupils will be expected to do.

LETTER CARDS

If you do not have the *Resource Box,* you can make your own *Letter Cards* by printing each letter on an index card.

POCKET CHART

If you do not have a *Pocket Chart,* you can make your own. Use a sheet of tagboard that is approximately 24 by 18 inches. Mark and score a line 4 inches from the top of the tagboard and another line 5 inches from the top. Accordion-fold along the lines to make a pocket. Staple the ends. Follow a similar procedure for other pockets. Then attach the Pocket Chart to a piece of corrugated cardboard cut to fit, approximately 18 by 18 inches, and tape the edges.

LETTER GAME

For Activity 10, use index cards to prepare two sets of alphabet cards. Print a small letter on each card of one set and print a capital letter on each card of the other set. Place the set of small letter cards in a container.

BIBLIOGRAPHY

Prepare a reading corner or reading table. It is important that this area be a comfortable, pleasant place where pupils will be encouraged to spend time enjoying books. You may want to provide pillows, carpet squares, or an area rug for pupils to sit on. A display of posters or colorful book covers can make the area bright and attractive. A suggested bibliography for this lesson follows. Suggestions for reading books aloud appear throughout the lesson. Annotations for the books appear in the activities.

Alda, Arlene. *Arlene Alda's ABC.* Celestial Arts, 1981.

Anno, Mitsumasa. *Anno's Mysterious Multiplying Jar.* Philomel Books, 1983.

Asch, Frank. *Country Pie.* Greenwillow Books, 1979.

Berenstain, Stanley, and Janice Berenstain. *Inside, Outside, Upside Down.* Random House, 1968.

Cohen, Miriam. *Bee My Valentine.* Greenwillow, 1978.

DeBrunhoff, Jean. *The Story of Babar.* Random House, 1961.

Fatio, Louise. *The Happy Lion.* McGraw Hill, 1954.

Hall, Derek. *Otter Swims.* Sierra Club/Knopf, 1986.

Hoban, Tana. *Over, Under & Through and Other Spacial Concepts.* Macmillan, 1973.

Kessler, Leonard. *The Worst Team Ever.* Greenwillow, 1985.

Kitchen, Bert. *Animal Alphabet.* Dial Books, 1984.

Kraus, Robert. *Where Are You Going, Little Mouse?* Greenwillow, 1986.

Lewellen, J. *Moon, Sun, and Stars.* Childrens Press, 1981.

Lionni, Leo. *Fish Is Fish.* Pantheon, 1970.

Mayer, Mercer. *A Boy, a Dog, and a Frog.* Dial Books, 1967.

Myrick, Mildred. *Ants Are Fun.* Harper & Row, 1968.

Pinkwater, Honest Dan'l. *Roger's Umbrella.* Dutton, 1985.

Potter, Beatrix. *The Tale of Peter Rabbit.* Frederick Warne, 1902.

Prelutsky, Jack. *The Random House Book of Poetry for Children.* Random House, 1983.

Seuss, Dr. *The Cat in the Hat.* Random House, 1957.

——— *The 500 Hats of Bartholomew Cubbins.* Vanguard, 1933.

Sharmat, Mitchell. *Gregory, the Terrible Eater.* Four Winds Press, 1980.

Steig, William. *Farmer Palmer's Wagon Ride.* Farrar, Strauss and Giroux, 1974.

Van Leeuwen, Jean. *Tales of Amanda Pig.* Dial Books, 1983.

Van Woerkom, Dorothy. *Harry and Shellburt.* Macmillan, 1977.

Wood, Audrey, *King Bidgood's in the Bathtub.* Harcourt Brace Jovanovich, 1985.

Young, Ed. *The Other Bone.* Harper & Row, 1984.

Zion, Gene. *Harry the Dirty Dog.* Harper & Row, 1956.

ACTIVITY 1 Listening to the Poem "Play"
page 1 (T12–T14)

Skill Strands

LANGUAGE

I Listening: poetry

READINESS CONCEPTS

M Concept vocabulary: direction words

Materials

Sundrops, Level 1: page 1
Big Book: page 1
Practice Masters: page 1
Teacher's Idea Book

Special Populations

See *Teacher's Idea Book* for additional suggestions to help pupils with limited English proficiency.

Key to Symbols
I Introduced in this lesson
R Reinforced from an earlier lesson in this level
M Maintained from previous levels
T Tested in this level

1 Preparing for the page

I Listening: poetry

Display page 1 of the *Big Book* and ask what is happening in the picture. (A child is flying a kite.) Explain that an artist drew this picture to go with the words on the page. Point to the printed words.

SAY **These words are a poem for us to read. It is fun to look at pictures, but when I want to know what a story or a poem says, I have to read the words.**

Play (To be read by the teacher)

Come play with me said the sun,
come play with me said the earth,
come play with me said the sky.
What shall we play said I?

Let's fly a kite said the sun,
stand on me said the earth,
I'll bring the wind said the sky,
I'll hold the string said I.

Frank Asch

● **Listening:** poetry
● **Directions:** Listen as the teacher reads the poem.
● **To the Parent:** Read and discuss the poem with your child.

2 Using the page

I Listening: poetry

Help pupils find page 1 in their books. Have pupils point first to the picture, then to the words.

SAY **When I look at the picture, I can tell that this tells about happy things because everything in the picture is smiling. Here is the name of the poem.** (Indicate.) **The name of this poem is "Play." Who do you think is playing in this poem?** (the boy) **Listen to the poem to see if anyone is playing with the boy.**

Move your hand under each line of the poem as you read it aloud. Then ask pupils to tell who is playing with the boy. (the sun, the sky, and the earth) Explain that you will read the first part of the poem and that when you point to the pupils, they can say the line "What shall we play said I?" Next, read the second part of the poem and have pupils say the line "I'll hold the string said I."

3 Developing the Skills

M Concept vocabulary: direction words

PM 1 Distribute copies of *Practice Masters* page 1. Ask pupils to look at the picture and to find the child flying a kite.

SAY Here is a child playing the way the child did in our poem. The other characters in this picture are similar to ones we will meet in our book, *Sundrops*. The people or animals in a book are called characters. Who can name some of the characters on this page? (a mouse, an ant, a dog, a turtle, a hen) Sometimes a thing, such as the sun, can be a character, too. We will be reading stories about each of the characters on this page.

I am going to tell you some things to do on this page. Listen carefully and then do as I say. First, circle the ant.

PRACTICE MASTERS

Name

Readiness Concepts
Use with Review Unit

- **Concept vocabulary:** direction words
- **Directions:** Follow the directions the teacher gives to color the page.
- **To the Parent:** Ask your child to tell about the characters in this picture.

Sundrops Level 1

Continue with the directions below.

1. **Trace the happy face on the sun.**
2. **Make a blue dot on the turtle's shell.**
3. **With your yellow crayon, draw a piece of cheese by the mouse.**
4. **The dog's name is Sam. Draw a line under Sam.**
5. **Color the hen red.**

✳ Practicing and Extending

The activities that follow provide practice and extension of skills developed in this lesson. Not every pupil needs to complete these activities. Choose only the activities that are needed to provide for the individual differences in your classroom.

Practicing Skills

M Concept vocabulary: direction words

ADDITIONAL PRACTICE Have volunteers perform each of the following directions:

1. **Make an X on the chalkboard.**
2. **Draw a line under the X.**
3. **Make a circle around the X and the line.**

Extending Selection Concepts

LITERATURE

LISTENING: POETRY Read aloud one or more poems and ask pupils to tell what they might put in a picture to go with each poem.

Asch, Frank. *Country Pie.* Greenwillow Books, 1979. This is a collection of poems inspired by the country, including "Play."

Prelutsky, Jack. *The Random House Book of Poetry for Children.* Random House, 1983. This is a treasury of poems for every occasion.

ACTIVITY 2 Following Directions
page 2 (T15–T17)

Skill Strands

READINESS CONCEPTS

M **Concept vocabulary:** position words
M **Concept vocabulary:** left-to-right
progression

Materials

Sundrops, Level 1: page 2
Big Book: page 2
Practice Masters: page 2
Teacher's Idea Book

Special Populations

See *Teacher's Idea Book* for additional suggestions to help pupils with limited English proficiency.

Key to Symbols
I   Introduced in this lesson
R Reinforced from an earlier lesson in this level
M Maintained from previous levels
T   Tested in this level

1 Preparing for the page

M **Concept vocabulary:** position words

Ask pupils to listen as you read this poem:

READ
I'll be the leader,
And you follow me.
Jump over the puddle
And skip 'round the tree.
Duck under the bushes
And when I am through,
You be the leader,
And I'll follow you!

Reread the poem and ask what the children were going to jump over. (the puddle) Ask what the children were going to skip around. (the tree) Then ask what the children were going to duck under. (the bushes)

SAY The children were playing a game called "Follow the Leader." Why is "Follow the Leader" a good name for this game? (One person is the leader, and another person follows what the leader does.)

Have pupils find page 2 in their books.

SAY The children in these pictures are playing different games. Which children might be playing "Follow the Leader" as in the poem? (the children crawling through the tunnel) Think about the poem "Play" on the first page of your books. What did the boy do in that poem? (He flew a kite.) Which picture goes with that poem? (the first picture)

Discuss each of the other pictures and have pupils suggest what games the children might be playing. (Possible answers are: "Hide-and-seek," "The Farmer in the Dell," "London Bridge.")

On the worksheet image:

Name

- **Concept vocabulary:** position words
- **Directions:** Follow the directions given by the teacher to mark the pictures that show over, through, around, behind, in, and under.
- **To the Parent:** Ask your child to tell about each picture. Encourage your child to use the words *over, under, in, through, behind.*

2

2 Using the page

M **Concept vocabulary:** position words
M **Concept vocabulary:** left-to-right progression

SAY Words such as *under, through, in,* and *behind* tell us where things are. What are children going through in this picture? (a tunnel) What is one child in? (a box) What is one child under? (other children's arms) What is flying over the children? (the kite) What are children going around? (a child in the middle)

I am going to ask you to use a crayon to mark these pictures. You will have to listen carefully to know where to make your marks.

Read aloud each of these sentences and allow time for pupils to complete the directions.

1. Make a blue circle around the child who is behind something.
2. Make a red circle around something children can go through.
3. Now make a green line under children who are going around someone.
4. Make a purple circle around someone who is under.
5. Color a big, red dot on something that a child is in.
6. Circle something that is over the children's heads.

Display *Big Book* page 2. Tell pupils that you will tell them how to make two paths on the page. Have them use a crayon to draw each path as you describe it. Demonstrate with your finger on the *Big Book.*

SAY The first path or line will start at the left at the boy with a kite. Then it will go over the tunnel to the circle of children on the right.

The second path will start at the tree on the left and will go under the box to the children playing on the right.

3 Developing the Skills

M   Concept vocabulary: position words

Tell pupils that you will pretend to be one of the children in the picture and that you will say a sentence that tells where you are. Then ask which child you are pretending to be.

SAY   **My friend Jerry will never find me. I'm glad I found something to hide in.**

Call on pupils to guess which child you are pretending to be. (the child in the box) Then ask volunteers to pretend to be other children in the picture and to say a sentence that gives a hint about where they are. Invite classmates to guess which child each pupil is pretending to be. Encourage pupils to use the position words *through, over, behind, under, around,* and *in.*

✳ Practicing and Extending

The activities that follow provide practice and extension of skills developed in this lesson. Not every pupil needs to complete these activities. Choose only the activities that are needed to provide for the individual differences in your classroom.

Practicing Skills

M   Concept vocabulary: position words

PM 2   **ADDITIONAL PRACTICE**   *Practice Masters* page 2 may be used as optional practice for reviewing position words. Make sure pupils understand the directions on the page.

CHALLENGE ACTIVITY   Ask questions using position words and have pupils answer in complete sentences, using the position word and an object in the classroom. For example, ask "What could you climb over?" A pupil might answer "I can climb over my desk." Remind pupils that these are imaginary sentences.

Extending Selection Concepts

LITERATURE

LISTENING: FICTION   Read a book in which position words are used. Discuss with pupils the many words that tell where.

Berenstain, Stanley, and Janice Berenstain. *Inside, Outside, Upside Down.* Random House, 1968. The well-known bears demonstrate words that tell where.

Hoban, Tana. *Over, Under & Through and Other Spacial Concepts.* Macmillan, 1973. Spatial concepts are illustrated with Hoban's excellent photographs.

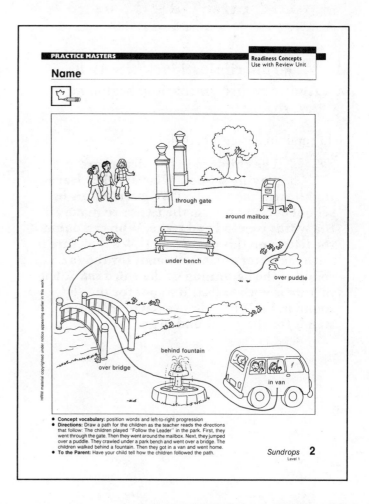

ACTIVITY 3 Reviewing the Alphabet
page 3 (T18–T20)

Skill Strands

READINESS CONCEPTS

M **Visual discrimination:** Letters *Aa, Bb, Cc*
M **Auditory discrimination:** beginning sounds /a/, /b/, /k/

Materials

Sundrops, Level 1: page 3
Practice Masters: page 3
Teacher's Idea Book

Special Populations

See *Teacher's Idea Book* for additional suggestions to help pupils with limited English proficiency.

Key to Symbols
I Introduced in this lesson
R Reinforced from an earlier lesson in this level
M Maintained from previous levels
T Tested in this level

1 Preparing for the page

M **Visual discrimination:** letters *Aa, Bb, Cc*
M **Auditory discrimination:** beginning sounds /a/, /b/, /k/

Help pupils find page 3 in their books.

SAY **The children in the picture are playing school. What are they learning?** (letters, the alphabet) **We learn letters in school because we use the letters to make all the words we read and write. Who can name the letters on this page?** (*a, b, c*) **What picture is with the letter *a*?** (ant) ***A* stands for the /a/ sound at the beginning of the word *ant*. What picture is with *b*?** (bat) ***B* stands for the /b/ sound in *bat*. What picture is with *c*?** (cat) ***C* stands for the /k/ sound in *cat*.**

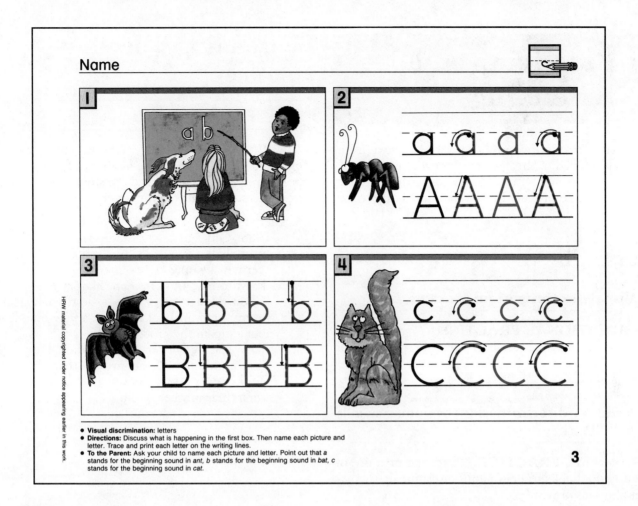

Name

- **Visual discrimination:** letters
- **Directions:** Discuss what is happening in the first box. Then name each picture and letter. Trace and print each letter on the writing lines.
- **To the Parent:** Ask your child to name each picture and letter. Point out that *a* stands for the beginning sound in *ant*, *b* stands for the beginning sound in *bat*, *c* stands for the beginning sound in *cat*.

HRW material copyrighted under notice appearing earlier in this work.

3

2 Using the page

M Visual discrimination: letters *Aa, Bb, Cc*

Demonstrate on the chalkboard the formation of the small *a* and the capital *A*. Have pupils trace and print the letter *a* on the writing line. Continue in the same manner with letters *b* and *c*.

3 Developing the Skills

M Auditory discrimination: beginning sounds /a/, /b/, /k/

Ask pupils to listen as you say this sentence:

Barney Bear ate a bunch of bananas.

Then ask pupils to repeat the sentence.

| SAY | The word *Barney* begins with the letter *b*. Letter *b* stands for the /b/ sound. |

Read the sentence again and ask pupils to name the other words that begin with /b/. (*bear, bunch, bananas*) Continue in the same manner with these sentences:

1. **Andy Alligator saw an ambulance.**
2. **Casey ran after Carla's cat.**

✳ Practicing and Extending

The activities that follow provide practice and extension of skills developed in this lesson. Not every pupil needs to complete these activities. Choose only the activities that are needed to provide for the individual differences in your classroom.

Practicing Skills

M **Visual discrimination:** letters *Aa, Bb, Cc*

PM 3 **ADDITIONAL PRACTICE** *Practice Masters* page 3 may be used as optional practice for identifying letters.

M **Auditory discrimination:** beginning sounds /a/, /b/, /k/

ADDITIONAL PRACTICE Read one or more of the following books to help pupils discriminate the beginning sounds of words:

Moncure, Jane Belk. *My "a" Sound Box.* Childrens Press, 1984.
———— *My "b" Sound Box.* Childrens Press, 1977.
———— *My "c" Sound Box.* Childrens Press, 1979.

Extending Selection Concepts

LISTENING: FICTION Choose a book with major characters that relate to the key word for a sound/symbol correspondence and read the story aloud. Ask pupils how this story relates to the letter.

Kessler, Leonard. *The Worst Team Ever.* Greenwillow, 1985. Old Turtle is called on to coach the worst swampball team ever. Will the Green Hoppers ever win a game?
Myrick, Mildred. *Ants Are Fun.* Harper & Row, 1968. When Don's ant farm is destroyed, Jack and Jimmy help him put together a new one, learning about ants in the process.
Seuss, Dr. *The Cat in the Hat.* Random House, 1957. This children's classic proves that the children should never allow the Cat in the Hat to come in when their mother is out.

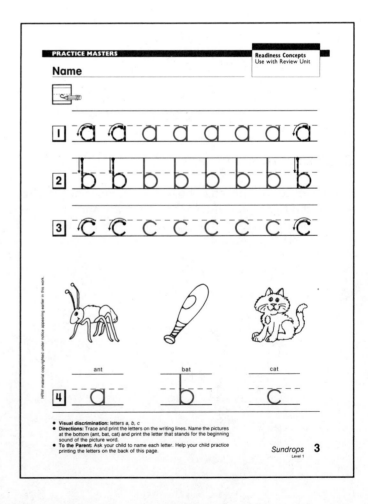

ACTIVITY 4 Reviewing the Alphabet
page 4 (T21–T23)

Skill Strands

READINESS CONCEPTS

M   **Visual discrimination:** letters *Dd, Ee, Ff, Gg*

M   **Auditory discrimination:** beginning sounds /d/, /e/, /f/, /g/

Materials

Sundrops, Level 1: page 4

Practice Masters: page 4
Teacher's Idea Book

Special Populations

See *Teacher's Idea Book* for additional suggestions to help pupils with limited English proficiency.

Key to Symbols
I   Introduced in this lesson
R   Reinforced from an earlier lesson in this level
M   Maintained from previous levels
T   Tested in this level

1 Preparing for the page

M   **Visual discrimination:** letters *Dd, Ed, Ff, Gg*

M   **Auditory discrimination:** beginning sounds /d/, /e/, /f/, /g/

Help pupils find page 4 in their books.

SAY **Here are some more letters for us to practice. Who can name the letters on this page?** (*d, e, f, g*) **What picture is with the letter *d*?** (dog) ***D* stands for the /d/ sound at the beginning of the word *dog*. What picture is with *e*?** (elephant) ***E* stands for the /e/ sound in *elephant*. What picture is with *f*?** (fish) ***F* stands for the /f/ sound in *fish*. What picture is with *g*?** (goat) ***G* stands for the /g/ sound in *goat*.**

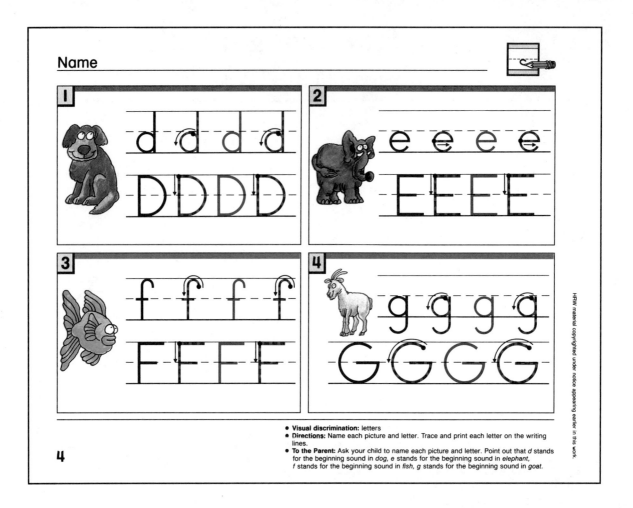

Name

1
2
3
4

- **Visual discrimination:** letters
- **Directions:** Name each picture and letter. Trace and print each letter on the writing lines.
- **To the Parent:** Ask your child to name each picture and letter. Point out that *d* stands for the beginning sound in *dog*, *e* stands for the beginning sound in *elephant*, *f* stands for the beginning sound in *fish*, *g* stands for the beginning sound in *goat*.

4

2 Using the page

M   Visual discrimination: letters *Dd, Ee, Ff, Gg*

Demonstrate on the chalkboard the formation of each letter on the page. Have pupils trace and print the letters on each writing line.

3 Developing the Skills

M   Auditory discrimination: beginning sounds /d/, /e/, /f/, /g/

Ask pupils to listen as you say this sentence:

Don dug for dinosaur bones.

Ask pupils to repeat the sentence.

SAY The word *Don* begins with the letter *d*. The letter *d* stands for the /d/ sound.

Read the sentence again and ask pupils to name the other words that begin with /d/. (*dug, dinosaur*) Continue in the same manner with these sentences:

1. **Ed the engineer rode the engine.**
2. **Fred caught five fish.**
3. **Gail gave me a goat.**

✳ Practicing and Extending

The activities that follow provide practice and extension of skills developed in this lesson. Not every pupil needs to complete these activities. Choose only the activities that are needed to provide for the individual differences in your classroom.

Practicing Skills

M Visual discrimination: letters *Dd, Ed, Ff, Gg*

PM 4 ADDITIONAL PRACTICE *Practice Masters* page 4 may be used as an optional practice for identifying letters.

M Auditory discrimination: beginning sounds /d/, /e/, /f/, /g/

ADDITIONAL PRACTICE Read one or more of the following books and ask pupils to listen for words that begin with the sound of letter *d, e, f,* or *g.*

Moncure, Jane Belk. *My "d" Sound Box.* Childrens Press, 1978.
———. *My "e" Sound Box.* Childrens Press, 1984.
———. *My "f" Sound Box.* Childrens Press, 1977.
———. *My "g" Sound Box.* Childrens Press, 1979.

Extending Selection Concepts

LITERATURE

LISTENING: FICTION Choose a book with major characters that relate to the key word for a sound/symbol correspondence and read the story aloud. Ask pupils how this story relates to the letter.

DeBrunhoff, Jean. *The Story of Babar.* Random House, 1961. This is the classic story of the elephant king and his lovely wife, Celeste.
Zion, Gene. *Harry the Dirty Dog.* Harper & Row, 1956. Harry becomes so dirty that even his family doesn't recognize him.

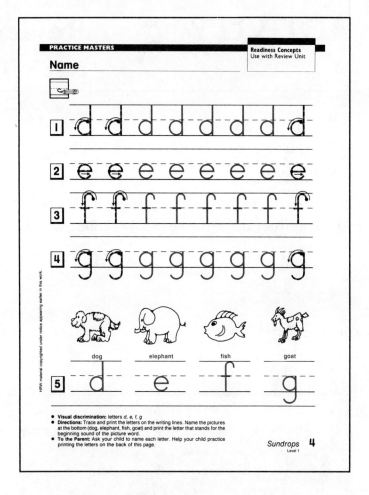

Lionni, Leo. *Fish Is Fish.* Pantheon, 1970. A little fish discovers that life on land is not what he thinks it will be.
Sharmat, Mitchell. *Gregory, the Terrible Eater.* Four Winds Press, 1980. Poor Gregory likes vegetables. Why won't he eat the things the other goats eat?

ACTIVITY 5 Reviewing the Alphabet
page 5 (T24–T26)

Skill Strands

M **Visual discrimination:** letters *Hh, Ii, Jj, Kk*
M **Auditory discrimination:** beginning sounds /h/, /i/, /j/, /k/

Special Populations

See *Teacher's Idea Book* for additional suggestions to help pupils with limited English proficiency.

Materials

Sundrops Level 1: page 5
Practice Masters: page 5
Teacher's Idea Book

Key to Symbols
I Introduced in this lesson
R Reinforced from an earlier lesson in this level
M Maintained from previous levels
T Tested in this level

1 Preparing for the page

M **Visual discrimination:** letters *Hh, Ii, Jj, Kk*
M **Auditory discrimination:** beginning sounds /h/, /i/, /j/, /k/

Help pupils find page 5 in their books.

SAY **Here are some more letters for us to practice. Who can name the letters on this page?** (*h, i, j, k*) **What picture is with the letter h?** (hat) *H* **stands for the /h/ sound at the beginning of the word** *hat.* **What picture is with i?** (igloo) *I* **stands for the /i/ sound in** *igloo.* **What picture is with j?** *(jar) J* **stands for the /j/ sound in** *jar.* **What picture is with k?** (king) *K* **stands for the /k/ sound in** *king.*

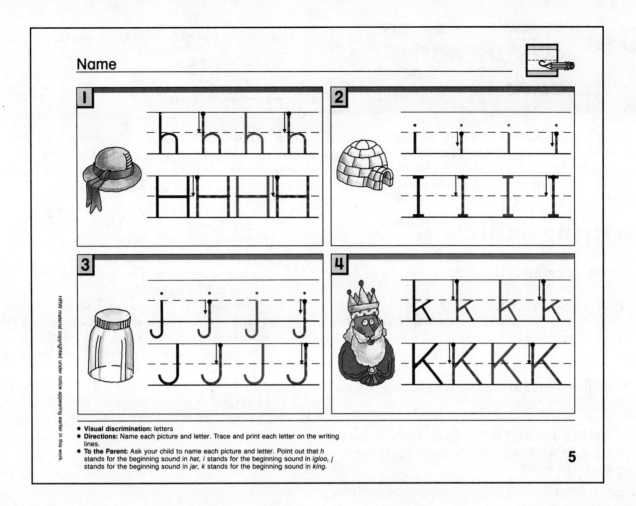

- **Visual discrimination:** letters
- **Directions:** Name each picture and letter. Trace and print each letter on the writing lines.
- **To the Parent:** Ask your child to name each picture and letter. Point out that *h* stands for the beginning sound in *hat*, *i* stands for the beginning sound in *igloo*, *j* stands for the beginning sound in *jar*, *k* stands for the beginning sound in *king*.

5

2 Using the page

M Visual discrimination: letters *Hh, Ii, Jj, Kk*

Demonstrate on the chalkboard the formation of each of the letters on the page. Then have pupils trace and print letters on each writing line.

3 Developing the Skills

M Auditory discrimination: beginning sounds /h/, /i/, /j/, /k/

Ask pupils to listen as you say this sentence: *Harry bumped his head.* Then ask pupils to repeat the sentence.

> **SAY** The word *Harry* begins with the letter *h*. The letter *h* stands for the /h/ sound.

Read the sentence again and ask pupils to name the other words that begin with /h/. (*his, head*) Continue in the same manner with these sentences:

1. **Isabel is never ill.**
2. **Jan jumped over the Jack-o'-lantern.**
3. **Kevin let the kitten kiss him.**

The activities that follow provide practice and extension of skills developed in this lesson. Not every pupil needs to complete these activities. Choose only the activities that are needed to provide for the individual differences in your classroom.

Practicing Skills

M Visual discrimination: letters *Hh, Ii, Jj, Kk*

PM 5 ADDITIONAL PRACTICE *Practice Masters* page 5 may be used as optional practice for identifying letters.

M Auditory discrimination: beginning sounds /h/, /i/, /j/, /k/

ADDITIONAL PRACTICE Read one or more of the following books to help pupils discriminate the beginning sounds of words:

Moncure, Jane Belk. *My "h" Sound Box.* Childrens Press, 1977.
————. *My "i" Sound Box.* Childrens Press, 1984.
————. *My "j" Sound Box.* Childrens Press, 1979.
————. *My "k" Sound Box.* Childrens Press, 1979.

Extending Selection Concepts

> **LITERATURE**

LISTENING: FICTION Choose a book with major characters that relate to the key word for a sound/symbol correspondence and read the story aloud. Ask pupils how this story relates to the letter.

Anno, Mitsumasa. *Anno's Mysterious Multiplying Jar.* Philomel Books, 1983. This beautifully illustrated book begins with one jar. The water in the jar becomes a sea with an island that has kingdoms, houses, and rooms. The book ends with an explanation of "10 factorial."

Seuss, Dr. *The 500 Hats of Bartholomew Cubbins.* Vanguard, 1933. When a peasant boy tries to remove his hat for the king, a new hat appears in its place. The only solution is to cut off the boy's head, or is it?

Wood, Audrey. *King Bidgood's in the Bathtub.* Harcourt Brace Jovanovich, 1985. The king is in the bathtub and won't come out. Only the court page has the solution.

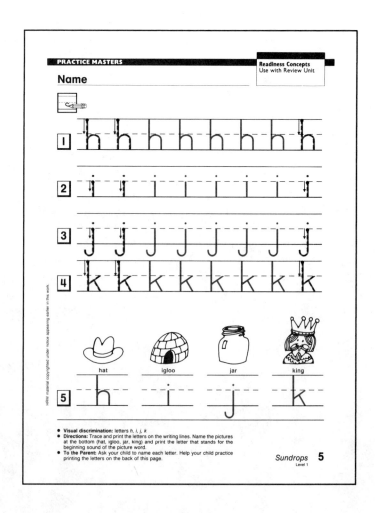

ACTIVITY 6 Reviewing the Alphabet
page 6 (T27–T29)

Skill Strands

READINESS CONCEPTS

M **Visual discrimination:** letters *Ll, Mm, Nn, Oo*

M **Auditory discrimination:** beginning sounds /l/, /m/, /n/, /o/

Materials

Sundrops, Level 1: page 6

Practice Masters: page 6
Teacher's Idea Book

Special Populations

See *Teacher's Idea Book* for additional suggestions to help pupils with limited English proficiency.

Key to Symbols
I Introduced in this lesson
R Reinforced from an earlier lesson in this level
M Maintained from previous levels
T Tested in this level

1 Preparing for the page

M **Visual discrimination:** letters *Ll, Mm, Nn, Oo*

M **Auditory discrimination:** beginning sounds /l/, /m/, /n/, /o/

Help pupils find page 6 in their books.

SAY **Here are some more letters for us to practice. Who can name the letters on this page?** (*l, m, n, o*) **What picture is with the letter l?** (lion) **L stands for the /l/ sound at the beginning of the word** *lion.* **What picture is with m?** (mouse) **M stands for the /m/ sound in** *mouse.* **What picture is with n?** (nut) **N stands for the /n/ sound in** *nut.* **What picture is with o?** (otter) **O stands for the /o/ sound in** *otter.*

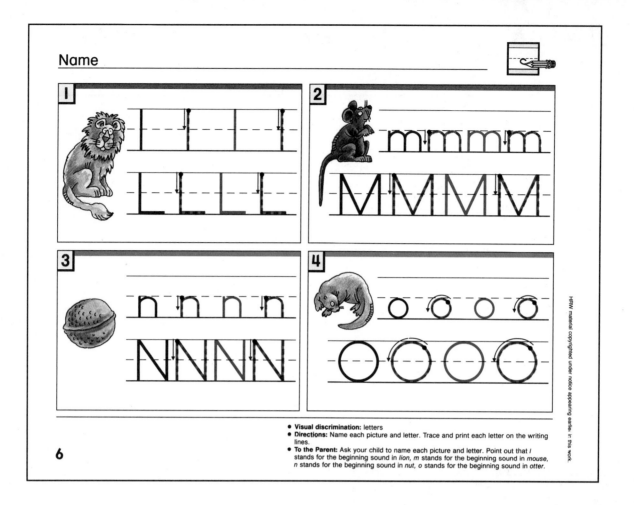

- **Visual discrimination:** letters
- **Directions:** Name each picture and letter. Trace and print each letter on the writing lines.
- **To the Parent:** Ask your child to name each picture and letter. Point out that *l* stands for the beginning sound in *lion*, *m* stands for the beginning sound in *mouse*, *n* stands for the beginning sound in *nut*, *o* stands for the beginning sound in *otter*.

6

2 Using the page

M Visual discrimination: letters *Ll, Mm, Nn, Oo*

Demonstrate on the chalkboard the formation of each letter on the page. Then have pupils trace and print the letters on each writing line.

3 Developing the Skills

M Auditory discrimination: beginning sounds /l/, /m/, /n/, /o/

Ask pupils to listen as you say this sentence: *The lazy lambs sniffed lemons.* Ask pupils to repeat the sentence.

> **SAY** **The word *lazy* begins with the letter *l*. The letter *l* stands for the /l/ sound.**

Read the sentence again and ask pupils to name the other words that begin with /l/. (*lambs, lemons*) Continue in the same manner with these sentences:

1. **My mom baked muffins.**
2. **Nancy never eats noodles.**
3. **Oscar caught an octopus in October.**

✳ Practicing and Extending

The activities that follow provide practice and extension of skills developed in this lesson. Not every pupil needs to complete these activities. Choose only the activities that are needed to provide for the individual differences in your classroom.

Practicing Skills

M   Visual discrimination: letters *Ll, Mm, Nn, Oo*

PM 6   **ADDITIONAL PRACTICE**   *Practice Masters* page 6 may be used as an optional practice for identifying letters.

M   Auditory discrimination: beginning sounds /l/, /m/, /n/, /o/

ADDITIONAL PRACTICE   Read one or more of the following books to help pupils discriminate the beginning sounds of words:

Moncure, Jane Belk. *My "l" Sound Box.* Childrens Press, 1978.
———. *My "m" Sound Box.* Childrens Press, 1979.
———. *My "n" Sound Box.* Childrens Press, l979.
———. *My "o" Sound Box.* Childrens Press, 1984.

Extending Selection Concepts

LISTENING: FICTION   Choose a book with major characters that relate to the key word for a sound/symbol correspondence and read the story aloud. Ask pupils how this story relates to the letter.

Fatio, Louise. *The Happy Lion.* McGraw Hill, 1954. The happy lion decides to see what the world is like outside his cage in the zoo.
Hall, Derek. *Otter Swims.* Sierra Club/Knopf, 1986. A fearful young otter stays away from the river until he accidentally falls in and discovers how much fun it is to swim.
Kraus, Robert. *Are You Going, Little Mouse?* Greenwillow, 1986. The little mouse from *Whose Mouse Are You?* sets out to go as far from home as he can. He wants another family that will give him unlimited attention, but soon realizes that home is best after all.

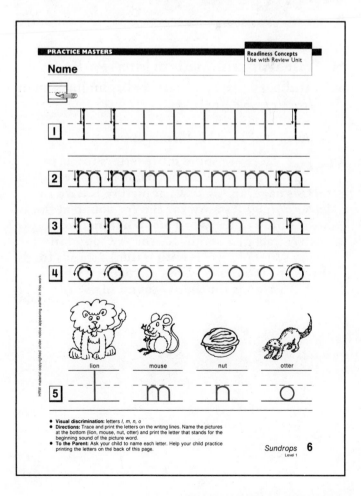

ACTIVITY 7 Reviewing the Alphabet
page 7 (T30–T32)

Skill Strands

READINESS CONCEPTS

M **Visual discrimination:** letters *Pp, Rr, Ss, Tt*
M **Auditory discrimination:** beginning sounds /p/, /r/, /s/, /t/

Materials

Sundrops, Level 1: page 7
Practice Masters: page 7
Teacher's Idea Book

Special Populations

See *Teacher's Idea Book* for additional suggestions to help pupils with limited English proficiency.

1 Preparing for the page

M **Visual discrimination:** letters *Pp, Rr, Ss, Tt*
M **Auditory discrimination:** beginning sounds /p/, /r/, /s/, /t/

Help pupils find page 7 in their books.

SAY Here are some more letters for us to practice. Who can name the letters on this page? (*p, r, s, t*) What picture is with the letter *p*? (pig) *P* stands for the /p/ sound at the beginnning of the word *pig.* What picture is with *r*? (rabbit) *R* stands for the /r/ sound in *rabbit.* What picture is with *s*? (sun) *S* stands for the /s/ sound in *sun.* What picture is with *t*? (turtle) *T* stands for the /t/ sound in *turtle.*

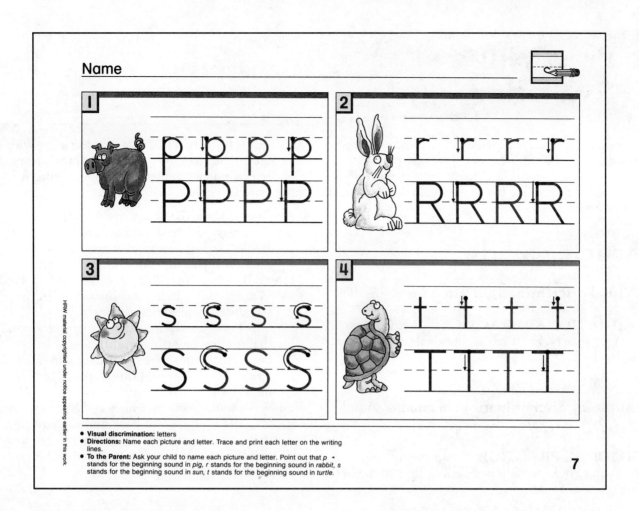

- **Visual discrimination:** letters
- **Directions:** Name each picture and letter. Trace and print each letter on the writing lines.
- **To the Parent:** Ask your child to name each picture and letter. Point out that *p* stands for the beginning sound in *pig, r* stands for the beginning sound in *rabbit, s* stands for the beginning sound in *sun, t* stands for the beginning sound in *turtle.*

7

2 Using the page

M Visual discrimination: letters *Pp, Rr, Ss, Tt*

Demonstrate on the chalkboard the formation of each letter on the page. Then have pupils trace and print the letters on each writing line.

3 Developing the Skills

M Auditory discrimination: beginning sounds /p/, /r/, /s/, /t/

Ask pupils to listen as you say this sentence: *Put the pennies in your pocket.* Ask pupils to repeat the sentence.

| SAY | The word *put* begins with the letter *p*. *The letter p* stands for the /p/ sound. |

Read the sentence again and ask pupils to name the other words that begin with /p/. (*pennies, pocket*) Continue in the same manner with these sentences:

1. **Randy ran after the red rabbit.**
2. **Sam the seal sits by the sea.**
3. **Terry's turtle was on top.**

* Practicing and Extending

The activities that follow provide practice and extension of skills developed in this lesson. Not every pupil needs to complete these activities. Choose only the activities that are needed to provide for the individual differences in your classroom.

Practicing Skills

M **Visual discrimination:** letters *Pp, Rr, Ss, Tt*

PM 7 **ADDITIONAL PRACTICE** *Practice Masters* page 7 may be used as optional practice for identifying letters.

M **Auditory discrimination:** beginning sounds /p/, /r/, /s/, /t/

ADDITIONAL PRACTICE Read one or more of the following books to help pupils discriminate the beginning sounds of words:

Moncure, Jane Belk. *My "p" Sound Box.* Childrens Press, 1978.
——. *My "r" Sound Box.* Childrens Press, 1978.
——. *My "s" Sound Box.* Childrens Press, 1977.
——. *My "t" Sound Box.* Childrens Press, 1977.

Extending Selection Concepts

LISTENING: FICTION Choose a book with major characters that relate to the key word for a sound/symbol correspondence and read the story aloud. Ask pupils how this story relates to the letter.

Lewellen, J. *Moon, Sun, and Stars.* Childrens Press, 1981. This easy to read book from the "New True Books" series, give an easy explanation of our sun's relationship to the moon and the stars.
Potter, Beatrix. *The Tale of Peter Rabbit.* Frederick Warne, 1903. Peter and his sisters are warned to stay away from Mr. McGreggor's garden, but curious Peter sneaks into the garden. He soon learns that mother rabbit was right.
Van Leeuwen, Jean. *Tales of Amanda Pig.* Dial Books, 1983. The chapters of this book tell the warm loving story of Amanda and her family.
Van Woerkom, Dorothy. *Harry and Shellburt.* Macmillan, 1977. Harry the hare finds it hard to believe that a turtle once beat a hare in a race, so he and his good friend Shellburt stage a race of their own.

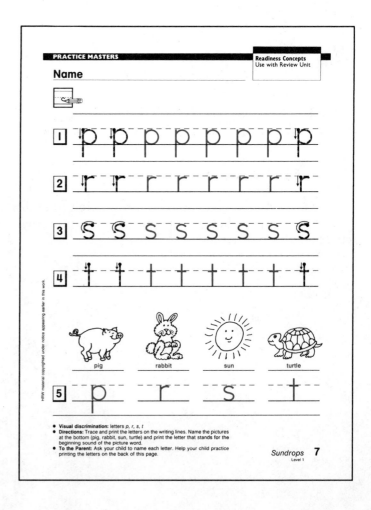

ACTIVITY 8 Reviewing the Alphabet
page 8 (T33–T35)

Skill Strands

READINESS CONCEPTS

M **Visual discrimination:** letters *Uu, Vv, Ww, Yy*

M **Auditory discrimination:** beginning sounds /u/, /v/, /w/, /y/

Materials

Sundrops, Level 1: page 8

Practice Masters: page 8
Teacher's Idea Book

Special Populations

See *Teacher's Idea Book* for additional suggestions to help pupils with limited English proficiency.

Key to Symbols
I Introduced in this lesson
R Reinforced from an earlier lesson in this level
M Maintained from previous levels
T Tested in this level

1 Preparing for the page

M **Visual discrimination:** letters *Uu, Vv, Ww, Yy*

M **Auditory discrimination:** beginning sounds /u/, /v/, /w/, /y/

Help pupils find page 8 in their books.

SAY **Here are some more letters for us to practice. Who can name the letters on this page?** (u, v, w, y) **What picture is with the letter *u*?** (umbrella) ***U* stands for the /u/ sound at the beginning of the word *umbrella*. What picture is with v?** (valentine) ***V* stands for the /v/ sound in *valentine*. What picture is with *w*?** (wagon) ***W* stands for the /w/ sound in *wagon*. What picture is with *y*?** (yo-yo) ***Y* stands for the /y/ sound in *yo-yo*.**

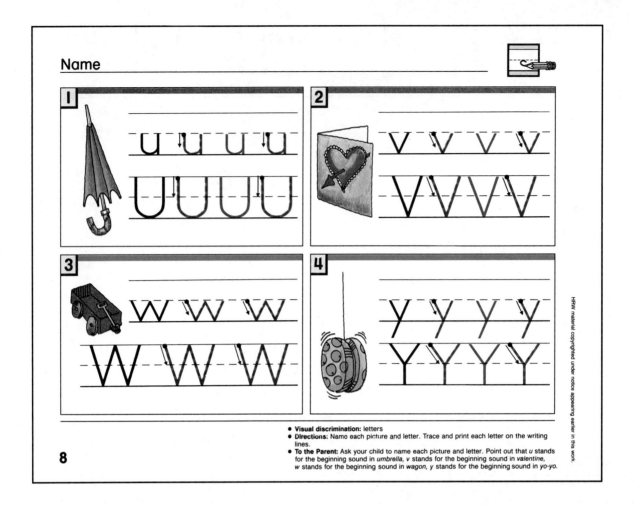

Name

- **Visual discrimination:** letters
- **Directions:** Name each picture and letter. Trace and print each letter on the writing lines.
- **To the Parent:** Ask your child to name each picture and letter. Point out that *u* stands for the beginning sound in *umbrella*, *v* stands for the beginning sound in *valentine*, *w* stands for the beginning sound in *wagon*, *y* stands for the beginning sound in *yo-yo*.

8

2 Using the page

3 Developing the Skills

M   Visual discrimination: letters *Uu, Vv, Ww, Yy*

Demonstrate on the chalkboard the formation of each letter on the page. Then have pupils trace and print the letters on each writing line.

M   Auditory discrimination: beginning sounds /u/, /v/, /w/, /y/

Ask pupils to listen as you say this sentence: *Uncle Bill has an ugly umbrella.* Ask pupils to repeat the sentence.

| SAY | The word *Uncle* begins with the letter *u*. The letter *u* stands for the /u/ sound. |

Read the sentence again and ask pupils to name the other words that begin with /u/. (*ugly, umbrella*) Continue in the same manner with these sentences:

1. **Valerie's valentine has purple violets.**
2. **William wants to wait until Wednesday.**
3. **Yes, you have a yellow yo-yo.**

✳ Practicing and Extending

The activities that follow provide practice and extension of skills developed in this lesson. Not every pupil needs to complete these activities. Choose only the activities that are needed to provide for the individual differences in your classroom.

Practicing Skills

M **Visual discrimination:** letters Uu, Vv, Ww, Yy

PM 8 **ADDITIONAL PRACTICE** *Practice Masters* page 8 may be used as optional practice for identifying letters.

M **Auditory discrimination:** beginning sounds

ADDITIONAL PRACTICE Read one or more of the following books to help pupils discriminate the beginning sounds of words:

Moncure, Jane Belk. *My "u" Sound Box.* Childrens Press, 1984.
————. *My "v" Sound Box.* Childrens Press, 1979.
————. *My "w" Sound Box.* Childrens Press, 1978.

Extending Selection Concepts

LISTENING: FICTION Choose a book with major characters that relate to the key word for a sound/symbol correspondence and read the story aloud. Ask pupils how this story relates to the letter.

Pinkwater, Honest Dan'l. *Roger's Umbrella.* Dutton, 1985. No one believes that Roger's wild umbrella lifts him up and dumps him in strange places. Life is maddening until the boy meets three lady alligators who teach him how to make the umbrella behave.

Cohen, Miriam. *Bee My Valentine.* Greenwillow, 1978. Everyone in first grade was to give a valentine to everyone else, but George felt bad because he didn't get many. The first graders found a way to cheer him up.

Steig, William. *Farmer Palmer's Wagon Ride.* Farrar, Strauss, and Giroux, 1974. Farmer Palmer starts out on a wagon ride to town, but he soon has more adventures, or misadventures than he bargained for.

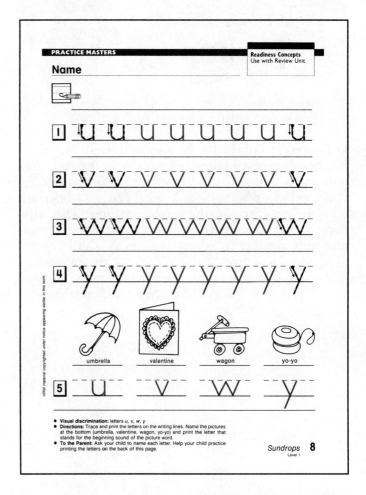

ACTIVITY 9 Telling a Story
page 9 (T36–T38)

Skill Strands

LANGUAGE

I **Speaking:** telling stories from pictures

READINESS CONCEPTS

M **Concept vocabulary:** sentences

Materials

Sundrops, Level 1: page 9
Big Book: page 9
Teacher's Idea Book

Special Populations

See *Teacher's Idea Book* for additional suggestions to help pupils with limited English proficiency.

Key to Symbols
I Introduced in this lesson
R Reinforced from an earlier lesson in this level
M Maintained from previous levels
T Tested in this level

1 Preparing for the page

I **Speaking:** telling a story from pictures

Display page 9 of the *Big Book* and tell pupils that these pictures show what happened one day in the park. Ask pupils to describe what is happening in the first picture. (Everyone is sad because the kite has crashed.) Then ask what is happening in the second picture. (The artist drew a kite and wants the children to come see it.) Call on pupils to tell what is happening in the third picture. (The artist is helping the children fly the new kite.) Then have pupils tell what is happening in the last picture. (The kite is flying, and everyone is happy. The artist is painting a picture.)

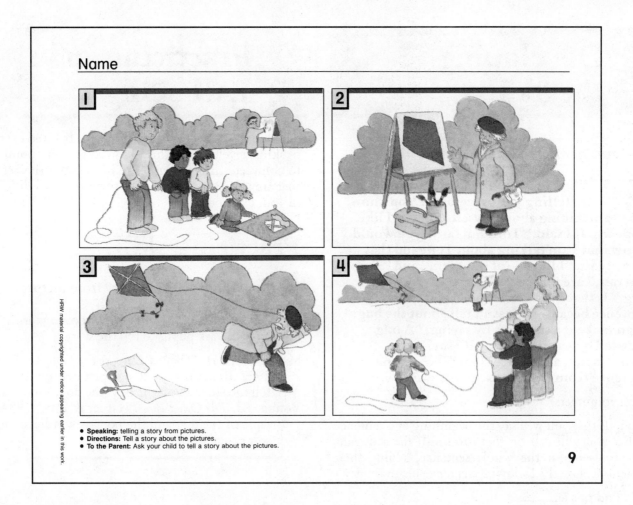

Name

● **Speaking:** telling a story from pictures.
● **Directions:** Tell a story about the pictures.
● **To the Parent:** Ask your child to tell a story about the pictures.

9

HRW material copyrighted under notice appearing earlier in this work.

2 Using the page

I   Speaking: telling a story from pictures

Help pupils find page 9 in their books.

SAY **We just told what is happening in each of these pictures. There are no words on this page, so we can tell our own story about the pictures. I will begin a story about these pictures, and you can help me finish it.**

   Once upon a time, a boy named Scott went to the park to fly his new kite. All Scott's friends were excited to see the kite go up, up in the air.

   Who can tell more of the story?

Call on volunteers to add to the story. You might have to guide the telling by asking questions, such as "What did the artist draw?" "Where did the children get their new kite?" "What did the artist draw then?" As you proceed with the story, it may be helpful for you to retell the story up to the point where something new is to be added. Encourage pupils to add as many details as possible. When pupils reach the end of the story, ask them to suggest names for their story. (Possible answers are: "A Day in the Park," "A New Kite.")

3 Developing the Skills

M   **Concept vocabulary:** sentences

SAY When I say, "I like to eat popcorn," I am telling you something. You know that I am talking about myself and that I like popcorn. If I said, "Tom ran fast," you would know that I am talking about Tom and that he ran fast. "I like to eat popcorn," and "Tom ran fast," are sentences. Suppose I say, "a bug." Is that a sentence? (no) No, it is not a sentence because it doesn't tell about the bug. I can make it a sentence by saying, "A bug crawled on the sidewalk." If I say, "two boys," is that a sentence? (no) Who can make a sentence from the words "two boys?"

Call on volunteers.

Tell pupils that you will say the beginning of a sentence and that you will call on them to finish the sentence. Have pupils repeat the whole sentence, adding their completions. Use the following sentence beginnings:

1. **My dad has a** ———.
2. **We always** ———.
3. **A brown dog** ———.

✳ Practicing and Extending

The activities that follow provide practice and extension of skills developed in this lesson. Not every pupil needs to complete these activities. Choose only the activities that are needed to provide for the individual differences in your classroom.

Practicing Skills

M   **Speaking:** telling a story from pictures

CHALLENGE ACTIVITY   Choose a wordless picture book and ask pupils to tell the story.

Mayer, Mercer. *A Boy, a Dog, and a Frog.* Dial Books, 1967. Remarkably detailed pictures invite pupils to tell the story about the boy, the dog, and the frog.

Young, Ed. *The Other Bone.* Harper & Row, 1984. The fable of the dog and the bone is wordlessly told in soft pencil drawings.

ACTIVITY 10

Matching Capital and Small Letters page 10 (T39–T41)

Skill Strands

READINESS CONCEPTS

M **Visual discrimination:** capital and small letters

Materials

Sundrops, Level 1: page 10
Practice Masters: page 9
Resource Box: Letter Cards b, f, g, n
Pocket Chart
Teacher's Idea Book
Letter Game (See page T11.)

Special Populations

See *Teacher's Idea Book* for additional suggestions to help pupils with limited English proficiency.

Key to Symbols
I Introduced in this lesson
R Reinforced from an earlier lesson in this level
M Maintained from previous levels
T Tested in this level

1 Preparing for the page

M **Visual discrimination:** capital and small letters

SAY **We have two ways to write every letter of the alphabet. One way is called the capital letter and the other way is called the small letter.** (Print capital *A* on the chalkboard.) **This is capital letter A.** (Print small *a* on the chalkboard.) **This is the small letter a. Capital A and small a are two ways to print letter a.**

Place *Letter Cards b, f, g,* and *n* along the chalk ledge. Print capital *F* on the chalkboard.

SAY **This is capital F. Who can show us the card that has the small f?**

Call on a volunteer. Print the capital forms of each of the remaining *Letter Cards* and call on a volunteer to find the small letter to go with each one.

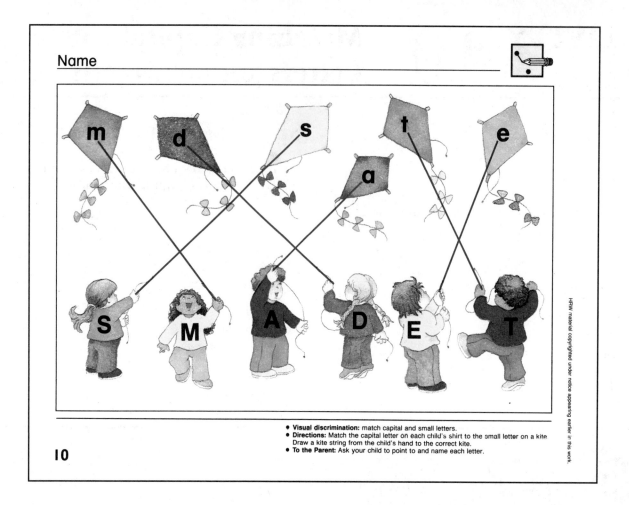

Name _____

m   d   s   t   e

a

S   M   A   D   E   T

- **Visual discrimination:** match capital and small letters.
- **Directions:** Match the capital letter on each child's shirt to the small letter on a kite. Draw a kite string from the child's hand to the correct kite.
- **To the Parent:** Ask your child to point to and name each letter.

10

2 Using the page

3 Developing the Skills

M   **Visual discrimination:** capital and sm~~...~~ letters

~~...~~rimination: capital and small

Help pupils find page 10 in their ~~...~~

Do after word sort as
Krushenky

SAY   **The children on this ~~...~~ kites, but I can't tell v~~...~~ belongs to each child because t~~...~~ missing. You can help each chil~~...~~ her kite. Draw a string from each~~...~~ hand to the correct kite. The capit~~...~~ on each child's shirt matches the smal~~...~~ letter on the child's kite.**

When pupils have completed the page, call on volunteers to name the capital letter on each child's shirt and to tell the color of the kite that belongs to that child.

~~...~~play the "Letter Match Game." ~~...~~ *Chart* and the container of small letter ~~...~~age T11.) Hold up a capital letter card and ~~...~~pupils to take turns choosing cards from the container until the small letter that matches the capital letter you are holding is found. The pupil who found the correct small letter may place both the capital and small letter cards in the *Pocket Chart*. Display a new capital letter and continue the game.

✳ Practicing and Extending

The activities that follow provide practice and extension of skills developed in this lesson. Not every pupil needs to complete these activities. Choose only the activities that are needed to provide for the individual differences in your classroom.

Practicing Skills

M   Visual discrimination: capital and small letters

PM 9   **ADDITIONAL PRACTICE**   *Practice Masters* page 9 may be used as optional practice for matching capital letters and small letters.

Extending Selection Concepts

LISTENING: FICTION   Read an alphabet book with large illustrations of letters. Discuss with pupils the letters used, either capital or small, and the pictures that illustrate each letter.

Alda, Arlene. *Arlene Alda's ABC.* Celestial Arts, 1981. This is a collection of photographs of objects that resemble letters of the alphabet.

Kitchen, Bert. *Animal Alphabet.* Dial Books, 1984. A magnificently drawn animal illustrates each letter of the alphabet.

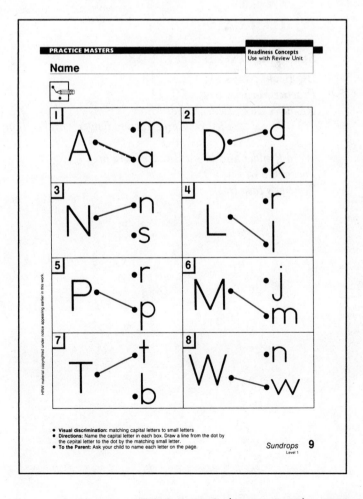

UNIT 1   "Mice"
pages 11–18 (T42–T71)

Skill Strands

DECODING/VOCABULARY

I, T   **Sound/symbol correspondence:** consonant /m/*m* (initial, final)

STUDY SKILLS

I   **Organizing information:** classification

COMPREHENSION/THINKING

I   **Critical thinking:** using prior knowledge

I, T   **Literal:** sequence

LANGUAGE

I   **Listening:** story comprehension
I   **Listening:** rhyming words
R   **Listening:** poetry
I   **Speaking:** retelling stories
I   **Writing:** language–experience stories

Materials

Sundrops, Level 1: pages 11–18
Big Book: pages 11, 13, 17, 18
Practice Masters: pages 10–14
Resource Box: Letter Cards M, m
           Picture Cards carrot, flower, giraffe, lion, mouse, tree
Word Builder and *Word Builder Card m*
Pocket Chart
Teacher's Idea Book

Language Applications

EXTENDING SELECTION CONCEPTS
Listening: fiction
Listening: poetry
Listening: rhymes
Listening: information

Special Populations

See *Teacher's Idea Book* for additional suggestions to help pupils with limited English proficiency.

Key to Symbols
I   Introduced in this lesson
R   Reinforced from an earlier lesson in this level
M   Maintained from previous levels
T   Tested in this level

Idea Center

PICTURE CARDS

If you do not have the *Resource Box,* you can make your own *Picture Cards.* Color and cut apart the pictures in the *Teacher's Idea Book* and paste each on a card. Or, you may prefer to find pictures in magazines or workbooks to paste on cards.

WORD BUILDER AND WORD BUILDER CARDS

If you do not have a *Word Builder* and *Word Builder Cards* for each pupil, you can make your own. Use a 12-by-9-inch sheet of tagboard for each *Word Builder.* Mark and score a line 1 inch from the bottom of the tagboard. Fold along the line to make a pocket. Staple the ends. Make *Word Builder Cards* approximately 2 by 3 inches. Print a capital letter on the upper half of one side of the card, and a lowercase letter on the other side. For each pupil, make two cards of each letter.

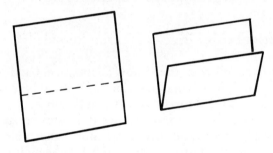

MOUSE

For Activity 1, make a paper mouse. Follow the directions in the *Teacher's Idea Book.* The mouse will be used to help pupils retell parts of the story "Moon Mouse."

SOUND/SYMBOL FOLDER

For Activity 8, make a sound/symbol folder for letter *m.* Print a large letter *m* on the front of a manila folder. Draw a line to divide the inside of the folder into two sections. Print m_____ at the top of the first section to represent /m/ at the beginning of words. Print _____m at the top of the other section to represent /m/ at the end of words. From magazines or catalogs, cut pictures of objects that have /m/ at the beginning or at the end of their names. Place the pictures in an envelope and store the envelope inside the folder. Invite pupils to place the pictures on the section of the folder that corresponds to where the /m/ sound is heard in the word. A similar folder may be made for each sound/symbol correspondence taught.

BIBLIOGRAPHY

The book below is the literary selection that has been reprinted for use in Activity 1. You may wish to have this book on display for pupils to enjoy after you have read the story.

Holl, Adelaide. *Moon Mouse.* Random House, 1969.

Add other books about mice or the moon to the reading corner or reading table. Encourage pupils to look at the books on their own. Suggestions for reading books aloud appear throughout this lesson. Listed below is a bibliography to choose from. Annotations for the books appear in the activities.

Barklem, Jill. *The Secret Staircase.* Philomel Books, 1983.

Branley, Franklyn M. *Is There Life in Outer Space?* Thomas Y. Crowell, 1984.

Brown, Marcia. *Once a Mouse.* Charles Scribner's Sons, 1961.

Friskey, Margaret. *Space Shuttles.* Childrens Press, 1982.

Keats, Ezra Jack. *Regards to the Man in the Moon.* Four Winds Press, 1981.

Kraus, Robert. *All the Mice Came.* Harper & Row, 1955.

Lionni, Leo. *Alexander and the Wind-up Mouse.* Pantheon Books, 1969.

—— *Frederick.* Pantheon Books, 1966.

—— *The Greentail Mouse.* Pantheon Books, 1973.

Numeroff, Laura J. *If You Give a Mouse a Cookie.* Harper & Row Junior Books, 1985.

Perkins, Al. *Hand, Hand, Fingers, Thumb.* Random House, 1969.

Taniguchi, Kazuko. *Monster Mary Mischief Maker.* McGraw-Hill Book Co., 1976.

Yolen, Jane. *Commander Toad in Space.* Coward-McCann, 1980.

ACTIVITY 1 Listening to "Moon Mouse"
page 11 (T44–T48)

Skill Strands

COMPREHENSION/THINKING

I **Critical thinking:** using prior knowledge

LANGUAGE

I **Listening:** story comprehension
I **Speaking:** retelling stories

Materials

Sundrops, Level 1: page 11
Big Book: page 11
Mouse from *Teacher's Idea Book*

Special Populations

See *Teacher's Idea Book* for additional suggestions to help pupils with limited English proficiency.

Key to Symbols
I   Introduced in this lesson
R   Reinforced from an earlier lesson in this level
M   Maintained from previous levels
T   Tested in this level

1 Preparing for the page

SUMMARY A little mouse named Arthur wants to go to the moon. He travels a long way until he sees the moon at the top of a building. Arthur climbs up the building and finds a big round cheese that he assumes is the moon. He eats a lot of the cheese and then returns home and tells his mother that he has eaten part of the moon. He is sure of this when, the next time he sees the moon, one side is missing.

I **Critical thinking:** using prior knowledge

Ask pupils to tell what they know about mice. Guide the discussion by asking what mice look like and where they live. (Mice are small furry animals that live in fields, deserts, or woods. Sometimes they live in houses or barns.) Then ask what mice eat. (Mice eat almost anything, including grain, meat, insects, and seeds.) If cheese has not been mentioned, point out that many people think cheese is a favorite food for mice.

Print the title "Moon Mouse" on the chalkboard and read it. Tell pupils that this is the title of a story that you are going to read. Explain that the story is about a mouse who wants to go to the moon because he thinks he will find cheese there. Ask why the mouse might think he will find cheese on the moon. If necessary, explain that there is an old saying that the moon is made of cheese.

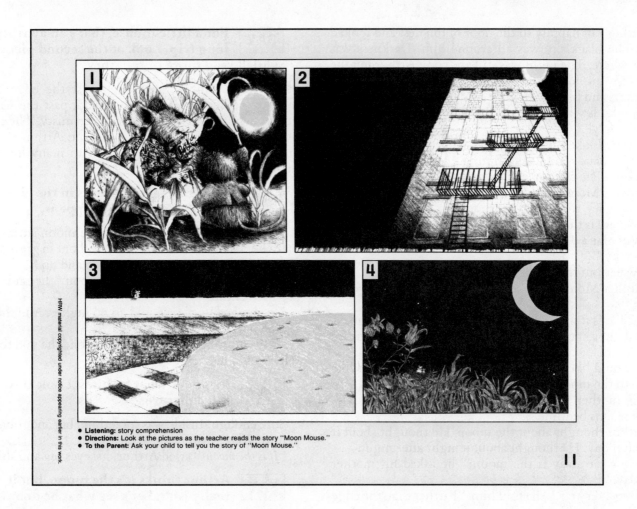

- **Listening:** story comprehension
- **Directions:** Look at the pictures as the teacher reads the story "Moon Mouse."
- **To the Parent:** Ask your child to tell you the story of "Moon Mouse."

11

2 Using the page

I Listening: story comprehension

Note: Successful readers make predictions about what will happen, evaluate and revise those predictions, draw inferences, relate previous knowledge to the text, and are aware of comprehension difficulties. The teacher should model these behaviors so that pupils can become aware of active comprehension strategies. One way to model these behaviors is to make comments as you read a story aloud. Suggested asides to be made by the teacher are indicated in the story "Moon Mouse." The asides should be presented as a natural response to the reading, without disrupting the flow of the story.

Help pupils find page 11 in their books. Explain that the pictures on this page are from the story "Moon Mouse" and that pupils can look at these pictures as you read the story. Ask if these pictures show real mice or make-believe mice. (make-believe mice) Then ask pupils to listen to find out if Arthur, the mouse in the story, really goes to the moon. The words in boldface type are possible aside comments to be read or stated by you as if you were thinking aloud.

Moon Mouse
by Adelaide Holl

SAY **Look at the first picture while I read part of the story.**

One evening Mother Mouse called to her baby.
"Come, Arthur," she said. "Now that you are old enough, you may stay up after dark. Let us watch the night."

Arthur ran happily to the door of the nest and looked out. The black sky was all around him. Darkness was everywhere. The night was still and cool. Arthur felt the coolness on his little, pointed nose. It touched his whiskers and his round, little ears.

"So this is what the night looks like!" he said happily. "It is lovely!"

Arthur looked up. There in the blackness was something big, and round, and shining.

"Look!" he cried in excitement. "Oh, look! Look!"

Mother Mouse smiled, "It is only the moon," she said. "It is the big, round, yellow moon."

"Where is the moon?" asked Arthur with bright eyes.

"Very far away," his mother told him. "Up, up, high in the sky."

"What is it for?" asked the little mouse.

Mother Mouse said, "It shines in the dark. It gives us light."

"What is it made of?" asked Arthur in excitement.

"I do not know," answered his mother. "I have heard that it is made of cheese, but I do not think so."

"I would like to go there," said Arthur. "I would like to go to the moon."

His mother smiled. "Well, not tonight," she said. "Come, it is bedtime."

Arthur thought about the moon. He thought about it day after day. He thought about it night after night.

"How far away is the moon?" he asked his mother one day.

"Very, very far," she told him. "Farther than the edge of the meadow. Farther than the farmer's cornfield. Farther than the fields of golden wheat."

One evening, Arthur said to himself, "I am old enough to stay up after dark. I must be old enough to go to the moon."

He looked up. The sky was dark and misty. He could not see the round, yellow moon anywhere.

"I will go look for the moon," said Arthur to himself. So he set off all alone.

SAY **For a little mouse, that's an awfully long trip. Look at the second picture while I read more of the story.**

He went a long, long way—past the edge of the meadow, past the farmer's cornfield, past the fields of golden wheat. The sky was black and misty. Then, little by little, the stars began to come out. Arthur went on and on until he came to a place with many lights and many noises.

SAY **It sounds as if Arthur is in the city now. Let's see what happens.**

And there, all at once, he saw the moon sitting high on top of a tall building. He looked about in great excitement. He saw steps going up and up and up.

"This must be the way to the moon," he said. So he began to climb.

He climbed until he could go no higher. And there he saw an open place for going in.

"This must be the door to the moon," he said to himself. And in he went.

SAY **I wonder what he finds. Look at the third picture.**

Sure enough! Inside was something big and round and yellow. And it was made of cheese!

"*It is the moon!*" cried Arthur, his eyes big and shining.

SAY **Arthur thinks it's the moon, but it really isn't. Let's see what he does.**

He scampered all about. He ran in and out of the little craters. He nibbled a bit here. He nibbled a bit there. At last, he was very full and very tired.

"The moon is a delicious place," he said to himself. "But I think I shall go home now."

He climbed down, all the way down to the ground. He went a long, long way—past the fields of golden wheat, past the farmer's cornfield, past the edge of the meadow. He went all the way home to his nest.

"Where on earth have you been?" asked Mother Mouse. "I have been looking for you."

"I have been all the way to the moon," said Arthur in excitement. "It *is* big, and round, and yellow. It *is* made of cheese. And it is very delicious!"

Mother Mouse smiled. "Funny little mouse!" she said kindly.

SAY | **I don't think Arthur's mother thinks he really went to the moon.**

Arthur looked up at the night sky. A soft rain was falling. There was darkness all about.

"Where is the moon?" he asked his mother.

"It is a rainy, cloudy night," she told him. "The moon is hiding."

Arthur watched for the moon the next night, and again the next. Night after night he waited. But there was only the blackness and the rain.

SAY | **Look at the fourth picture and listen as I read.**

Then one evening the rain stopped. The clouds began to drift away. All at once, the moon came out. It was shiny. It was bright. But it was not big and round. It was only a small, thin slice. One whole side was missing.

"Look!" Arthur called to his mother in excitement. "See what a lot of the moon I nibbled!"

"So you did," said his mother with a smile. "It was a good thing you did not eat it *all up!*"

SAY | **Did Arthur really go to the moon?** (no) **What happened to the moon?** (It changed.) **What made Arthur think he had gone to the moon?** (He climbed up high; he found something big and round and yellow; he ate a lot of cheese and the next time he saw the moon, part of it was gone.)

3 Developing the Skills

I Speaking: retelling stories

The questions that follow have been designed to help pupils reconstruct the story "Moon Mouse." The questions are both literal and inferential in nature, as basic understanding of a story requires recalling specific events as well as making inferences. Repeated use of this questioning technique will help pupils learn to distinguish the important parts of a story. Display the *Big Book* and call attention to the pictures on page 11 as you ask the questions.

Picture 1: **What did Arthur's mother tell him about the moon?** (It is far away; it gives light; some people think it is made of cheese.)

What did Arthur decide to do when he couldn't see the moon? (He decided to look for it.)

Picture 2: **Where did Arthur think he found the moon?** (He saw it on top of a building.)

Picture 3: **What did Arthur find inside the building?** (He found a big, round cheese.)

What did Arthur think it was? (He thought it was the moon.) **Why?** (It was big, round, yellow, and far away.)

What did Arthur do to the "moon" he found? (He ate a lot of it.)

Picture 4: **What did Arthur think the next time he saw the real moon?** (He thought he had eaten part of it.)

Encourage volunteers to retell the parts of the story that they enjoyed most.

✳ Practicing and Extending

The activities that follow provide practice and extension of skills developed in this lesson. Not every pupil needs to complete these activities. Choose only the activities that are needed to provide for the individual differences in your classroom.

Practicing Skills

I   Speaking: retelling stories

CHALLENGE ACTIVITY   Make the mouse shown in the *Teacher's Idea Book*. Use it to help pupils retell parts of the story "Moon Mouse." For example, give the mouse to a pupil and ask the pupil to pretend to be Arthur. Ask "Arthur" to tell how he felt when he first saw the moon. Then give the mouse to another pupil to pretend to be Arthur's mother. Ask "Arthur's mother" to tell Arthur what the moon is like. If you wish, duplicate copies of the page for pupils to make their own mouse.

Extending Selection Concepts

LISTENING: POETRY   Ask pupils to listen to a poem written by Rose Fyleman. Explain that a person who writes a poem is called a poet, so Rose Fyleman is a poet. Ask pupils if they agree with what the poet says about mice. Reread the poem several times and ask pupils to join in on the last two lines.

Mice

I think mice
Are rather nice.

  Their tails are long,
  Their faces small,
  They haven't any
  Chins at all.
  Their ears are pink,
  Their teeth are white,
  They run about
  The house at night.
  They nibble things
  They shouldn't touch
  And no one seems
  To like them much.

But *I* think mice
Are nice.

Rose Fyleman

HOW AM I DOING?

Many pupils need help in clarifying their ideas so they can begin establishing a well-organized approach to creative writing. Ask yourself the following questions to gauge your teaching effectiveness in this area.

	Yes	No	Some-times
1. Do I respond positively to pupils' questions?	☐	☐	☐
2. Did I help them understand the importance of writing clear descriptions?	☐	☐	☐
3. Do I share well written articles or books with the class?	☐	☐	☐
4. As I read aloud, do I point out good examples of descriptive writing as models for them to emulate?	☐	☐	☐

ACTIVITY 2 Recognizing Sequence
page 12 (T49–T52)

Skill Strands

COMPREHENSION/THINKING

I, T   Literal: sequence

Materials

Sundrops, Level 1: page 12

Practice Masters: page 10
Teacher's Idea Book

Special Populations

See *Teacher's Idea Book* for additional suggestions to help pupils with limited English proficiency.

Key to Symbols
I   Introduced in this lesson
R   Reinforced from an earlier lesson in this level
M   Maintained from previous levels
T   Tested in this level

1 Preparing for the page

I, T   Literal: sequence

Draw a circle on the chalkboard. Tell pupils that when Moon Mouse first saw the cheese it was big and round, like a circle. Then explain that as Moon Mouse started eating the cheese, the cheese started to get smaller. Next to the circle, draw a half-circle. Explain that Moon Mouse ate and ate until the cheese was almost gone. Draw a crescent shape after the half-circle. Point to each picture.

SAY **This is how the cheese looked first.** (Write a number 1 under the circle.) **This is how the cheese looked next.** (Write a number 2 under the half-circle.) **This is how the cheese looked last.** (Write a number 3 under the crescent.) **First, the cheese was whole. Next, Moon Mouse ate some of it. Then Moon Mouse ate until he was too full to eat any more.**

- **Literal:** sequence
- **Directions:** Number the pictures in each row to show what happened first, next, and last.
- **To the Parent:** Ask your child to tell what happened first, next, and last in each row of pictures.

12

2 Using the page

I, T   Literal: sequence

Help pupils find page 12 in their books. Call attention to the three pictures across the top of the page. Explain that these pictures show a mouse eating a big cheese, the way Moon Mouse did. Tell pupils to look at the three pictures in their books and to compare them to the three pictures on the chalkboard.

SAY These pictures are not in the correct order, but you can put them in order with the numbers 1, 2, and 3.

Call on pupils to tell which of the pictures in their books shows what happened first. (the first picture) Tell pupils to trace number 1 on the line under the first picture. Ask which picture shows what happened second, or next. (the last picture) Tell pupils to trace number 2 under the last picture. Then ask which picture shows what happened last. (the middle picture) Tell pupils to trace number 3 under the middle picture. Remind pupils that the pictures on this page are not in order and call attention to the next row of pictures. Have pupils tell what is happening in these pictures. (A snow figure is melting.) Then ask what is happening in the last row of pictures. (A boy is growing flowers.) Explain that pupils are to decide what happened first, next, and last in each row of pictures and to number the pictures in each row 1, 2, and 3. Have pupils tell what happened in each row of pictures using the words *first, next,* and *then.*

3 Developing the Skills

I, T Literal: sequence

Tell pupils that you will describe the steps in doing something and that you will ask them to tell what should happen next.

SAY First, I get up. Next, I get dressed. Then _____.

Call on a volunteer to name a third activity. Accept any logical suggestion, such as "Then I make my bed," or "Then I eat breakfast." Ask a volunteer to repeat the entire series, including the suggested final action. Continue with these series:

1. **First, Mary puts on her socks. Next, she puts on her shoes. Then _____.**
2. **First, I throw a stick. Next, my dog runs after it. Then _____.**
3. **First, Juan mixes the batter. Next, he bakes the muffins. Then _____.**

You may want to give only the first event and have two pupils add succeeding events before having the series repeated. Suggested first events are: First, I put on my coat; First, Kelly opens the box; First, Matt gets on the bus.

✳ Practicing and Extending

The activities that follow provide practice and extension of skills developed in this lesson. Not every pupil needs to complete these activities. Choose only the activities that are needed to provide for the individual differences in your classroom.

Practicing Skills

I, T Literal: sequence

PM 10 **ADDITIONAL PRACTICE** *Practice Masters* page 10 may be used as an optional practice for sequencing events.

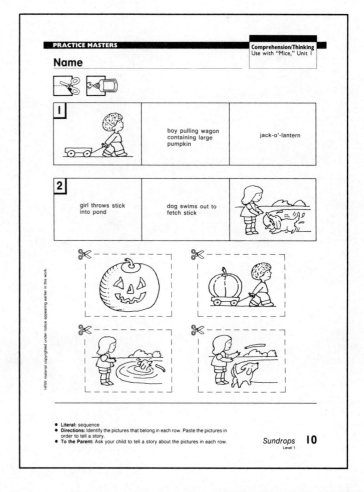

PRACTICE MASTERS

Comprehension/Thinking
Use with "Mice," Unit 1

Name

1 | boy pulling wagon containing large pumpkin | jack-o'-lantern

2 | girl throws stick into pond | dog swims out to fetch stick

• Literal: sequence
• **Directions:** Identify the pictures that belong in each row. Paste the pictures in order to tell a story.
• **To the Parent:** Ask your child to tell a story about the pictures in each row.

Sundrops Level 1 **10**

HRW material copyrighted under notice appearing earlier in this work.

Extending Selection Concepts

LISTENING: FICTION Choose a book about a mouse and read it aloud. Discuss with pupils what the mouse does in the story.

Krause, Robert. *All the Mice Came.* Harper & Row, 1955. All the mice are delighted to go to a party until they find out who invited them.

Lionni, Leo. *Alexander and the Wind-up Mouse.* Pantheon, 1969. This is a fantasy about the friendship between a real mouse and a mechanical mouse.

ACTIVITY 3 Relating Initial /m/ to *m*
page 13 (T53–T56)

Skill Strands

DECODING/VOCABULARY

I, T **Sound/symbol correspondence:** consonant /m/*m* (initial)

Materials

Sundrops, Level 1: page 13
Big Book: page 13
Practice Masters: page 11
Resource Box: Letter Cards M, m
Word Builder Card m
Pocket Chart
Teacher's Idea Book

Special Populations

See *Teacher's Idea Book* for additional suggestions to help pupils with limited English proficiency.

Key to Symbols
I Introduced in this lesson
R Reinforced from an earlier lesson in this level
M Maintained from previous levels
T Tested in this level

1 Preparing for the page

I, T **Sound/symbol correspondence:** consonant /m/*m* (initial)

Note: Learning to read requires understanding the alphabetic principle. This principle is that a written symbol—a letter or letters—is associated with a unit of speech—a sound. Direct teaching of sound/symbol correspondences makes gaining understanding of the alphabetic principle easier. Associating a sound with a letter (or letters) helps pupils quickly gain independent decoding strategies. In pronouncing an isolated consonant sound, such as /m/, avoid adding a vowel sound either before or after the consonant. The sound should be *mmm,* not *emm* or *muh.*

SAY When Moon Mouse ate the cheese, he probably said, "*Mmm* this is good cheese." Say *mmm* with me: mmm.

Place *Letter Card m* in the *Pocket Chart.*

SAY The name of this letter is *m.* The letter *m* stands for the /m/ sound in words. When we see the letter *m* we make the /m/ sound. When I touch the letter *m,* you make the /m/ sound. Keep making the sound as long as I am touching the letter. Stop making the sound when I lift my finger.

Make a game of touching the letter and lifting your finger at various intervals, sometimes touching the letter for several seconds, sometimes touching it very quickly.

SAY The letter *m* stands for the /m/ sound at the beginning of the word *mouse.* Say *mouse* with me: *mouse.* Now say *moon* with me: *moon.* What sound do you hear at the beginning of *moon?* (/m/) Yes, *moon* begins with the /m/ sound. I'll say some other words that begin with the /m/ sound and you say each word after me.

Use the following words: *monkey, motorcycle.*

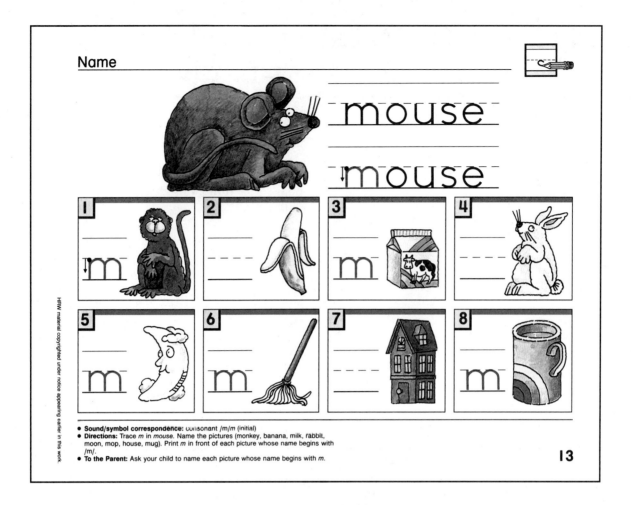

- **Sound/symbol correspondence:** consonant /m/*m* (initial)
- **Directions:** Trace *m* in *mouse*. Name the pictures (monkey, banana, milk, rabbit, moon, mop, house, mug). Print *m* in front of each picture whose name begins with /m/.
- **To the Parent:** Ask your child to name each picture whose name begins with *m*.

13

Make sure each pupil has a *Word Builder Card m*. Have pupils name the letter.

> **SAY** I am going to say some words that begin with /m/ and some words that do not begin with /m/. Each time you hear a word that begins with the /m/ sound, hold up your letter *m*. If a word does not begin with /m/, do not hold up your card.

Use the following words: *mouse, magic, rabbit, man, popcorn, marbles, milk.* Call on pupils to name other words that begin with the /m/ sound.

Place *Letter Card M* in the *Pocket Chart* beside letter *m*.

> **SAY** The name of this letter is capital *M*. Capital *M* stands for the same sound as the small *m*. What sound is that? (/m/) We use capital *M* at the beginning of names such as *Mary* and *Moon Mouse*.

If you have pupils whose names (first or last) begin with the /m/ sound, invite them to say their names. Tell pupils whose names begin with /m/ to make the /m/ sound when you point to the capital *M*. Tell the other pupils to make the /m/ sound when you point to the small *m*. Point to each letter several times.

2 Using the page

I, T Sound/symbol correspondence: consonant /m/*m* (initial)

Display page 13 of the *Big Book* and call attention to the picture of a mouse at the top. Tell pupils that the word beside the picture is *mouse*. Have pupils point to the first letter in the word *mouse*. Then call on volunteers to tell the name of the letter. (*m*) Ask what sound this letter stands for. (/m/) Have pupils look at the second word *mouse* and trace the *m* at the beginning of the word. Call attention to the direction symbol at the top of the page and explain that the symbol means to trace and print letters.

Have the picture in the first box identified. (monkey)

ASK Does *monkey* begin with the /m/ sound? (yes) Since *monkey* begins with the /m/ sound, trace the *m* on the writing line in front of the picture.

Have pupils name the second picture. (banana)

ASK Does *banana* begin with the /m/ sound? (no) Since *banana* does not have the /m/ sound at the beginning, do not print *m* on the line.

Help pupils find page 13 in their books. Tell pupils that they are to print the letter *m* on the line in front of each picture whose name begins with the /m/ sound. Identify the remaining pictures as milk, rabbit, moon, mop, house, mug.

3 Developing the Skills

I, T Sound/symbol correspondence: consonant /m/*m* (initial)

Tell pupils that you will say some sentences that have missing words and that each of the missing words begins with the /m/ sound. Then read each of the following sentences and have pupils guess the missing word. Encourage volunteers to repeat the complete sentences.

1. **I like to drink _____.** (milk)
2. **My hands were cold, so I put on my _____.** (mittens)
3. **I like to listen to _____.** (music)
4. **We go to the zoo to see the _____.** (monkeys)
5. **After the rain, Jim stepped in the _____.** (mud)
6. **We wake up in the _____.** (morning)

✳ Practicing and Extending

The activities that follow provide practice and extension of skills developed in this lesson. Not every pupil needs to complete these activities. Choose only the activities that are needed to provide for the individual differences in your classroom.

Practicing Skills

I, T Sound/symbol correspondence: consonant /m/*m* (initial)

PM 11 ADDITIONAL PRACTICE *Practice Masters* page 11 may be used as optional practice for identifying the letter *m* with the /m/ sound in words.

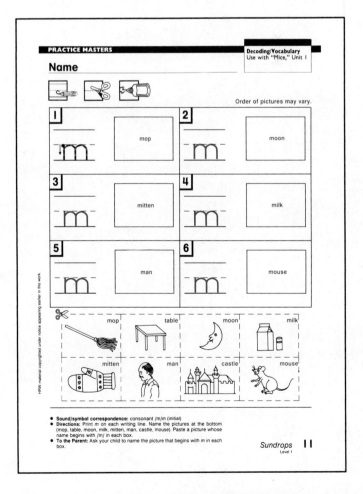

CHALLENGE ACTIVITY   Have pupils join hands and stand in a circle to represent the full moon. Tell pupils that they will play a game to see how much of the moon Moon Mouse nibbled. Each pupil will have a turn to say "Moon Mouse nibbled a _____" and then to complete the sentence by naming any word that begins with the /m/ sound. If the pupil correctly names a word beginning with /m/, he or she may sit down, leaving a hole in the moon.

Extending Selection Concepts

LITERATURE

LISTENING: FICTION   Choose a book about mice, the moon, or a book that has /m/ in the title and read it aloud. Discuss with pupils what the characters did in each story.

Brown, Marcia. *Once a Mouse.* Charles Scribner's Sons, 1961. This is a fable about a hermit who turns a mouse into a cat, then a dog, and finally a tiger.

Numeroff, Laura J. *If You Give a Mouse a Cookie.* Harper & Row Junior Books, 1985. This is a humorous account of other things a mouse will want once he is given a cookie.

Taniguchi, Kazuko. *Monster Mary Mischief Maker.* McGraw-Hill, 1976. Monster Mary discovers that it is much better to be helpful and loving than to be lazy and mischievous.

ACTIVITY 4 Relating Final /m/ to *m*
page 14 (T57–T59)

Skill Strands

DECODING/VOCABULARY

I, T **Sound/symbol correspondence:** consonant /m/*m* (final)

LANGUAGE

I **Listening:** rhyming words

Materials

Sundrops, Level 1: page 14
Practice Masters: page 12
Word Builder and *Word Builder Card m*
Teacher's Idea Book

Special Populations

See *Teacher's Idea Book* for additional suggestions to help pupils with limited English proficiency.

Key to Symbols

I Introduced in this lesson
R Reinforced from an earlier lesson in this level
M Maintained from previous levels
T Tested in this level

1 Preparing for the page

I, T **Sound/symbol correspondence:** consonant /m/*m* (final)

Print letter *m* on the chalkboard. Have pupils name the letter and tell what sound the letter stands for. Ask pupils to name words that begin with the /m/ sound.

SAY **Now I am going to say a word that has the /m/ sound at the end:** *room.* **Say** *room* **with me:** *room.* **I will say some other words that have /m/ at the end and you say them after me:** *plum, ham, arm.*

Make sure each pupil has *Word Builder Card m.*

SAY **I am going to say some words that have /m/ at the end and some words that do not have /m/ at the end. When you hear a word that has /m/ at the end, hold up your *m* card. Do not hold up a card if you do not hear /m/ at the end of a word.**

Use the following words: *broom, wall, jam, ram, scoot, bottom.*

Make sure each pupil has a *Word Builder.* Explain that they will be using the *Word Builder* to practice sounds and to read words. Indicate the pocket in the *Word Builder* and demonstrate how *Word Builder Card m* will fit in the pocket. Then point to the left side of a *Word Builder* and explain that this is the beginning of the *Word Builder.* Move your finger to the right to the end of the *Word Builder* and explain that this is the end of the *Word Builder.*

SAY *Mouse* **has the /m/ sound at the beginning, so I will put an *m* card in the beginning of my *Word Builder* for *mouse.* (Demonstrate.)** *Room* **has the /m/ sound at the end, so I will put the *m* card at the end of the *Word Builder* for *room.* (Demonstrate.)**

Tell pupils that you will say some words that have the /m/ sound at the beginning and some words that have the /m/ sound at the end. Pupils should place their *m* card at the beginning of the *Word Builder* if they hear /m/ at the beginning of the word, and they should place their *m* card at the end of the *Word Builder* if they hear /m/ at the end of the word. Use these words: *moon, drum, man, home, mountain, dream, hum, steam, money.*

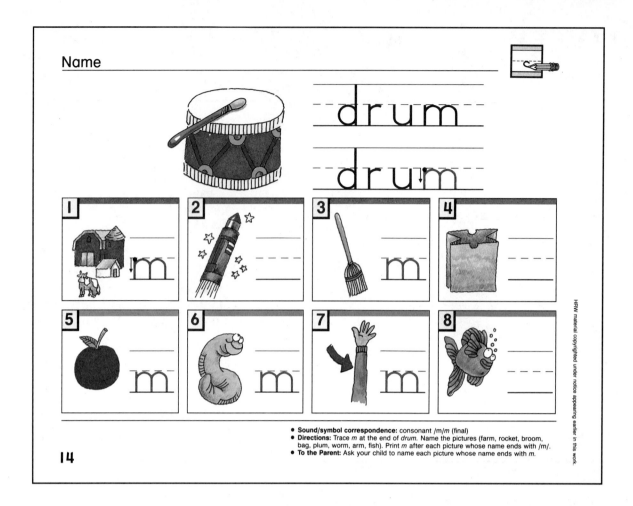

Name _____

drum

drum

1 | 2 | 3 | 4
5 | 6 | 7 | 8

- **Sound/symbol correspondence:** consonant /m/m (final)
- **Directions:** Trace m at the end of *drum*. Name the pictures (farm, rocket, broom, bag, plum, worm, arm, fish). Print m after each picture whose name ends with /m/.
- **To the Parent:** Ask your child to name each picture whose name ends with m.

14

HRW material copyrighted under notice appearing earlier in this work.

2 Using the page

I, T   Sound/symbol correspondence: consonant /m/m (final)

Ask pupils to open their books to page 14 and to name the picture at the top of the page. (a drum)

SAY The word beside the picture is *drum.* Where do you hear the /m/ sound in *drum?*

Have pupils point to the letter *m* in the word *drum* and tell where they see the *m* in *drum.* (at the end) Have pupils trace the *m* in the second word *drum.*

SAY Look at the picture in the first box. It is a picture of a farm. Say *farm* with me: *farm.* Do you hear /m/ at the end of *farm?* (yes) Print letter *m* on the line after the picture to show that *farm* has the /m/ sound at the end.

Continue in the same manner with the next picture. (rocket) Explain that since *rocket* does not have the /m/ sound at the end, they should not print *m.* Identify the remaining pictures as broom, bag, plum, worm, arm, and fish. Then have pupils complete the page by printing *m* on the line after each picture that has the /m/ sound at the end of its name.

3 Developing the Skills

I   Listening: rhyming words

Tell pupils that you will say some rhymes that have the last word missing and that each missing word ends with /m/. Then read each of the following rhymes and ask pupils to guess the missing word. Encourage pupils to repeat the completed rhymes.

1. **I must sweep this little room.
   I will go and get the _____.** (broom)

2. **Can you hear the rum-tum-tum
   As the drummer plays the _____?** (drum)

3. **No matter how far away I roam
   I always like to come back _____.** (home)

4. **Here's my friend, his name is Tom
   I want him to meet my _____.** (mom)

✳ Practicing and Extending

The activities that follow provide practice and extension of skills developed in this lesson. Not every pupil needs to complete these activities. Choose only the activities that are needed to provide for the individual differences in your classroom.

Practicing Skills

I, T   Sound/symbol correspondence: consonant /m/*m* (final)

PM 12   ADDITIONAL PRACTICE   *Practice Masters* page 12 may be used as an optional practice for identifying final /m/.

Extending Selection Concepts

LITERATURE

LISTENING: RHYMES Read aloud the book *Hand, Hand, Fingers, Thumb* by Al Perkins (Random House, 1969). Then reread passages and have pupils name words that begin or end with the /m/ sound. Invite pupils to join you in reciting some of the nonsense rhymes.

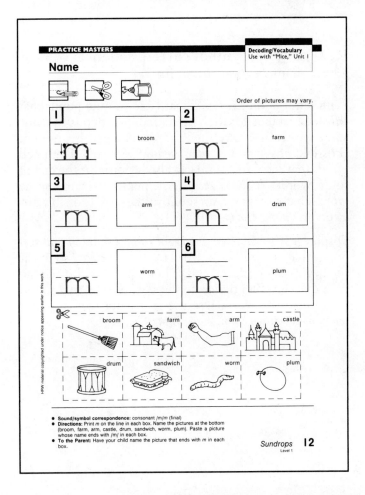

ACTIVITY 5 Discriminating Initial and Final /m/ page 15 (T60–T62)

Skill Strands

DECODING/VOCABULARY

R, T **Sound/symbol correspondence:** consonant /m/ *m* (initial, final)

Materials

Sundrops, Level 1: page 15

Practice Masters: page 13
Word Builder and *Word Builder Card m*
Teacher's Idea Book

Special Populations

See *Teacher's Idea Book* for additional suggestions to help pupils with limited English proficiency.

Key to Symbols
I Introduced in this lesson
R Reinforced from an earlier lesson in this level
M Maintained from previous levels
T Tested in this level

1 Preparing for the page

R, T **Sound/symbol correspondence:** consonant /m/ *m* (initial, final)

Print letter *m* on the chalkboard and remind pupils that this letter stands for the /m/ sound. Ask pupils to name some words that have the /m/ sound at the beginning. (Possible answers are: *man, many, Monday.*) Then tell pupils that the /m/ sound can also be found at the end of some words, such as *room.* Ask pupils to name some words that have the /m/ sound at the end. (Possible answers are: *ham, broom, stem.*)

Display a *Word Builder* and *Word Builder Card m* and tell pupils that you will say a word that has the /m/ sound at the beginning or at the end. Then a pupil will place the *m* card in the *Word Builder* to show where the /m/ sound is heard in the word. Use the following words: *magic, roam, ham, mitten, slim, map, hum, mice, milk.*

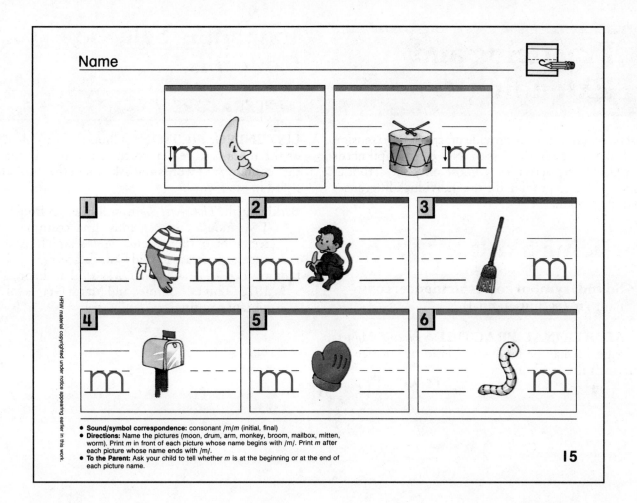

Name _____

- **Sound/symbol correspondence:** consonant /m/m (initial, final)
- **Directions:** Name the pictures (moon, drum, arm, monkey, broom, mailbox, mitten, worm). Print m in front of each picture whose name begins with /m/. Print m after each picture whose name ends with /m/.
- **To the Parent:** Ask your child to tell whether m is at the beginning or at the end of each picture name.

15

HRW material copyrighted under notice appearing earlier in this work.

2 Using the page

3 Developing the Skills

R, T Sound/symbol correspondence: consonant /m/m (initial, final)

Help pupils find page 15 in their books and ask someone to identify the first picture. (moon)

SAY **Is the /m/ sound at the beginning of the word *moon* or at the end of the word *moon*?** (at the beginning) **Trace letter *m* on the line in front of the picture to show that the /m/ sound is at the beginning of the word *moon*. The next picture is a drum. Is the /m/ sound heard at the beginning or at the end of the word *drum*?** (end) **Trace *m* on the line after the drum to show that the /m/ sound is at the end of the word *drum*.**

Have pupils print *m* in front of each picture that has /m/ at the beginning and print *m* after each picture that has /m/ at the end. Identify the pictures as arm, monkey, broom, mailbox, mitten, worm.

R, T Sound/symbol correspondence: consonant /m/m (initial, final)

Tell pupils that you will begin a game by saying either "Moon Mouse has a _____ (word that begins with /m/)" or "Tom Ram wants a (word that ends with /m/)." Then you will call on a pupil to repeat the sentence you said and to add another word that either begins or ends with /m/. You may wish to continue the same sentence until as many as four elements are repeated before starting a new sentence. Examples follow.

Teacher: **Moon Mouse has a mitten.**
Pupil: **Moon Mouse has a mitten and a mop.**
Teacher: **Tom Ram wants a stem.**
Pupil: **Tom the ram wants a stem, a ham, and a home.**

✳ Practicing and Extending

The activities that follow provide practice and extension of skills developed in this lesson. Not every pupil needs to complete these activities. Choose only the activities that are needed to provide for the individual differences in your classroom.

Practicing Skills

I, T **Sound/symbol correspondence:** consonant /m/*m* (initial, final)

PM 13 **ADDITIONAL PRACTICE** *Practice Masters* page 13 may be used as an optional practice for identifying initial and final *m*.

Extending Selection Concepts

LITERATURE

LISTENING: FICTION Choose a book about mice or the moon and read it to the class. Reread sentences that contain /m/ words and ask where the /m/ sound is heard in each word.

Barklem, Jill. *The Secret Staircase.* Philomel Books, 1983. Two mouse children must find costumes for the recitation of their poem. Their search leads them to a secret staircase in Old Oak Palace.

Lionni, Leo. *The Greentail Mouse.* Pantheon Books, 1973. This tale of mice and Mardi Gras is told with vibrant paintings.

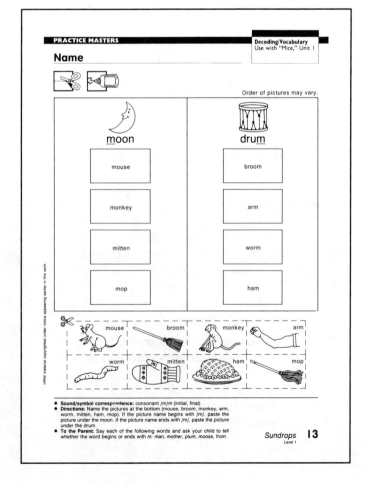

ACTIVITY 6 Classifying Pictures
page 16 (T63–T65)

Skill Strands

STUDY SKILLS

I Organizing information: classification

Materials

Sundrops, Level 1: page 16

Practice Masters: page 14

Resource Box: Picture Cards carrot, flower, giraffe, lion, mouse, tree

Pocket Chart

Teacher's Idea Book

Special Populations

See *Teacher's Idea Book* for additional suggestions to help pupils with limited English proficiency.

Key to Symbols
I Introduced in this lesson
R Reinforced from an earlier lesson in this level
M Maintained from previous levels
T Tested in this level

1 Preparing for the page

I Organizing information: classification

Place *Picture Cards mouse* and *lion* in the *Pocket Chart* and ask pupils to name each picture.

> **SAY** **A mouse is a very small animal. A lion is a large animal. How are a lion and a mouse alike?** (They both have four legs; they both have fur; they are both animals.)

Display *Picture Cards giraffe* and *tree.*

> **ASK** **Which picture goes with the pictures in the *Pocket Chart?*** (the giraffe) **Why?** (It is an animal.)

Have a pupil place the Picture *Card giraffe* with the other pictures in the *Pocket Chart.*

> **SAY** **Now we have a group of animal pictures in the *Pocket Chart.***

Display *Picture Cards carrot, flower, giraffe, lion, mouse, tree* in random order.

> **SAY** **Some of these pictures show animals, and some show things that are not animals. Who can put the pictures that are not animals in the *Pocket Chart?*** (tree, flower, carrot)

Have pupils explain how the pictures in the *Pocket Chart* are alike. (They are not animals; they are plants.)

Display the cards in random order again and ask pupils to group the pictures of things that are small. (flower, mouse, carrot) Then have pupils group the pictures of things that are big. (lion, giraffe, tree)

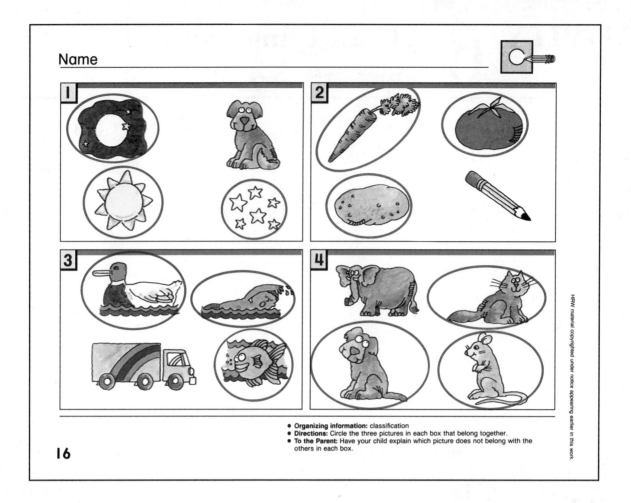

Name

1

2

3

4

- **Organizing information:** classification
- **Directions:** Circle the three pictures in each box that belong together.
- **To the Parent:** Have your child explain which picture does not belong with the others in each box.

16

2 Using the page

I Organizing information: classification

Help pupils find page 16 in their books.

SAY **Each box on this page has four pictures. Three of the pictures go together, and one picture does not belong. Look at the first box. Who can name the pictures?** (moon, dog, sun, stars) **Three of the pictures belong together. What are they?** (moon, sun, stars) **Why do these pictures belong together?** (They are all things you see in the sky.) **Circle the moon, the sun, and the stars to show that they belong together.**

Have pupils circle the pictures in each box that belong together. Ask pupils why the three pictures in each box belong together.

3 Developing the Skills

I Organizing information: classification

Tell pupils that you will say the names of three things. Explain that one of the things will not belong with the others and that you will ask them to tell which two things go together. Have pupils explain why the two things go together.

Use these groups: *shoe, sock, table; chair, hat, desk; hamburger, pizza, crayon; truck, dog, cat; pencil, pumpkin, crayon.*

✳ Practicing and Extending

The activities that follow provide practice and extension of skills developed in this lesson. Not every pupil needs to complete these activities. Choose only the activities that are needed to provide for the individual differences in your classroom.

Practicing Skills

I Organizing information: classification

PM 14 ADDITIONAL PRACTICE *Practice Masters* page 14 may be used as an optional practice for classifying pictures.

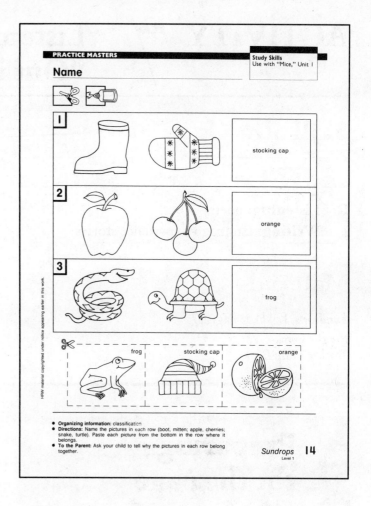

ACTIVITY 7 Listening to the Poem "Out in Space" page 17 (T66–T68)

Skill Strands

LANGUAGE

R **Listening:** poetry
I **Writing:** language-experience stories

Materials

Sundrops, Level 1: page 17
Big Book: page 17
Teacher's Idea Book

Special Populations

See *Teacher's Idea Book* for additional suggestions to help pupils with limited English proficiency.

Key to Symbols
I Introduced in this lesson
R Reinforced from an earlier lesson in this level
M Maintained from previous levels
T Tested in this level

1 Preparing for the page

R **Listening:** poetry

Display page 17 of the *Big Book* and ask what is happening in the picture. (A child is flying on a bed.) Explain that "Out in Space" is a poem and ask if pupils think the poem will tell about real or make-believe things. (make-believe) Have pupils explain why they think this. (The moon is winking; a bed cannot fly; the creatures on the planet are imaginary.)

Out in Space (To be read by the teacher)

When Mom and Dad turn out the lights
and I'm tucked in my room,
I pretend my bed's a rocket ship
And out in space I zoom.

I always wave to the man in the moon.
He'd like for me to stay,
But I pretend my friends on Mars
Want me to come and play.

Linda Cave

• **Listening:** poetry
• **Directions:** Listen as the teacher reads the poem.
• **To the Parent:** Read and discuss the poem with your child.

17

2 Using the page

R   Listening: poetry

Help pupils find page 17 in their books. Ask pupils to listen as you read the poem to find out where the child is going. Run your hand under the words as you read the poem aloud.

ASK   **When does the child pretend to fly on a rocket?** (when she goes to bed) **Why is the man-in-the-moon winking?** (He wants the child to stay.) **Why won't the child stay with the man-in-the-moon?** (She wants to play with her friends on Mars.)

Reread the poem, leaving off the last word of each stanza and ask pupils to supply the rhyming word. (*zoom, play*) Then read the poem a third time and ask pupils to join you.

SAY   **I will read each line of the poem. You tell me what word or words in the line have the /m/ sound.** (line 1: *Mom;* line 2: *I'm, my, room;* line 3: *my;* line 4: *zoom;* line 5: *man, moon;* line 6: *me;* line 7: *my, Mars;* line 8: *me, come*)

3 Developing the Skills

* Practicing and Extending

I Writing: language-experience stories

Remind pupils of the poem about a child's pretend trip into space. Display chart paper and tell pupils that they can work together to make up a story about a pretend trip into space. Explain that you will write the story on the chart paper for them. Tell pupils to think about who will travel in space in their story. Have them suggest names for their space travelers and tell where they might like to go. If necessary, help organize the story by asking questions such as the following:

> **How should our story start?**
> **What will (character's name) use to travel?**
> **What might happen when (character) gets to (place)?**
> **Will there be any space creatures there?**
> **What will we call the creatures?**
> **What might the creatures do?**
> **What will (character) do?**
> **What might happen when (character) comes home?**

As pupils dictate to you, write on the chart the words pupils use. Read back each sentence and invite pupils to join you. When the story is finished, read it aloud several times, running your hand under the words and encouraging pupils to join in. Then encourage volunteers to read parts of the story. Invite pupils to illustrate the story and display the illustrations near the chart paper where pupils can enjoy the story on their own.

The activities that follow provide practice and extension of skills developed in this lesson. Not every pupil needs to complete these activities. Choose only the activities that are needed to provide for the individual differences in your classroom.

Extending Selection Concepts

LITERATURE

LISTENING: FICTION   Choose a book about an imaginary trip into space to read aloud. Discuss with pupils what happens to the characters in space.

Keats, Ezra Jack. *Regards to the Man in the Moon.* Four Winds Press, 1981. Louie learns that his imagination can take him anywhere, even into space.

Yolen, Jane. *Commander Toad in Space.* Coward-McCann, 1980. A band of space explorers board the ship Star Warts for a funny adventure.

ACTIVITY 8 Reviewing /m/m
page 18 (T69–T71)

Skill Strands

DECODING/VOCABULARY

R, T Sound/symbol correspondence: consonant /m/m (initial, final)

LANGUAGE

R Listening: rhyming words

Materials

Sundrops, Level 1: page 18
Big Book: page 18
Teacher's Idea Book
Sound/Symbol folder (See page T43 for instructions.)

Special Populations

See *Teacher's Idea Book* for additional suggestions to help pupils with limited English proficiency.

Key to Symbols
I Introduced in this lesson
R Reinforced from an earlier lesson in this level
M Maintained from previous levels
T Tested in this level

1 Preparing for the page

R, T Sound/symbol correspondence: consonant /m/m (initial, final)

Remind pupils of Moon Mouse's "trip" to the moon. Ask pupils what they might need to make a real trip to the moon. (a rocket ship) Display page 18 of the *Big Book* and call attention to the rocket ships. Ask where the rockets are going (to the moon) and what letter stands for the beginning sound in the word *moon.* (m)

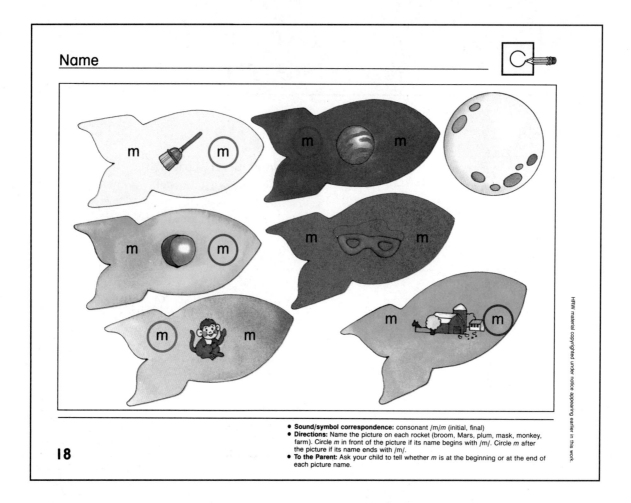

Name

- **Sound/symbol correspondence:** consonant /m/*m* (initial, final)
- **Directions:** Name the picture on each rocket (broom, Mars, plum, mask, monkey, farm). Circle *m* in front of the picture if its name begins with /m/. Circle *m* after the picture if its name ends with /m/.
- **To the Parent:** Ask your child to tell whether *m* is at the beginning or at the end of each picture name.

18

2 Using the page

R, T Sound/symbol correspondence: consonant /m/*m* (initial, final)

Help pupils find page 18 in their books. Point out that a picture is on each rocket, with a letter *m* in front of the picture and a letter *m* after the picture. The first *m* in each rocket stands for /m/ at the beginning of a word and the last *m* on the rocket stands for /m/ at the end of a word. Tell pupils to circle the first *m* if the /m/ sound is at the beginning of the picture name and to circle the last *m* if the /m/ sound is at the end of the picture name. Identify the pictures as broom, Mars, plum, mask, monkey, farm.

3 Developing the Skills

R Listening: rhyming words

Say the words *broom* and *zoom* and ask pupils what is the same about these words. (They both end with /m/; they rhyme.) Point out that *broom* and *zoom* are rhyming words because they sound alike at the end.

SAY | **Listen to two more rhyming words: *ham, slam.***

Explain that you will say a word that ends with the /m/ sound and then you will ask a volunteer to name a word that rhymes. Use the following words (possible answers shown in parentheses): *ram (ham), trim (slim), room (zoom), beam (seam), ham (slam), brim (him), sum (drum).*

✳ Practicing and Extending

The activities that follow provide practice and extension of skills developed in this lesson. Not every pupil needs to complete these activities. Choose only the activities that are needed to provide for the individual differences in your classroom.

Practicing Skills

DECODING/VOCABULARY

R, T   Sound/symbol correspondence: consonant /m/*m*

ADDITIONAL PRACTICE   Invite pupils to work in pairs or in small groups to discriminate the /m/ sound in the pictures in the Sound/Symbol folder for *m*. (See page T43.)

Extending Selection Concepts

SCIENCE

LISTENING: INFORMATION   Choose a book about space travel or astronauts and read it to the class. Discuss with pupils how real astronauts compare to the traveler in the story they composed.

Branley, Franklyn M. *Is There Life in Outer Space?* Thomas Y. Crowell, 1984. This simply-written account explains what investigations have shown about the moon and Mars, and what probably exists of life in other galaxies.

Friskey, Margaret. *Space Shuttles.* Childrens Press, 1982. Color photographs and simple text explain space shuttles.

UNIT 2 "Ants"
pages 19–26 (T72–T101)

Skill Strands

DECODING/VOCABULARY

I, T **Sound/symbol correspondence:** vowel /a/a (initial, medial)

R, T **Sound/symbol correspondence:** consonant /m/m, vowel /a/a (initial)

COMPREHENSION/THINKING

I **Critical thinking:** using prior knowledge

I, T **Literal:** cause and effect

LANGUAGE

R **Listening:** story comprehension

R **Speaking:** retelling stories

R **Speaking:** telling stories from pictures

Materials

Sundrops, Level 1: pages 19–26
Big Book: pages 19, 25–26
Practice Masters: pages 15–19
Resource Box: Letter Cards A, a
Word Builder and *Word Builder Cards a, m*
Pocket Chart
Teacher's Idea Book

Language Applications

EXTENDING SELECTION CONCEPTS

Listening: fiction
Listening: poetry
Writing: poetry
Listening: information

Special Populations

See *Teacher's Idea Book* for additional suggestions to help pupils with limited English proficiency.

Key to Symbols
I Introduced in this lesson
R Reinforced from an earlier lesson in this level
M Maintained from previous levels
T Tested in this level

Idea Center

ANT

For Activity 1, follow the directions in the *Teacher's Idea Book* to make an ant that can be used to play the game "The Ant Is Hiding."

THE SENTENCE GAME

For Activity 3, color and cut apart the picture cards in the *Teacher's Idea Book*. Place the pictures in a container decorated with the letter *a*.

BIBLIOGRAPHY

The book below is the literary selection that has been reprinted in Activity 1. You may wish to have this book on display for pupils to enjoy after you have read the story.

Quackenbush, Robert. *Henry's Awful Mistake*. Parents Magazine Press, 1980.

Add other books about ants to the reading corner or reading table. Encourage pupils to look at the books on their own. Suggestions for reading books aloud appear throughout this unit. Listed below is a bibliography to choose from. Annotations for the books appear in the activities.

Brandenberg, Franz. *No School Today!* Scholastic, 1978.

Brenner, Barbara, and Fred Brenner. *If You Were an Ant*. Harper & Row, 1973.

Cameron, Polly. *"I Can't," Said the Ant*. Coward-McCann, 1961.

Freschet, Berniece. *The Ants Go Marching*. Scribner's, 1973.

Guilfoile, Elizabeth. *Nobody Listens to Andrew*. Modern Curriculum Press, 1957.

Keller, Beverly. *The Bee Sneeze*. Coward-McCann, 1982.

Mizumura, Kazue. *The Way of an Ant*. Thomas Y. Crowell, 1970.

Moncure, Jane Belk. *Word Bird Makes Words with Cat: A Short Vowel Adventure*. Childrens Press, 1984.

Seuss, Dr. *The Cat in the Hat*. Random House, 1957.

ACTIVITY 1 Listening to "Henry's Awful Mistake" page 19 (T74–T77)

Skill Strands

COMPREHENSION/THINKING

I **Critical thinking:** using prior knowledge

LANGUAGE

R **Listening:** story comprehension
R **Speaking:** retelling stories

Materials

Sundrops, Level 1: page 19
Big Book: page 19
Ant from *Teacher's Idea Book*

Special Populations

See *Teacher's Idea Book* for additional suggestions to help pupils with limited English proficiency.

Key to Symbols
I Introduced in this lesson
R Reinforced from an earlier lesson in this level
M Maintained from previous levels
T Tested in this level

1 Preparing for the page

SUMMARY Henry is preparing dinner for his friend Clara when he discovers an ant in the kitchen. Henry's determination to rid his house of the ant causes problem after problem until at last there is a disaster. The next time Henry sees an ant, he looks away.

I **Critical thinking:** using prior knowledge

Ask pupils what they know about ants. Then explain that many insects can be pests, that is, they can bother people. Ask some ways that ants might be pests. (Ants can get in food; they can crawl on you; they can get in the house.) Ask how people might try to get rid of ants in their houses. (Use insect spray; try to catch them; try to hit them.) Tell pupils that in the story you are going to read, Henry the Duck tries to get rid of an ant in his house.

● **Listening:** story comprehension
● **Directions:** Look at the pictures as the teacher reads the story "Henry's Awful Mistake."
● **To the Parent:** Ask your child to tell the story of "Henry's Awful Mistake."

19

2 Using the page

R   Listening: story comprehension

Help pupils find page 19 in their books. Ask pupils to look at the pictures and to tell if this will be a real story or a make-believe story and why. (It is a make-believe story because the duck is wearing clothes and cooking on a stove.) Then ask if pupils think this will be a sad story or a funny story and why. (It is a funny story because the pictures are like cartoons.) Tell pupils that the title of this story is "Henry's Awful Mistake" and that Robert Quackenbush wrote the story and also drew the pictures. Ask pupils to listen to find out what Henry's awful mistake was. The words in boldface type are possible aside comments to be read or stated by you as if you were thinking aloud.

Henry's Awful Mistake
by Robert Quackenbush

SAY   **Look at the first picture as I begin the story.**

The day Henry the Duck asked his friend Clara over for supper, he found an ant in the kitchen.

Henry was worried that Clara would see the ant. She might think his house was not clean. The ant had to go.

Henry reached for a can of ant spray. But he didn't want to spray near the food he was cooking. So he chased the ant with a frying pan.

Henry ran around the kitchen, chasing after the ant. But the ant got away and hid behind the stove.

SAY Do you think Henry will be able to get the ant now? (Allow time for response.)

Henry took the food he was cooking off the stove. Then he shut off the flame and pulled the stove away from the wall. He saw the ant!

The ant saw Henry and ran into a small crack in the wall. Henry went and got a hammer.

SAY Henry *really* wants to get that ant!

Henry pounded a big hole in the wall where the crack was. But he couldn't find the ant. So he kept on pounding.

The hole got bigger and bigger. At last, Henry saw the ant sitting on a pipe inside the wall.

Henry aimed the hammer at the ant—and missed. The blow of the hammer broke the pipe.

SAY Uh-oh. Now what will happen? Look at the second picture.

Water came shooting out of the pipe. Henry couldn't stop it.

Henry grabbed a towel. He tied it around the pipe, and the water stopped shooting out.

But Henry hadn't stopped the water soon enough. It had sprayed all over the kitchen. Everything was soaking wet, except for Clara's supper, thank goodness.

Henry began mopping the puddles of water. All at once he slipped and banged against the kitchen table. Everything came crashing down. Henry was covered with pots and pans and food.

The supper was ruined. There was nothing Henry could do now but to call Clara and tell her not to come.

While Henry was talking on the telephone, the towel came loose from the pipe. The water came shooting out and flooded the whole house. Henry was carried right out the front door by the flood.

SAY Poor Henry! The ant ruined everything.

There was no going back. Poor Henry's house was washed away by the flood. He saved what he could and moved into a new house.

SAY Henry made a real mess chasing that ant!

When Henry was settled in his new house, he again asked Clara over for supper. Just as he went to the door to let Clara in, he saw an ant.

SAY Oh no! Not again! What do you think Henry will do? Let's find out.

He looked the other way!

ASK Why do you think he looked the other way? (because he didn't want to chase the ant) **Of all the things that Henry did, what was the really awful mistake?**

Pupils may suggest breaking the pipe or hammering a hole in the wall. Help them understand that Henry's biggest mistake was chasing the ant in the first place.

3 Developing the Skills

R Speaking: retelling stories

The questions that follow have been designed to help pupils reconstruct the story "Henry's Awful Mistake." Have pupils refer to the pictures on page 19 in their books or the *Big Book* as you ask the questions.

Picture 1: **Why was Henry so upset about an ant in the kitchen?** (Henry didn't want Clara to see the ant and think his house was not clean.)
In what ways did Henry try to catch the ant? (First he chased it behind the stove; then he hammered a hole in a wall; then he made a hole in a water pipe trying to hit the ant.)

Picture 2: **Why did Henry have to move to a new house?** (The flood from the water pipe washed his old house away.)
Did Henry chase the next ant he saw? (no)
Why? (He did not want to have all the trouble he had last time.)

✳ Practicing and Extending

The activities that follow provide practice and extension of skills developed in this lesson. Not every pupil needs to complete these activities. Choose only the activities that are needed to provide for the individual differences in your classroom.

Practicing Skills

M Concept vocabulary: position words

CHALLENGE ACTIVITY Use the ant from the *Teacher's Idea Book* to play "The Ant Is Hiding." Ask one pupil to hide his or her eyes, while a second pupil hides the ant somewhere in the classroom. The first pupil must then try to find the ant as other pupils give clues such as "Look under something big and brown," or "Look on top of something gray." All clues must be given in complete sentences. When the ant is found, the first pupil gets to hide it for a new player.

Extending Selection Concepts

> LITERATURE

LISTENING: FICTION Choose a book in which one of the characters is an ant. Discuss with pupils how the ant in this story is different from the one in "Henry's Awful Mistake."

Cameron, Polly. *"I Can't," Said the Ant.* Coward-McCann, 1961. A nonsense rhyme about how the ant and others in the kitchen replace the fallen teakettle.

ACTIVITY 2 Recognizing Cause and Effect

page 20 (T78–T80)

Skill Strands

COMPREHENSION/THINKING

I Literal: cause and effect

Materials

Sundrops, Level 1: page 20
Teacher's Idea Book

Special Populations

See *Teacher's Idea Book* for additional suggestions to help pupils with limited English proficiency.

Key to Symbols
I Introduced in this lesson
R Reinforced from an earlier lesson in this level
M Maintained from previous levels
T Tested in this level

1 Preparing for the page

I Literal: cause and effect

Remind pupils of the story "Henry's Awful Mistake" and ask why Henry made a hole in the pipe. (He was trying to hit the ant.)

SAY **Henry made the hole in the pipe** *because* **he wanted to hit the ant.**

Then ask why Henry moved to a new house. (His old house was flooded.)

SAY **Henry moved to a new house** *because* **his old house was flooded. Sometimes in a story one thing** *causes,* **or makes, another thing happen. The word** *because* **is often used to tell that one thing makes another happen. When you know what makes things happen, you can understand the story better.**

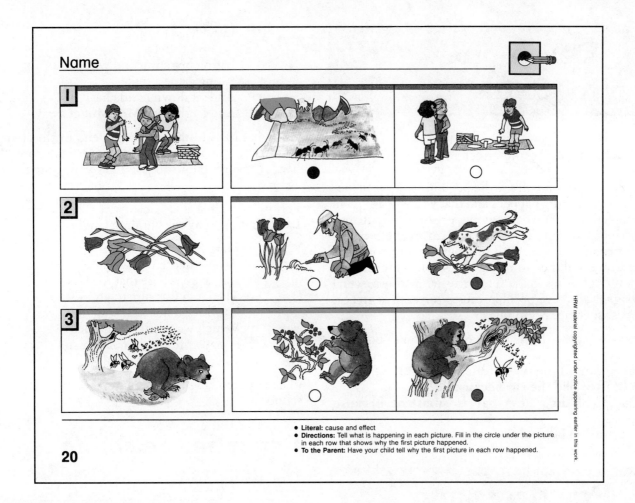

- **Literal:** cause and effect
- **Directions:** Tell what is happening in each picture. Fill in the circle under the picture in each row that shows why the first picture happened.
- **To the Parent:** Have your child tell why the first picture in each row happened.

20

2 Using the page

I Literal: cause and effect

Help pupils find page 20. Call attention to the first picture in the first row and ask what is happening in this picture. (The children are having a picnic; they are brushing something off their clothes.)

ASK **What does the second picture show?** (It shows ants crawling on a blanket.) **What does the third picture show?** (It shows children coming to a picnic.) **Which picture shows why the children in the first picture are brushing off their clothes?** (the middle picture) **Why?** (because the ants crawled all over them)

Tell pupils to darken the circle under the middle picture to show that this is why the children are brushing themselves off. Then have pupils look at the other rows of pictures and fill in the circle under the picture in each row that shows why the first picture happened.

Call on volunteers to look at each row of pictures again and to complete each of the following sentences:

1. **The children brushed themselves off because _____.** (the ants crawled on them)
2. **The flowers were trampled because _____.** (the big dog ran through the flower bed)
3. **The bees chased the bear because _____.** (the bear tried to take their honey)

3 Developing the Skills

I, T Literal: cause and effect

Tell pupils that you will say the beginning of a sentence in which something happens and that you will ask them to complete the sentence, giving a reason why it may have happened. For example, say **Kim broke her toy truck because** _____ . Call on volunteers to complete the sentence and then to repeat the whole sentence. Accept any logical response. You may wish to let several pupils give different possible causes for each sentence. Use these sentence beginnings:

1. **Steven can't find his new mittens because** _____ .
2. **Laura ran all the way home because** _____ .
3. **Mom stopped the car because** _____ .
4. **The elephant's new hat is smashed because** _____ .
5. **The ant ran behind the stove because** _____ .

* Practicing and Extending

The activities that follow provide practice and extension of skills developed in this lesson. Not every pupil needs to complete these activities. Choose only the activities that are needed to provide for the individual differences in your classroom.

Practicing Skills

I, T Literal: cause and effect

ADDITIONAL PRACTICE To review cause and effect, ask pupils to listen to the nursery rhyme "Little Miss Muffet."

> Little Miss Muffet
> Sat on a tuffet
> Eating her curds and whey.
> Along came a spider
> And sat down beside her
> And frightened Miss Muffet away.

Ask what Miss Muffet did at the end of the rhyme and why. (She ran away because a spider sat down beside her.) Then ask pupils to join in as you recite the rhyme again.

Follow the same procedure with "Mary Had a Little Lamb" asking why the children laughed and played.

> Mary had a little lamb
> Whose fleece was white as snow,
> And everywhere that Mary went
> The lamb was sure to go.
> It followed her to school one day
> Which was against the rule.
> It made the children laugh and play
> To see a lamb in school.

(The children laughed and played because a lamb was in school.)

Extending Selection Concepts

LITERATURE

LISTENING: FICTION Read aloud a book that has a clear cause and effect. Discuss with pupils what happened and why.

Brandenberg, Franz. *No School Today!* Scholastic, 1978. Arriving early for school and finding no one there, the kitten announces that there is no school today.

Keller, Beverly. *The Bee Sneeze.* Coward-McCann, 1982. Fiona rescues a bee from some lemonade, thus beginning a series of hilarious catastrophes.

ACTIVITY 3

Relating Initial /a/ to *a*

page 21 (T81–T83)

Skill Strands

DECODING/VOCABULARY

I, T   **Sound/symbol correspondence:** vowel /a/*a* (initial)

Materials

Sundrops, Level 1: page 21

Practice Masters: page 15

Resource Box: Letter Cards A, a

Word Builder Cards a

Pocket Chart

"The Sentence Game" (See page T73 for instructions.)

Special Populations

See *Teacher's Idea Book* for additional suggestions to help pupils with limited English proficiency.

Key to Symbols

I   Introduced in this lesson

R   Reinforced from an earlier lesson in this level

M   Maintained from previous levels

T   Tested in this level

1 Preparing for the page

I, T   **Sound/symbol correspondence:** vowel /a/*a* (initial)

Ask what Henry was chasing when he made his awful mistake. (an ant)

SAY   **Henry was chasing an ant. Listen as I say the word *ant*: *ant*. The sound at the beginning of the word *ant* is /a/. Say *ant* with me: *ant*.** (Place Letter Card *a* in the *Pocket Chart*.) **This is the letter *a*. Letter *a* stands for the /a/ sound in many words. When I touch the letter *a*, you make the /a/ sound. Keep making the sound as long as I am touching the letter. Stop making the sound when I lift my finger.**

Touch the letter several times, sometimes holding your finger on it for several seconds, sometimes lifting your finger very quickly.

SAY   **I'll say some other words that begin with the /a/ sound, and you say each word after me.**

Use the following words: *actor, alligator, accident.*

Make sure each pupil has *Word Builder Card a*. Ask pupils to name the letter. (*a*)

SAY   **I am going to say some words that begin with /a/ and some words that do not begin with /a/. Each time you hear a word that begins with the /a/ sound, hold up your letter *a*. When you hear a word that does not begin with /a/, do not hold up your card.**

Use the following words: *ambulance, clown, apple, answer, doctor, alligator, animal.*

Place *Letter Card A* in the *Pocket Chart* with letter *a*.

SAY   **The name of this letter is capital *A*. Capital *A* stands for the same sound as the small *a*. What sound does capital *A* stand for?** (/a/) **We use the capital letter *A* at the beginning of names, such as *Ann* or *Anthony*.**

Tell pupils to say the /a/ sound when you touch capital *A* or small *a*. Touch each letter several times.

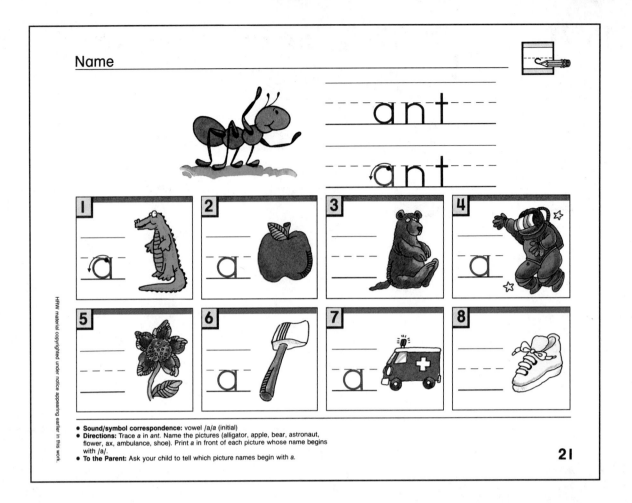

Name

ant

ant

1 a [alligator]	2 a [apple]	3 [bear]	4 a [astronaut] ☆
5 [flower]	6 a [ax]	7 a [ambulance]	8 [shoe]

- **Sound/symbol correspondence:** vowel /a/*a* (initial)
- **Directions:** Trace *a* in *ant*. Name the pictures (alligator, apple, bear, astronaut, flower, ax, ambulance, shoe). Print *a* in front of each picture whose name begins with /a/.
- **To the Parent:** Ask your child to tell which picture names begin with *a*.

21

2 Using the page

I, T Sound/symbol correspondence: vowel /a/*a* (initial)

Call attention to the picture of an ant at the top of page 21 and tell pupils that the word beside the picture is *ant*. Have pupils point to the first letter in the word *ant* and to name the letter. (*a*) Ask what sound this letter stands for. (/a/) Then have pupils look at the second word *ant* and trace the beginning letter.

Indicate the picture in the first box and ask pupils to name the picture. (alligator)

ASK Does *alligator* begin with the /a/ sound as in *ant*? (yes) Since *alligator* begins with the /a/ sound, trace an *a* on the writing line in front of the picture.

Tell pupils that they are to print *a* on the line in front of each picture whose name begins with /a/.

3 Developing the Skills

I, T Sound/symbol correspondence: vowel /a/*a* (initial)

Tell pupils they will play "The Sentence Game." (See page T73.)

Display the container and tell pupils that there are several pictures in the container. Each pupil will have a chance to choose two pictures from the container, to name the pictures, and to tell what letter stands for the sound at the beginning of each picture name. Then the pupil may call on another pupil to make up a sentence, using both picture words. For example, *The alligator ate an apple.* The pupil who makes up a sentence may then select two more pictures. Have the pictures returned to the container after each sentence.

✳ Practicing and Extending

The activities that follow provide practice and extension of skills developed in this lesson. Not every pupil needs to complete these activities. Choose only the activities that are needed to provide for the individual differences in your classroom.

Practicing Skills

I, T   Sound/symbol correspondence: vowel /a/*a* (initial)

PM 15   ADDITIONAL PRACTICE   *Practice Masters* page 15 may be used as an optional practice for identifying /a/.

Extending Selection Concepts

LITERATURE

LISTENING: FICTION   Read aloud a book about ants or a book with /a/ in its title. Discuss with pupils what caused a problem in the story.

Guilfoile, Elizabeth. *Nobody Listens to Andrew.* Modern Curriculum Press, 1957. Everyone is too busy to pay attention to Andrew until they discover he really has something to tell.

Mizumura, Kazue. *The Way of an Ant.* Thomas Y. Crowell, 1970. A young ant wants to climb as high as the sky, but no matter how high it climbs, there is always something higher.

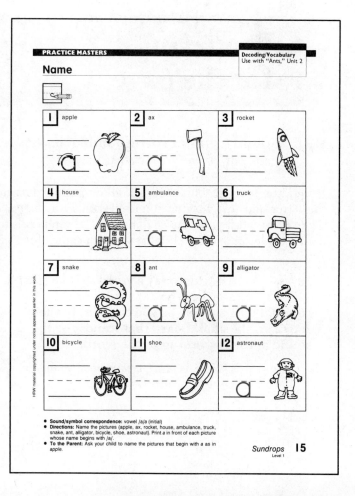

ACTIVITY 4 Discriminating Initial /a/ and /m/ page 22 (T84–T87)

Skill Strands

DECODING/VOCABULARY

R, T   Sound/symbol correspondence: consonant /m/*m*, vowel /a/*a* (initial)

LANGUAGE

R   Listening: poetry

Materials

Sundrops, Level 1: page 22
Practice Masters: page 16
Word Builder Cards a, *m*
Teacher's Idea Book

Special Populations

See *Teacher's Idea Book* for additional suggestions to help pupils with limited English proficiency.

Key to Symbols
I   Introduced in this lesson
R   Reinforced from an earlier lesson in this level
M   Maintained from previous levels
T   Tested in this level

1 Preparing for the page

R, T   Sound/symbol correspondence: consonant /m/*m*, vowel /a/*a* (initial)

Print letter *a* on the chalkboard. Call on pupils to name the letter and to tell what sound it stands for. (*a*, /a/) Then print letter *m* on the chalkboard. Call on pupils to name this letter and to tell what sound it stands for. (*m*, /m/)

SAY   I am going to say a word that begins with either the /a/ sound or the /m/ sound. I will ask one of you to point to the letter on the chalkboard that stands for the sound at the beginning of the word.

Use these words: *apple, monster, action, mud, mountain, ax.*

Make sure pupils have *Word Builder Cards a* and *m.*

SAY   I will say some more words that begin with /a/ or /m/. If you hear the /a/ sound at the beginning, hold up your *a* card. If you hear the /m/ sound at the beginning, hold up your *m* card.

Use these words: *alligator, antler, monkey, alphabet, apple, moose, mother, antelope, magazine, animal, milk, acrobat.*

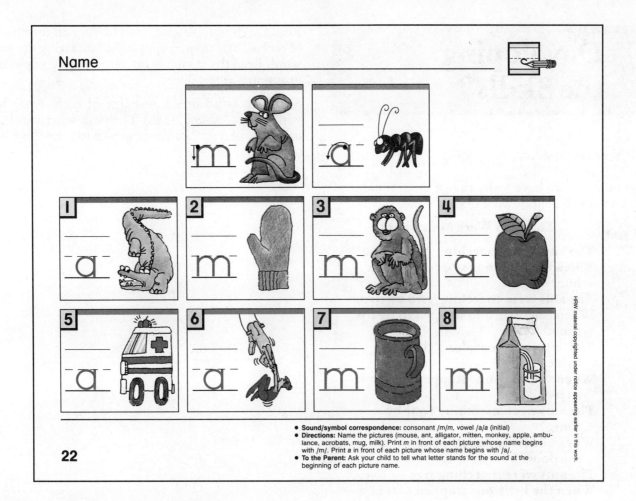

- **Sound/symbol correspondence:** consonant /m/m, vowel /a/a (initial)
- **Directions:** Name the pictures (mouse, ant, alligator, mitten, monkey, apple, ambulance, acrobats, mug, milk). Print *m* in front of each picture whose name begins with /m/. Print *a* in front of each picture whose name begins with /a/.
- **To the Parent:** Ask your child to tell what letter stands for the sound at the beginning of each picture name.

22

2 Using the page

R, T Sound/symbol correspondence: consonant /m/m, vowel /a/a (initial)

Help pupils find page 22 in their books. Call attention to the first sample box and have the picture identified. (mouse) Ask pupils to name the letter that stands for the beginning sound in *mouse*. (*m*) Tell pupils to trace the letter *m* on the line in front of the mouse.

Have the picture in the next sample box identified. (ant) Call on volunteers to name the letter that stands for the beginning sound in *ant*. (*a*) Tell pupils to trace the letter *a* on the line in front of the ant. Tell pupils to complete the page by printing letter *a* in front of each picture whose name begins with the /a/ sound and by printing letter *m* in front of each picture whose name begins with the /m/ sound. Help pupils identify the pictures as alligator, mitten, monkey, apple, ambulance, acrobats, mug, milk.

3 Developing the Skills

R   Listening: poetry

Tell pupils that you have a silly rhyme about some ants. Then read aloud the following rhyme:

READ   **The Ants Were Marching**

**The ants were marching one by one,
When the little one stopped to eat a
 bun.
The ants were marching two by two,
When the little one stopped to tie his
 shoe.
The ants were marching three by
 three,
When the little one stopped to climb
 a tree.
The ants were marching four by
 four,
When the little one stopped to shut
 the door.
The ants were marching five by five,
When the little one stopped to take a
 dive.**

Read the rhyme a second time, leaving off the final word of each stanza. Invite pupils to join in, saying the missing word. Read the rhyme again, encouraging pupils to join in as much as possible.

Ask what word in the first line of each stanza begins with the /a/ sound. (*ants*) Then ask what word in the first line of each stanza begins with the /m/ sound. (*marching*)

✳ Practicing and Extending

The activities that follow provide practice and extension of skills developed in this lesson. Not every pupil needs to complete these activities. Choose only the activities that are needed to provide for the individual differences in your classroom.

Practicing Skills

R, T   Sound/symbol correspondence: consonant /m/*m,* vowel /a/*a* (initial)

PM 16   **ADDITIONAL PRACTICE**   *Practice Masters* page 16 may be used as an optional practice for discriminating /a/ and /m/.

Extending Selection Concepts

LANGUAGE

WRITING: POETRY   Reread the rhyme "The Ants Were Marching." Then add the line "The ants were marching six by six," and invite pupils to complete the stanza. Print the pupils' suggestions on chart paper. Continue until you reach the number ten. You might print the entire poem on chart paper, adding the pupils' verses.

LISTENING: FICTION   Read *The Ants Go Marching* by Berniece Freschet. (Scribner's, 1973) Discuss with pupils how the ants in the story are like the ants in the rhyme.

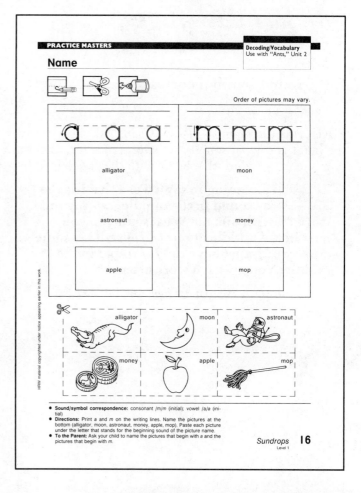

ACTIVITY 5 Relating Medial /a/ to *a*

Skill Strands

DECODING/VOCABULARY

I, T **Sound/symbol correspondence:** vowel /a/a (medial)

Materials

Sundrops, Level 1: page 23

Practice Masters: page 17
Resource Box: Letter Card a
Word Builder Card a
Pocket Chart
Teacher's Idea Book

Special Populations

See *Teacher's Idea Book* for additional suggestions to help pupils with limited English proficiency.

Key to Symbols
I Introduced in this lesson
R Reinforced from an earlier lesson in this level
M Maintained from previous levels
T Tested in this level

1 Preparing for the page

I, T **Sound/symbol correspondence:** vowel /a/a (medial)

Place *Letter Card a* in the *Pocket Chart.* Ask the name of the letter and what sound the letter stands for. Call on pupils to name words that begin with the /a/ sound.

> **SAY** I am going to say a word that has the /a/ sound in the middle: *cat.* Say the word *cat* with me: *cat.* What sound do you hear in the middle of *cat?* (/a/) I will say some other words that have the /a/ sound in the middle. You say each word after me.

Use the following words: *hat, fan, cap, ran, sad.*

Make sure each pupil has *Word Builder Card a.*

> **SAY** I am going to say some words that have /a/ in the middle and some words that do not have /a/ in the middle. When you hear a word that has /a/ in the middle, hold up your *a* card. Do not hold up a card if you do not hear /a/ in the middle of a word.

Use the following words: *bag, moon, man, bird, dad, can, fish, fat.*

Name

cat

cat

1	2	3	4
a		a	a

5	6	7	8
	a		a

- **Sound/symbol correspondence:** vowel /a/*a* (medial)
- **Directions:** Trace *a* in the middle of *cat*. Name the pictures (hat, bee, fan, bag, cup, can, dog, grass). Print *a* under each picture whose name has /a/ in the middle.
- **To the Parent:** Ask your child to tell which pictures have *a* in the middle of their names.

23

HRW material copyrighted under notice appearing earlier in this work.

2 Using the page

I, T   **Sound/symbol correspondence:** vowel /a/*a* (medial)

Help pupils find page 23 in their books. Call on a volunteer to name the picture at the top of the page. (cat) Tell pupils that the word beside the picture is *cat.* Have pupils find letter *a* in the word *cat* and tell where the letter *a* appears. (in the middle) Have pupils trace letter *a* in the second word *cat.* Then have pupils look at the picture in the first box.

SAY **What is this picture?** (a hat) **Do you hear /a/ in the middle of *hat*?** (yes) **Since you hear /a/ in the middle of *hat*, trace *a* on the line under the picture.**

Tell pupils to print *a* on the line under each picture that has /a/ in the middle of its name. Do not print *a* if the picture does not have /a/ in the middle of its name. Help pupils identify the pictures as bee, fan, bag, cup, can, dog, grass.

3 Developing the Skills

I, T   Sound/symbol correspondence: vowel /a/a (medial)

Tell pupils that you will play a game called "What Might You Call It?" Explain that you will ask a question and that they should try to guess the answer. Each answer must have two words that rhyme.

> **SAY**   **I'll do the first one so that you can see how to play. The first question is "What might you call a hat that has been smashed?" The answer is "a flat hat."**

Use the following questions:

1. **What might you call a chubby kitten?** (a fat cat)
2. **What might you call an unhappy father?** (a sad dad)
3. **What might you call a plant with ants on it?** (an ant plant)
4. **What might you call a hat for a cat?** (a cat hat)

After each answer is given, have pupils tell what sound is heard in the middle of the rhyming words. (/a/)

* Practicing and Extending

The activities that follow provide practice and extension of skills developed in this lesson. Not every pupil needs to complete these activities. Choose only the activities that are needed to provide for the individual differences in your classroom.

Practicing Skills

I, T   Sound/symbol correspondence: vowel /a/a (medial)

PM 17   **ADDITIONAL PRACTICE**   *Practice Masters* page 17 may be used as an optional practice for identifying medial /a/.

ADDITIONAL PRACTICE   Read the book *Word Bird Makes Words with Cat: A Short Vowel Adventure* by Jane Belk Moncure (Childrens Press, 1984) aloud to the class. Ask pupils to name words from the story that have the /a/ sound.

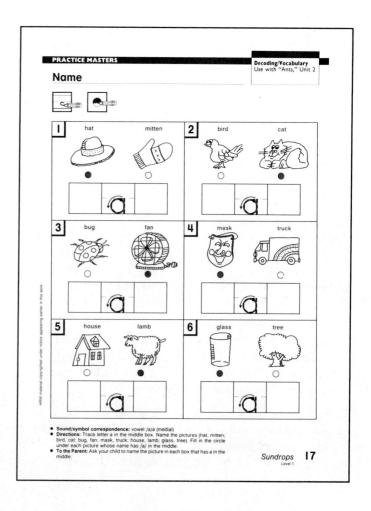

ACTIVITY 6 Discriminating Initial and Medial /a/ page 24 (T91–T93)

Skill Strands

DECODING/VOCABULARY

R, T Sound/symbol correspondence: vowel /a/*a* (initial, medial)

Materials

Sundrops, Level 1: page 24
Practice Masters: page 18
Word Builder and *Word Builder Card a*
Teacher's Idea Book

Special Populations

See *Teacher's Idea Book* for additional suggestions to help pupils with limited English proficiency.

Key to Symbols
I Introduced in this lesson
R Reinforced from an earlier lesson in this level
M Maintained from previous levels
T Tested in this level

1 Preparing for the page

R, T Sound/symbol correspondence: vowel /a/*a* (initial, medial)

Print letter *a* on the chalkboard and remind pupils that this letter stands for the /a/ sound. Ask pupils to name some words that begin with the /a/ sound. (Possible answers are *alligator, ant, accident.*) Then remind pupils that the /a/ sound can also be in the middle of words, as in *cat* and *man.* Ask pupils to name some words that have the /a/ sound in the middle.

Make sure each pupil has a *Word Builder* and *Word Builder Card a.* Hold up a *Word Builder* and indicate the left side.

SAY **We put a card here to show that a sound is heard at the beginning of a word.**

Then indicate the right side.

SAY **We put a card here to show that a sound is heard at the end of a word. If we want to show that a sound is heard in the middle of a word, we put the card here.** (Indicate the middle of the *Word Builder.*) **In the word *ant*, the /a/ sound is in the beginning, so I will put my *a* card at the beginning of the *Word Builder.*** (Demonstrate.) **In the word *cat*, the /a/ sound is in the middle, so I will put my *a* card in the middle of the *Word Builder.*** (Demonstrate.) **I will say some words that have /a/ at the beginning and some words that have /a/ in the middle. Put your *a* card in the beginning or in the middle of your *Word Builder* to show where you hear the /a/ sound.**

Use the following words: *apple, mat, sack, antler, fat, stamp, snap, action.*

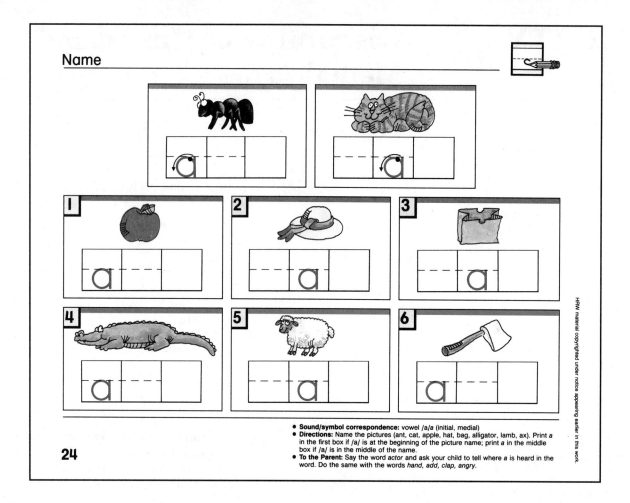

Name

1 2 3

4 5 6

24

- **Sound/symbol correspondence:** vowel /a/a (initial, medial)
- **Directions:** Name the pictures (ant, cat, apple, hat, bag, alligator, lamb, ax). Print *a* in the first box if /a/ is at the beginning of the picture name; print *a* in the middle box if /a/ is in the middle of the name.
- **To the Parent:** Say the word *actor* and ask your child to tell where *a* is heard in the word. Do the same with the words *hand, add, clap, angry.*

2 Using the page

R, T **Sound/symbol correspondence:** vowel /a/*a* (initial, medial)

Help pupils find page 24 and ask them to identify the first picture. (ant)

> **SAY** **Is the /a/ sound at the beginning or in the middle of the word *ant*?** (at the beginning) **Trace letter *a* in the first box under the picture to show that the /a/ sound is at the beginning of *ant*.**

Continue in the same manner with the next picture. (cat) Explain that pupils are to trace *a* in the middle box under the picture to show that the /a/ sound is in the middle of *cat*. Identify the remaining pictures as apple, hat, bag, alligator, lamb and ax.

3 Developing the Skills

R, T **Sound/symbol correspondence:** vowel /a/*a* (initial, medial)

Tell pupils that you are going to read some sentences. Explain that each sentence will have some /a/ words in it.

> **SAY** **First, I'll read the sentence. Then we will say the sentence together. After that, I will call on one of you to name the /a/ words from the sentence.**

1. **Ann has two hats.**
2. **Pam's fan is tan.**
3. **An alligator ran after me.**
4. **That cat is fat.**
5. **The mat has ants on it.**
6. **Anthony has my toy ambulance.**

✳ Practicing and Extending

The activities that follow provide practice and extension of skills developed in this lesson. Not every pupil needs to complete these activities. Choose only the activities that are needed to provide for the individual differences in your classroom.

Practicing Skills

I, T **Sound/symbol correspondence:** vowel /a/*a* (initial, medial)

PM 18 **ADDITIONAL PRACTICE** *Practice Masters* page 18 may be used as an optional practice for identifying sound/symbol correspondence /a/*a*.

CHALLENGE ACTIVITY Reread each of the sentences from "Developing the Skills" and ask where the /a/ sound is heard in each /a/ word.

Extending Selection Concepts

LITERATURE

LISTENING: POETRY Read aloud "The Pancake" by Christina Rossetti. Then encourage pupils to recite it with you. Pupils may make up actions to go along with the words. Ask pupils to name the /a/ words in the poem.

The Pancake
Mix a pancake,
Stir a pancake,
    Pop it in the pan;
Fry the pancake,
Toss the pancake—
    Catch it if you can!
Christina Rossetti

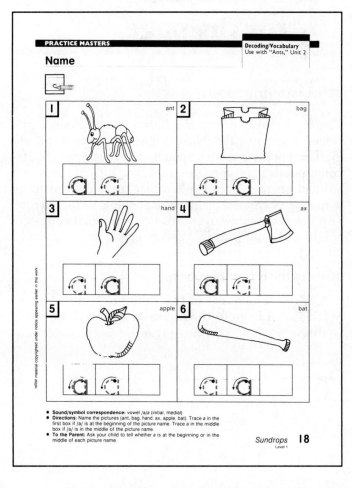

ACTIVITY 7 Listening to the Poem "Ant"

page 25 (T94–T97)

Skill Strands

COMPREHENSION/THINKING

R, T   **Literal:** cause and effect

LANGUAGE

R   **Listening:** poetry

Materials

Sundrops, Level 1: page 25
Big Book: page 25
Teacher's Idea Book

Special Populations

See *Teacher's Idea Book* for additional suggestions to help pupils with limited English proficiency.

Key to Symbols
I   Introduced in this lesson
R   Reinforced from an earlier lesson in this level
M   Maintained from previous levels
T   Tested in this level

---

1 Preparing for the page

R   **Listening:** poetry

Display page 25 of the *Big Book* and tell pupils that a poem is on this page. Have volunteers come to the *Big Book* and point first to the poem, then to the picture. Remind pupils that when you read, you look at the words printed on the page. Explain that the picture is to go with the poem. Ask what is happening in the picture. (An ant is crawling over a turtle.) Ask what the poem might be about. (Possible answers include: an ant and a turtle.)

Point to the title of the poem.

| SAY | **The name of this poem is "Ant."** **Listen to the poem to see what the ant** |

does.

Ant (To be read by the teacher)

Ant
sighs
and climbs
over the rock in her path
tickling
turtle.

Joanne Ryder

• **Listening:** poetry
• **Directions:** Listen as the teacher reads the poem.
• **To the Parent:** Read and discuss the poem with your child.

25

2 Using the page

R Listening: poetry

Help pupils find page 25 in their books.

Move your hand under each line of the poem as you read it aloud. Ask if the ant was really crawling over a rock. (No, the rock was a turtle.) Ask why the ant might think the turtle was a rock. (Possible answers include: The turtle is all closed up; the shape of the turtle's shell looks like a rock.) Ask how the ant tickled the turtle. (The ant tickled the turtle's shell when it crawled over it.)

Read the poem a second time.

| SAY | **This is a sigh.** (Demonstrate.) **Why might the ant sigh as it crawls over a rock?** (Possible answers include: The rock seemed so big that crawling over it would be a big job, but the ant would have to climb over it anyway.) |

Invite pupils to say the words with you as you read the poem again.

3 Developing the Skills

R, T Literal: cause and effect

Ask pupils to tell if they think the ant would discover that the rock was really a turtle. (Answers will vary.) Ask what might cause the ant to find out that it had crawled over a turtle. (Possible answers include: The turtle might stick its head out to see what was tickling it; the turtle might move.) Remind pupils that sometimes one thing causes another thing to happen.

Tell pupils you will read a story about some ants and then ask what caused some things to happen in the story.

READ **The little ant explored the ground under the picnic table. It found lots of delicious crumbs. It carried one crumb back to the nest because it wanted to show the other ants what it had found. The other ants were excited when the little ant told them about all the crumbs it had found. The other ants followed the little ant back to the picnic table because they wanted to get more crumbs to take back to the nest.**

Ask why the little ant carried a crumb back to the nest. (because it wanted to show the other ants) Then ask why the ants in the nest were excited. (because the little ant told them about all the crumbs it had found) Ask why the ants followed the little ant to the picnic table. (because they wanted to take more crumbs back to the nest)

SAY **You could tell why everything in the story happened. When you read, it is important to know why things happen. This will help you understand the stories you read.**

HOW AM I DOING?

Pupils need time to express their opinions and to listen to others. Ask yourself the following questions to gauge your teaching effectiveness in this area.

	Yes	No	Some-times
1. Have I encouraged pupils to respect each other's opinions?	☐	☐	☐
2. Have I provided enough time for pupils to share ideas?	☐	☐	☐
3. Have I given pupils opportunity to express their opinions?	☐	☐	☐
4. Have I provided feedback about pupils' ideas?	☐	☐	☐
5. Have I presented activities in which pupils can express their opinions?	☐	☐	☐

✳ Practicing and Extending

The activities that follow provide practice and extension of skills developed in this lesson. Not every pupil needs to complete these activities. Choose only the activities that are needed to provide for the individual differences in your classroom.

Practicing Skills

R, T Sound/symbol correspondence: consonant /m/*m;* vowel /a/*a* (initial)

ADDITIONAL PRACTICE Print letters *a* and *m* on the chalkboard or display the *Letter Cards.* Explain that you will say a word and that you will ask a pupil to repeat the word and to point to the letter that stands for the beginning sound in the word. Use the following words: *apple, mustard, alligator, ambulance, magazine, animal, midnight, margarine, accident, marshmallow.*

Extending Selection Concepts

LITERATURE

LISTENING: POETRY Ask if pupils have ever watched ants or other insects crawling on the ground. Explain that you will read a poem about a child who is watching insects on the ground. Read aloud the poem "Hey Bug!"

Hey Bug!

Hey, bug, stay!
Don't run away.
I know a game that we can play.

I'll hold my fingers very still
and you can climb a finger-hill.

No, no.
Don't go.

Here's a wall—a tower, too,
a tiny bug town, just for you.
I've a cookie. You have some.
Take this oatmeal cookie crumb.

Hey, bug, stay!
Hey, bug!
Hey!

Lilian Moore

Reread the poem and ask what the child wanted the bug to do. (The child wanted the bug to stay and play.) Ask what the child offered the bug. (a cookie crumb) Ask what the child wanted to make for the bug. (a hill, a wall, a tower, a bug town)

ACTIVITY 8

Reviewing /a/ a
page 26 (T98–T101)

Skill Strands

DECODING/VOCABULARY

R, T   **Sound/symbol correspondence:** vowel /a/ a (initial, medial)

LANGUAGE

R   **Speaking:** telling stories from pictures

Materials

Sundrops, Level 1: page 26
Big Book: page 26
Practice Masters: page 19
Teacher's Idea Book

Special Populations

See *Teacher's Idea Book* for additional suggestions to help pupils with limited English proficiency.

Key to Symbols
I   Introduced in this lesson
R   Reinforced from an earlier lesson in this level
M   Maintained from previous levels
T   Tested in this level

1 Preparing for the page

R, T   **Sound/symbol correspondence:** vowel /a/ a (initial, medial)

Print letter *a* on the chalkboard and ask the sound this letter stands for. (/a/) Ask what Henry the Duck chased that had /a/ at the beginning of its name. (an ant)

SAY   **Let's look at a picture of some ants.** (Display page 26 of the *Big Book* and help pupils find page 26 in their books.) **The ants on this page are traveling all over. Name some of the places the ants are going.** (The ants use a map to go from the anthill, across the alligator, by a cat's paw, over a cap, to an apple.)

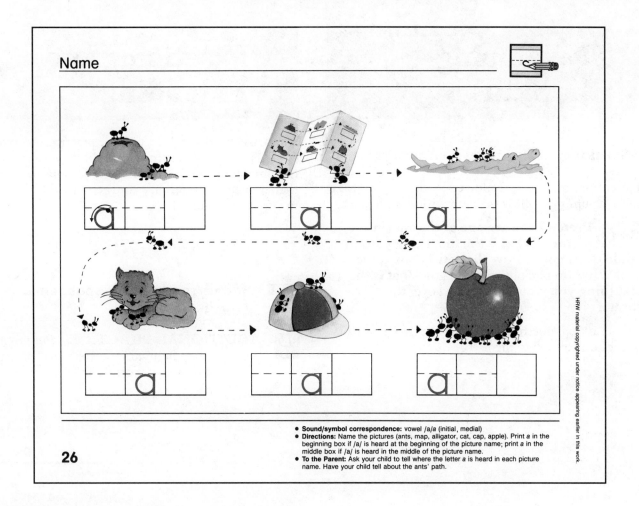

Name _____

- **Sound/symbol correspondence:** vowel /a/*a* (initial, medial)
- **Directions:** Name the pictures (ants, map, alligator, cat, cap, apple). Print *a* in the beginning box if /a/ is heard at the beginning of the picture name; print *a* in the middle box if /a/ is heard in the middle of the picture name.
- **To the Parent:** Ask your child to tell where the letter *a* is heard in each picture name. Have your child tell about the ants' path.

26

2 Using the page

Help pupils identify the pictures on page 26 that have boxes by them. (ants, map, alligator, cat, cap, apple) Tell pupils to print *a* at the beginning of the box if they hear /a/ at the beginning of the picture name and to print *a* in the middle of the box of they hear /a/ in the middle of the picture name.

R, T Sound/symbol correspondence: vowel /a/*a* (initial, medial)

Call attention to the boxes that appear under the objects on page 26. Draw a similar box on the chalkboard.

SAY The word *ant* begins with the /a/ sound. I will print an *a* in the beginning of this box to show that the /a/ sound is at the beginning of the word *ant.* (Demonstrate.) **Where is the /a/ sound in the word *cat*?** (in the middle) **I will print an *a* in the middle of this box to show that there is an /a/ sound in the middle of *cat.*** (Erase the first *a* and print new *a* in the middle box.)

3 Developing the Skills

R   **Speaking:** telling stories from pictures

Call attention to the path followed by the ants on page 26 and ask pupils to follow the path with their fingers.

SAY **Pretend you are one of the ants in the picture. What is the first thing you would do as you follow the path?** (look at the map) **Why?** (to find out where to go) **What is the next thing you would do?** (crawl over the alligator)

Continue asking questions to help pupils tell a story about the ants following the path.

✳ Practicing and Extending

The activities that follow provide practice and extension of skills developed in this lesson. Not every pupil needs to complete these activities. Choose only the activities that are needed to provide for the individual differences in your classroom.

Practicing Skills

R, T   **Sound/symbol correspondence:** vowel /a/a (initial, medial)

PM 19   **ADDITIONAL PRACTICE**   *Practice Masters* page 19 may be used as an optional practice for identifying sound/symbol correspondence /a/a.

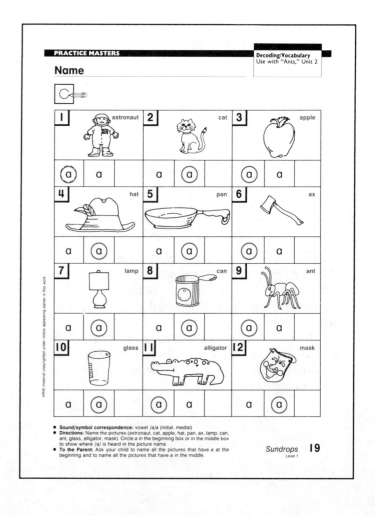

Extending Selection Concepts

LITERATURE

LISTENING: FICTION   Read *The Cat in the Hat* by Dr. Seuss (Random House, 1957) or another book with /a/ words and ask pupils to listen for the /a/ words.

SCIENCE

LISTENING: INFORMATION   Read a factual book about ants. Discuss with pupils how real ants behave.

Brenner, Barbara, and Fred Brenner. *If You Were an Ant.* Harper & Row, 1973. The factual information in this book is presented in the form "If you were an ant, you would . . ."

UNIT 3 "The Sun"
pages 27–36 (T102–T136)

Skill Strands

DECODING/VOCABULARY

I, T   **Sound/symbol correspondence:** consonant /s/*s* (initial, final)

R, T   **Sound/symbol correspondence:** consonants /s/*s*, /m/*m;* vowel /a/*a* (initial)

I   **Vocabulary:** word building

I, T   **Vocabulary:** word meaning

I   **Vocabulary:** words in context

STUDY SKILLS

I   **Graphic aids:** illustrations

COMPREHENSION/THINKING

I   **Critical thinking:** using prior knowledge

I, T   **Inferential:** main idea

LANGUAGE

I   **Listening:** specific information

R   **Speaking:** telling stories from pictures

I   **Conventions of language:** end punctuation (period)

R   **Writing:** language–experience stories

Materials

Sundrops, Level 1: pages 27–36
Big Book: page 35
Practice Masters: pages 20–26
Resource Box: Picture Cards baseball, breakfast, clothes
        Letter Cards a, m, S, s
        Word Cards am, I, Sam
        Punctuation Card period
Word Builder and *Word Builder Cards* a, m, S, s
Pocket Chart
Teacher's Idea Book

Language Applications

EXTENDING SELECTION CONCEPTS

Listening: poetry
Listening: fiction
Listening: tongue twisters
Speaking: telling about observations
Listening: information
Singing: songs

Special Populations

See *Teacher's Idea Book* for additional suggestions to help pupils with limited English proficiency.

Key to Symbols
I   Introduced in this lesson
R   Reinforced from an earlier lesson in this level
M   Maintained from previous levels
T   Tested in this level

Idea Center

SOUND/SYMBOL FOLDER

For activity 10, make a Sound/Symbol Folder for letter *s*. See page T43 for directions.

BIBLIOGRAPHY

The book below is the literary selection that has been slightly abridged for use in Activity 1. You may wish to have this book on display for pupils to enjoy after you have read the story.

Gibbons, Gail. *Sun Up, Sun Down.* Harcourt Brace Jovanovich, 1983.

Add other books about the sun or books that have /s/ in the title to the reading corner or reading table. Encourage pupils to look at the books on their own. Suggestions for reading books aloud appear throughout this lesson. Listed below is a bibliography to choose from. Annotations for the books appear in the activities.

Cartwright, Sally. *Sunlight.* Coward, McCann & Geoghegan, 1974.

Fujikawa, Gyo. *Sam's All Wrong Day.* Putnam Publishing Group, 1982.

Ginsburg, Mirra. *The Sun's Asleep Behind the Hill.* Greenwillow Books, 1982.

Greene, Carol. *Shine, Sun!* Childrens Press, 1983.

Hart, Jane. *Singing Bee.* Lothrop Lee Shepard Books, 1982.

Lobel, Arnold. *Frog and Toad Together.* Harper & Row, 1972.

Marshall, James. *George and Martha Tons of Fun.* Houghton Mifflin, 1980.

Palazzo, Janet. *Our Friend the Sun.* Troll Associates, 1982.

Petty, Kate. *The Sun.* Franklin Watts, 1985.

Potter, Charles Francis. *Tongue Tanglers.* World Publishing, 1962.

Schwartz, Alvin. *A Twister of Twists, a Tangler of Tongues.* Lippincott, 1972.

Scott, Ann Herbert. *Sam.* McGraw-Hill, 1967.

ACTIVITY 1 Listening to "Sun Up, Sun Down" page 27 (T104–T107)

Skill Strands

COMPREHENSION/THINKING

I **Critical thinking:** using prior knowledge

LANGUAGE

I **Listening:** specific information

STUDY SKILLS

I **Graphic aids:** illustrations

Materials

Sundrops, Level 1: page 27
Teacher's Idea Book

Special Populations

See *Teacher's Idea Book* for additional suggestions to help pupils with limited English proficiency.

Key to Symbols
I Introduced in this lesson
R Reinforced from an earlier lesson in this level
M Maintained from previous levels
T Tested in this level

1 Preparing for the page

SUMMARY A young girl shares what she has learned about the sun from her own observations and from information her parents have given her.

I **Critical thinking:** using prior knowledge

Ask pupils to tell what they know about the sun. Guide the discussion by encouraging pupils to tell where we see the sun in the sky in the morning and in the evening. Ask pupils if they feel warm or cold in the sun.

Print the title "Sun Up, Sun Down" on the chalkboard and read it. Tell pupils that this is the title of a story that you are going to read. Explain that this is a true story. Tell pupils that the author wrote this story to teach us about the sun. Ask when the sun comes up (in the morning) and when the sun goes down. (at night) Explain that in this story a young girl tells us what she finds out about the sun.

ASK **What questions would you ask if you wanted to know about the sun?**

Encourage pupils to ask questions. (Possible questions are: How big is the sun? How far away is the sun? What is the sun made of?)

You may want to list pupils' questions on the chalkboard to discuss after reading the story.

- **Listening:** information
- **Directions:** Look at the pictures as the teacher reads the story "Sun Up, Sun Down."
- **To the Parent:** Ask your child to tell what he or she learned about the sun.

27

2 Using the page

I Listening: specific information

Help pupils find page 27 in their books and explain that the pictures on this page are from the story "Sun Up, Sun Down." Pupils can look at the pictures as you read. Ask pupils to listen to find out what the sun does. The words in boldface type are possible aside comments to be read or stated by you, as if you were thinking aloud.

Sun Up, Sun Down
by Gail Gibbons

Point out the girl in the second picture and explain that she is telling the story.

> **SAY** **Look at the first picture while I read the first part of the girl's story.**

The sun wakes me up. It rises in the east and shines through my window. It lights up my room and makes patterns on my floor.

Its brightness colors the clouds and the sky, but the sun itself is too bright to look at. It could hurt my eyes.

> **SAY** **Yes, you should never look straight at the sun because it is bad for your eyes.**

I go down to breakfast. My cereal is made of wheat. My dad tells me the sun made the wheat grow. He says the sun gives power and energy to make plants and trees grow big and tall.

> **SAY** **Now I know one way the sun helps us, don't you? How does the sun help?**
(It makes plants grow.) **Look at the second picture.**

It is summer. Because it is hot, I don't need to wear a coat or sweater today. The sun is high in the sky, and the days are long.

When the sun is low in the sky, the days are shorter. It is winter, and it is cold. That is when I need my coat, hat, and mittens. But on a summer morning like this, I see my shadow on the ground. The sun is behind me in the east. When I move, my shadow moves, too. It points west. By noontime, the sun is shining right above me. My shadow is gone. It is a hot time of day, and I am glad when my mother calls me inside for lunch.

| SAY | **See the shadows in this picture. Point to the girl's shadow. Then point to the cat's shadow. Let's look at the third picture.** |

While I'm eating, I ask my parents a question. "How far away is the sun?"

My mother tells me it is very far away . . . 93 million miles from our planet, earth.

She says it is a very big star. It looks bigger than the other stars because it is closer to us.

My dad says the sun is a ball of very hot, glowing gases. It keeps our planet warm. He says our earth would be dark and very cold if there were no sun. It would also be empty. Nothing could live on it.

| SAY | **What did her mom tell her?** (The sun is very far away; it is a star.) **How did her dad say the sun helps us?** (It keeps us warm.) **Look at the fourth picture.** |

After lunch I go outside. My shadow is back again, but now it points east. The sun is moving west behind me.

| SAY | **See how the shadows have moved. The picture shows how the sun has moved, too. Look at the fifth picture.** |

Suddenly, big clouds begin to cover the sun. My shadow is gone again. Over in the valley, the sun peeks through the clouds, making shadows on the ground. More clouds come. They are gray and black. It becomes dark. A raindrop hits my nose, and I run home.

I hear the rain on the roof of my house. My dad says the sun helps make rain. He tells me that when the sun shines on water, some of the water goes into the air and makes clouds. Later, rain falls from the clouds so that we can have fresh water to drink and so that plants and trees can grow.

Soon, the storm clouds begin to drift away. Although it is still sprinkling, the sun appears once again and shines through the raindrops. I see a beautiful rainbow. My mom says the light of the sun shining through the raindrops makes the rainbow. She tells me the sunlight looks white, but it really isn't. It is made up of many colors. When sunbeams shine through the raindrops, what we see is a rainbow.

| SAY | **Now what do we know about the sun?** (The sun makes rainbows.) **Look at the last picture.** |

When I go outside, my shadow is long and skinny. The sun is setting in the western sky. It is getting cool outside. The sun is leaving for today, and the sky is getting dark.

My dad tells me the sun will shine on the other side of our planet while I'm asleep. He says the earth spins round and round and makes a complete turn once every twenty-four hours. When our part of the earth faces the sun, it is day. When it is turned away from the sun, it is night.

It is night now. The sun is down. The sky is dark. It is time to sleep.

| SAY | **This story told us many things that the sun does. Who can tell some things the sun does?** (The sun makes plants grow; the sun keeps us warm; the sun makes rainbows; the sun makes day and night.) |

3 Developing the Skills

I Graphic aids: illustrations

Ask pupils to look at the pictures on page 27 and explain that sometimes we call the pictures in a book illustrations.

SAY **The illustrations in a book can help us understand the story. Some books tell us stories. Some books are written to teach us something. In books that teach, the illustrations help us to understand. Let's look at the illustrations from "Sun Up, Sun Down" to see what they teach us.**

Direct pupils' attention to the pictures as you ask the questions that follow.

ASK **What does the first picture show us about the sun?** (The sun makes plants grow.) **Which two pictures show shadows?** (the second and the third) **How are the shadows different in each picture?** (They go in different directions.) **How is the sun different in these pictures?** (It is in different places in the sky.) **What does this tell us about the sun?** (The sun seems to move across the sky.) **What can you tell about the sun from the last picture?** (The sun makes rainbows.)

Encourage pupils to tell something they learned about the sun that they did not know before they heard the story.

✳ Practicing and Extending

The activities that follow provide practice and extension of skills developed in this lesson. Not every pupil needs to complete these activities. Choose only the activities that are needed to provide for the individual differences in your classroom.

Practicing Skills

I Graphic aids: illustrations

ADDITIONAL PRACTICE: Ask pupils to draw a picture to illustrate something about the sun; for example, that the sun helps plants grow or that the sun keeps us warm. Invite volunteers to show their pictures and to explain what they have illustrated.

Extending Selection Concepts

SCIENCE

SPEAKING: TELLING ABOUT OBSERVATIONS To demonstrate how the sun moves in the sky, take pupils outdoors in the morning on a sunny day and have them stand in a specific area. Tell pupils to stand so that they are facing their shadows and to look at a specific object, such as the building or a piece of playground equipment. Before pupils go home, take them to the same place and have them once again stand facing their shadows. Ask why the same object is no longer in front of them.

LITERATURE

LISTENING: POETRY Read "The Sun" and ask pupils to listen to find out how the poet felt on a sunny day.

The Sun

I told the sun that I was glad
 I'm sure I don't know why;
Somehow the pleasant way he had
 Of shining in the sky,
Just put a notion in my head
 That wouldn't it be fun
If walking on a hill, I said
 "I'm happy" to the sun.

John Drinkwater

ACTIVITY 2 Recognizing Main Idea
page 28 (T108–T110)

Skill Strands

| COMPREHENSION/THINKING |

I, T **Inferential:** main idea

Materials

Sundrops, Level 1: page 28
Picture Cards: baseball, breakfast, clothes
Pocket Chart
Teacher's Idea Book

Special Populations

See *Teacher's Idea Book* for additional suggestions to help pupils with limited English proficiency.

Key to Symbols
I Introduced in this lesson
R Reinforced from an earlier lesson in this level
M Maintained from previous levels
T Tested in this level

---

1 Preparing for the page

I, T **Inferential:** main idea

ASK **What was the story "Sun Up, Sun Down" about?** (the sun) **The title of a story often tells us what the story is about. What could you tell about this story from the title?** (The story was about the sun.)

I will show you some pictures. Look at each picture and tell me what the picture is about. (Show *Picture Card breakfast*.) **What is this picture about?** (breakfast or things you eat for breakfast) **Yes, this picture is about breakfast.**

Show *Picture Card baseball* and ask what this picture is about. (It is about baseball or things used to play baseball.)

Show *Picture Card clothes* and ask what this picture is about. (It is about clothes or things you wear.)

SAY **I will tell you a story. After I finish telling the story, I will ask you to tell me which picture the story is about. Then tell me a title for the story.**

Place *Picture Cards clothes, baseball,* and *breakfast* in the *Pocket Chart.*

READ **It is the perfect day for a game. The sun is shining, and the birds are chirping outside my bedroom window. Today is Saturday, and my friends and I are going to the park to play with our bats and balls.**

Ask which picture goes with the story and why. (*baseball, because the story is about playing ball*)

Then ask volunteers to give a title for the story. (Possible answers are: "Playing Baseball," "A Day for Baseball.")

Continue in the same manner with the following story:

READ **It is morning, and I smell something delicious. I follow my nose into the kitchen, and there is Dad with a big platter of pancakes, hot off the griddle. I sit down to a big plate of pancakes.**

ASK **Which picture goes with this story?** (breakfast) **Why?** (because the story is about Dad fixing breakfast) **What might be a title for this story?** (Possible answers are: "A Pancake Breakfast," "Breakfast with Dad.")

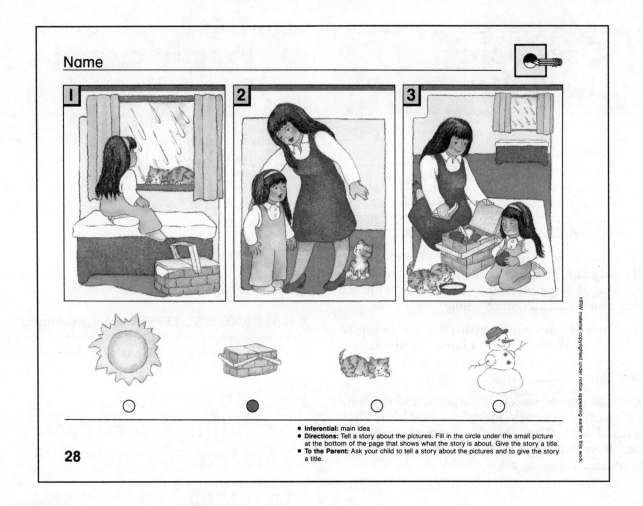

Name _____

28

- **Inferential:** main idea
- **Directions:** Tell a story about the pictures. Fill in the circle under the small picture at the bottom of the page that shows what the story is about. Give the story a title.
- **To the Parent:** Ask your child to tell a story about the pictures and to give the story a title.

2 Using the page

I, T   Inferential: main idea

Help pupils find page 28 in their books and call attention to the three large pictures on the page.

SAY **These pictures tell a story. Look at the first picture. What is happening?** (A sad girl is looking out a window at the rain.) **Why do you suppose the girl is sad?** (She wants to go on a picnic, but it is raining.) **Now look at the second picture. What is happening in this picture?** (The girl's mother is talking to her; the girl looks happier.) **Now look at the last picture. Tell me what is happening in this picture.** (The girl and her mother are having a picnic in their living room.)

Ask pupils to think about the story that they just read in pictures.

SAY **Now look at the four little pictures at the bottom of the page.**

Have the pictures identified as the sun, a picnic basket, a kitten, and a snow figure. Tell pupils to fill in the circle under the little picture that shows what the story was about. (the picnic basket) Call on volunteers to give a title for the story. (Possible answers are: "A Rainy-Day Picnic," "A Picnic at Home.")

3 Developing the Skills

I, T **Inferential:** main idea

Tell pupils that you will tell some stories. They should listen to each story and then you will say "This is a story about _____." Have pupils complete the sentence by telling what they think the story is about.

1. **Mom and I are going fishing. We have our bait all ready and we are getting up very early in the morning. I hope we catch lots of fish. This is a story about _____.** (going fishing)

2. **Grandma is coming to visit. We are going to pick her up at the airport. I hope the airplane is on time. I can't wait to see Grandma. This is a story about _____.** (Grandma's visit)

3. **I got a bucket of water, some soap, and the hose to give my dog a bath. First, I washed him. Then I rinsed him. Then he shook off the water. I guess it was his turn to get me wet! This is a story about _____.** (giving a dog a bath)

✳ Practicing and Extending

The activities that follow provide practice and extension of skills developed in this lesson. Not every pupil needs to complete these activities. Choose only the activities that are needed to provide for the individual differences in your classroom.

Practicing Skills

I, T **Inferential:** main idea

CHALLENGE ACTIVITY Ask a volunteer to tell a story about a time when he or she went to the zoo, got an exciting present, or played in the sun. When each story is finished, ask other pupils to think of titles for the stories.

Extending Selection Concepts

> LITERATURE

LISTENING: FICTION Choose a book with short stories or titled episodes. Read each episode aloud. Have pupils suggest titles for each episode. Then read the title the author gave it.

Lobel, Arnold. *Frog and Toad Together.* Harper & Row, 1972. Frog and Toad share five short, but sometimes daring, adventures.

Marshall, James. *George and Martha Tons of Fun.* Houghton Mifflin, 1980. Pupils will have tons of fun hearing about these two hippopotamuses and their friendship.

ACTIVITY 3 Relating Initial /s/ to s

page 29 (T111–T113)

Skill Strands

DECODING/VOCABULARY

I, T **Sound/symbol correspondence:** consonant /s/s (initial)

Materials

Sundrops, Level 1: page 29
Practice Masters: page 20
Resource Box: Letter Cards S, s
Word Builder Card s
Pocket Chart
Teacher's Idea Book

Special Populations

See *Teacher's Idea Book* for additional suggestions to help pupils with limited English proficiency.

Key to Symbols
I Introduced in this lesson
R Reinforced from an earlier lesson in this level
M Maintained from previous levels
T Tested in this level

1 Preparing for the page

I, T **Sound/symbol correspondence:** consonant /s/s (initial)

Note: In pronouncing an isolated consonant sound, such as /s/, avoid adding /h/ or a vowel sound after the consonant. The sound should be *sss*, not *shh* or *suh*.

SAY On a hot day when the sun has made you feel very warm, you might cook your food over an outside barbecue grill. When the meat is placed on the hot grill, it makes a sizzling sound, /ss/. Say /ss/ with me: /ss/.

Place Letter Card *s* in the *Pocket Chart.*

SAY The name of this letter is *s*. The letter *s* stands for the /s/ sound in words. When we see the letter *s*, we say the /s/ sound. When I point to the letter *s*, you say the /s/ sound. Keep making the sound as long as I am pointing to the letter. Stop making the sound when I lift my finger.

Make a game of pointing to the letter and lifting your finger at various intervals, sometimes pointing to the letter for several seconds, sometimes pointing very briefly.

SAY The letter *s* stands for the /s/ sound at the beginning of the word *sun.* Say *sun* with me: *sun.* Now say *sail* with me: *sail.* What sound do you hear at the beginning of *sail?* (/s/) Yes, *sail* begins with the /s/ sound. I'll say some other words that begin with the /s/ sound, and you say each word after me.

Use the following words: *sandwich, six.*

Make sure each pupil has *Word Builder Card s.* Have pupils name the letter.

SAY I am going to say some words that begin with /s/ and some words that do not begin with /s/. Each time you hear a word that begins with the /s/ sound, hold up your letter *s*. When you hear a word that does not begin with /s/, do not hold up a card.

Use the following words: *sidewalk, button, silk, sat, hand, some, supper.* Then call on pupils to name other words that begin with the /s/ sound.

Place Letter Card *S* in the *Pocket Chart.*

SAY The name of this letter is capital *S*. Capital *S* stands for the same sound as the small *s*. What sound is that? (/s/) We use capital *S* at the beginning of names such as Susan, Simon, and Sarah.

Ask pupils to say the /s/ sound as you point to the small *s* and to the capital *S* several times.

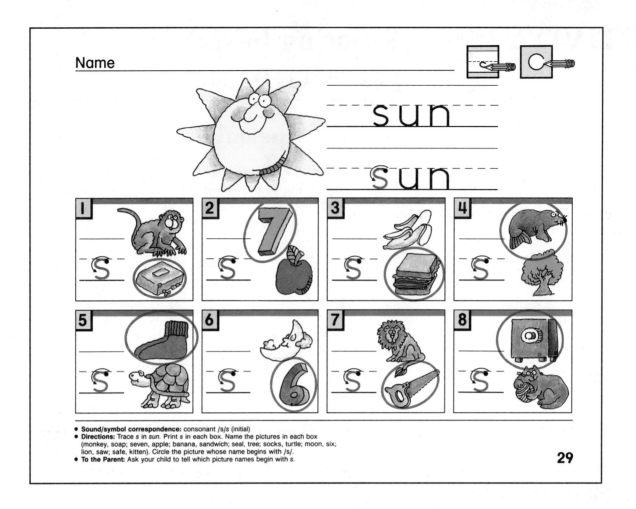

Name _____

sun

sun

1 s • monkey, soap	**2** s • seven, apple	**3** s • banana, sandwich	**4** s • seal, tree
5 s • socks, turtle	**6** s • moon, six	**7** s • lion, saw	**8** s • safe, kitten

- **Sound/symbol correspondence:** consonant /s/s (initial)
- **Directions:** Trace s in *sun*. Print s in each box. Name the pictures in each box (monkey, soap; seven, apple; banana, sandwich; seal, tree; socks, turtle; moon, six; lion, saw; safe, kitten). Circle the picture whose name begins with /s/.
- **To the Parent:** Ask your child to tell which picture names begin with *s*.

29

2 Using the page

I, T   Sound/symbol correspondence: consonant /s/s (initial)

Call attention to the picture of the sun at the top of page 29 and tell pupils that the word beside the picture is *sun*. Have them point to the first letter in the word *sun* and to name the letter. (s) Ask what sound this letter stands for. (/s/) Then have pupils trace the letter *s* at the beginning of the second word *sun*.

Have pupils look at the first box and tell them to trace the letter *s* on the writing line. Ask pupils to name the two pictures in the box. (monkey, soap)

ASK   **Which picture name begins with the /s/ sound?** (soap)

Have pupils circle the picture of soap to show that *soap* begins with the /s/ sound. Explain that they should trace letter *s* on the writing line in each box and then circle the picture in the box whose name begins with /s/. Identify the pictures as seven, apple; banana, sandwich; seal, tree; socks, turtle; moon, six; lion, saw; safe, kitten.

3 Developing the Skills

I, T   Sound/symbol correspondence: consonant /s/*s* (initial)

Tell pupils that you will say some riddles and that the answer to each riddle begins with the /s/ sound. Then read each of the riddles and have pupils guess the answer.

1. I am found on the beach.
   People like to build castles with me.
   My name begins with /s/.
   What am I? (sand)

2. I am a number.
   I come after five.
   My name begins with /s/.
   What am I? (six)

3. I am put on a horse's back.
   A rider sits on me.
   My name begins with /s/.
   What am I? (saddle)

4. I am planted in the soil.
   I grow into a flower.
   My name begins with /s/.
   What am I? (seed)

✳ Practicing and Extending

The activities that follow provide practice and extension of skills developed in this lesson. Not every pupil needs to complete these activities. Choose only the activities that are needed to provide for the individual differences in your classroom.

Practicing Skills

I, T   Sound/symbol correspondence: consonant /s/*s* (initial)

PM 20   ADDITIONAL PRACTICE   *Practice Masters* page 20 may be used as optional practice for identifying the letter *s* with the /s/ sound in words.

CHALLENGE ACTIVITY   Tell pupils that they will play a game to see what the sun shines on. Each pupil will complete the phrase "The sun shines on _____" by naming any word that begins with the /s/ sound.

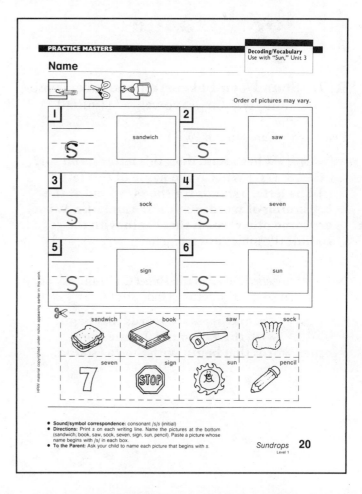

ACTIVITY 4 Discriminating Initial /s/s, /a/a, and /m/m page 30 (T114–T116)

Skill Strands

DECODING/VOCABULARY

R, T **Sound/symbol correspondence:** consonants /s/s, /m/m; vowel /a/a (initial)

Materials

Sundrops, Level 1: page 30

Practice Masters: page 21
Resource Box: Letter Cards a, m, s
Word Builder Cards a, m, s
Pocket Chart
Teacher's Idea Book

Special Populations

See *Teacher's Idea Book* for additional suggestions to help pupils with limited English proficiency.

Key to Symbols
I   Introduced in this lesson
R   Reinforced from an earlier lesson in this level
M   Maintained from previous levels
T   Tested in this level

---

1 Preparing for the page

R, T **Sound/symbol correspondence:** consonants /s/s, /m/m; vowel /a/a (initial)

Place *Letter Card s* in the *Pocket Chart.*

> **SAY** **What sound does this letter stand for?** (/s/) **What is the name of this letter?** (s) **The letter s stands for the /s/ sound at the beginning of words such as** *sun* **and** *silly.* **What are some other words that begin with the /s/ sound?** (Possible answers include: *sorry, sip,* and *soda.*

Now place *Letter Card a* in the *Pocket Chart* and ask pupils to tell what sound this letter stands for. (/a/)

> **SAY** *Ant* **and** *apple* **are words that begin with the /a/ sound. Name some other words that begin with the /a/ sound.**

Place *Letter Card m* in the *Pocket Chart* and continue in the same manner. Ask what sound the letter stands for and then ask pupils to name some words that begin with the /m/ sound. (Possible answers include: *meat, market,* and *man.*

Make sure each pupil has *Word Builder Cards s, a,* and *m.*

> **SAY** **I am going to say some words that begin with /s/, /a/, or /m/. Hold up the letter that stands for the sound that you hear at the beginning of each word.**

Use the following words: *motorcycle, size, man, said, astronaut.*

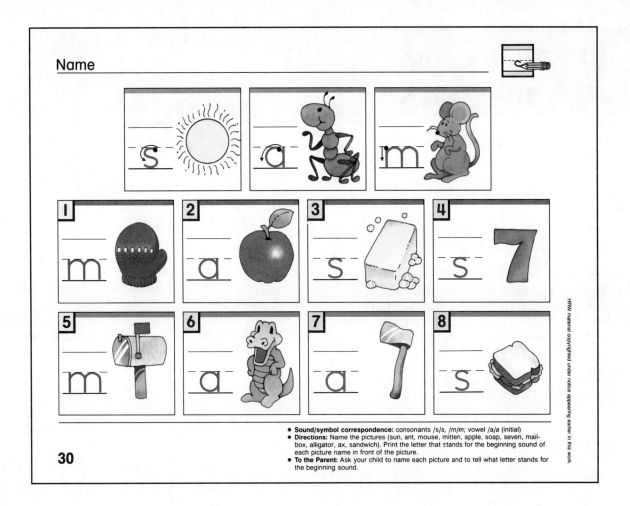

Name

HRW material copyrighted under notice appearing earlier in this work.

• **Sound/symbol correspondence:** consonants /s/s, /m/m; vowel /a/a (initial)
• **Directions:** Name the pictures (sun, ant, mouse, mitten, apple, soap, seven, mailbox, alligator, ax, sandwich). Print the letter that stands for the beginning sound of each picture name in front of the picture.
• **To the Parent:** Ask your child to name each picture and to tell what letter stands for the beginning sound.

30

2 Using the page

R, T   **Sound/symbol correspondence:** consonants /s/s, /m/m; vowel /a/a (initial)

Have pupils identify the pictures in the example boxes at the top of page 30. (sun, ant, mouse)

SAY   **What letter stands for the sound at the beginning of the word *sun*?** (*s*) **Trace the letter *s* on the writing lines. What letter stands for the sound at the beginning of the word *ant*?** (*a*) **Trace the letter *a* on the writing lines. What letter stands for the sound at the beginning of the word *mouse*?** (*m*) **Trace the letter *m* on the writing lines.**

Tell pupils to complete the page by printing the letter that stands for the beginning sound of each picture name. Identify the remaining pictures as mitten, apple, soap, seven, mailbox, alligator, ax, sandwich.

3 Developing the Skills

R, T   **Sound/symbol correspondence:** consonants /s/s, /m/m; vowel /a/a (initial)

SAY   **I will read a sentence that has some words that begin with the /a/ sound. Then I will ask you to tell me the words that begin with /a/. Listen to the first sentence: Andy Alligator saw an astronaut.**

Now listen for words that begin with /s/: Sammy slipped on the sidewalk.

Continue with the following sentences:

1. (/m/)   **Many marbles fell in the mud.**
2. (/s/)   **Six sisters saw the seals sing.**
3. (/a/)   **Aunt Ann gave me an apple.**
4. (/m/)   **Mary and Mike made my lunch.**

✳ Practicing and Extending

The activities that follow provide practice and extension of skills developed in this lesson. Not every pupil needs to complete these activities. Choose only the activities that are needed to provide for the individual differences in your classroom.

Practicing Skills

R, T   Sound/symbol correspondence: consonants /s/*s,* /m/*m;* vowel /a/*a* (initial)

PM 21 **ADDITIONAL PRACTICE**   *Practice Masters* page 21 may be used as optional practice for discriminating /s/, /a/ and /m/.

Extending Selection Concepts

LITERATURE

LISTENING: TONGUE TWISTERS Choose tongue twisters with words beginning with /s/, /a/, or /m/. Ask pupils to repeat the tongue twisters and to name the words that begin with /s/, /a/, or /m/. You might use the following tongue twister or select some from the books listed below:

Sarah sat on a silken seat.

Potter, Charles Francis. *Tongue Tanglers.* World Publishing, 1962. Your tongue will be tangled in no time with this book.

Schwartz, Alvin. *A Twister of Twists, A Tangler of Tongues.* Lippincott, 1972. These teasing tongue twisters tangle tongues to your mouth's delight.

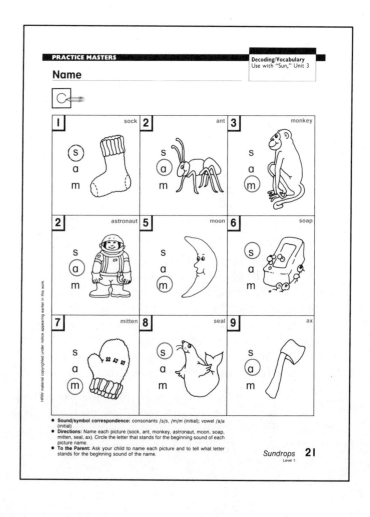

ACTIVITY 5 Relating Final /s/ to s
page 31 (T117–T119)

Skill Strands

DECODING/VOCABULARY

I, T   Sound/symbol correspondence: consonant /s/s (final)

Materials

Sundrops, Level 1: page 31
Practice Masters: page 22
Resource Box: Letter Card s
Word Builder and *Word Builder Card s*
Pocket Chart
Teacher's Idea Book

Special Populations

See *Teacher's Idea Book* for additional suggestions to help pupils with limited English proficiency.

Key to Symbols
I   Introduced in this lesson
R   Reinforced from an earlier lesson in this level
M   Maintained from previous levels
T   Tested in this level

---

1 Preparing for the page

I, T   Sound/symbol correspondence: consonant /s/s (final)

Place *Letter Card s* in the *Pocket Chart.* Ask pupils to name the letter and to tell what sound the letter stands for. (*s,* /s/) Ask pupils to name words that begin with the /s/ sound. (Possible answers include: *son, sun,* and *supper.*)

> **SAY** **I am going to say a word that has the /s/ sound at the end: *bus.* Say the word *bus* after me: *bus.* I will say some other words that have /s/ at the end, and you say each word after me.**

Use the following words: *yes, across, mess, pass.*

Make sure each pupil has *Word Builder Card s.*

> **SAY** **I am going to say some words that have /s/ at the end and some words that do not have /s/ at the end. When you hear a word that has /s/ at the end, hold up your *s* card. Do not hold up your card if you do not hear /s/ at the end of a word.**

Use the following words: *cross, cat, class, this, bone, walrus.*

Give each pupil a *Word Builder* and point to the left side of the *Word Builder.*

> **SAY** **This is the beginning of the *Word Builder.* (Move your finger to the end of the *Word Builder.*) This is the end of the *Word Builder. Sun* has the /s/ sound at the beginning, so I put my *s* card at the beginning of the *Word Builder.* (Demonstrate.) *Glass* has the /s/ sound at the end, so I put my *s* card at the end of the *Word Builder.* (Demonstrate.)**

Explain that you will say some words that have the /s/ sound at the beginning and some words that have the /s/ sound at the end. Pupils should place their *s* card in the *Word Builder* to show if the /s/ sound is at the beginning or at the end of each word. Use these words: *set, less, sometime, sand, miss, grass, sick, same, gas.*

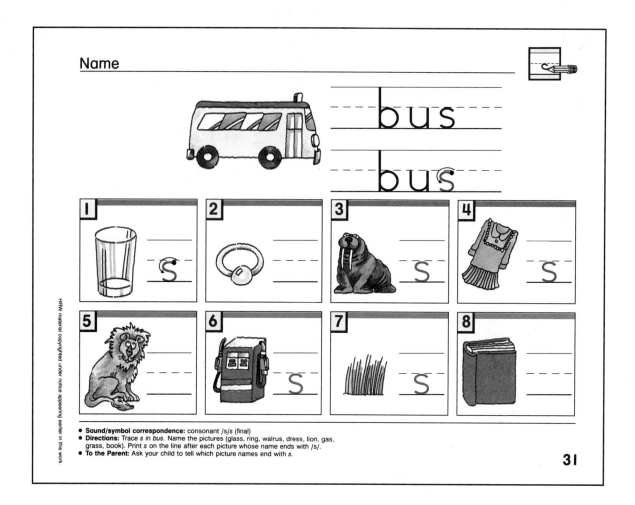

- **Sound/symbol correspondence:** consonant /s/s (final)
- **Directions:** Trace *s* in *bus*. Name the pictures (glass, ring, walrus, dress, lion, gas, grass, book). Print *s* on the line after each picture whose name ends with /s/.
- **To the Parent:** Ask your child to tell which picture names end with *s*.

31

2 Using the page

I, T Sound/symbol correspondence: consonant /s/s (final)

Ask pupils to open their books to page 31 and to identify the picture at the top of the page. (bus) Ask where the /s/ sound is heard in *bus*. (at the end) Have pupils point to the letter *s* in the word *bus* and tell where the letter is found. (at the end) Have pupils trace the letter *s* in the second word *bus*. Call on a volunteer to identify the first picture with a writing line. (glass) Ask where the /s/ sound is heard in the word *glass*. (at the end)

SAY Trace letter *s* on the line after the picture to show that *glass* has the /s/ sound at the end.

Have the next picture identified. (ring)

SAY Do you hear the /s/ sound at the end of *ring?* (no) Because *ring* does not have the /s/ sound at the end, do not print the letter.

Help pupils identify the remaining pictures as walrus, dress, lion, gas, grass, book. Have pupils complete the page by printing *s* after each picture whose name ends with /s/.

3 Developing the Skills

I, T Sound/symbol correspondence: consonant /s/s (final)

Tell pupils that you will say some rhymes that have missing words that end with the /s/ sound. Then read each rhyme and invite pupils to guess the missing word. Ask pupils to repeat the completed rhymes and to name the two words that rhyme.

1. **My best friend's name is Gus.**
   We sit together on the _____. (bus)

2. **Every day after class**
   I drink milk in a _____. (glass)

3. **I got mud on my new dress.**
   Now my dress is a _____. (mess)

* Practicing and Extending

The activities that follow provide practice and extension of skills developed in this lesson. Not every pupil needs to complete these activities. Choose only the activities that are needed to provide for the individual differences in your classroom.

Practicing Skills

I, T Sound/symbol correspondence: consonant /s/s (final)

PM 22 ADDITIONAL PRACTICE *Practice Masters* page 22 may be used as optional practice for identifying the /s/ sound at the end of words.

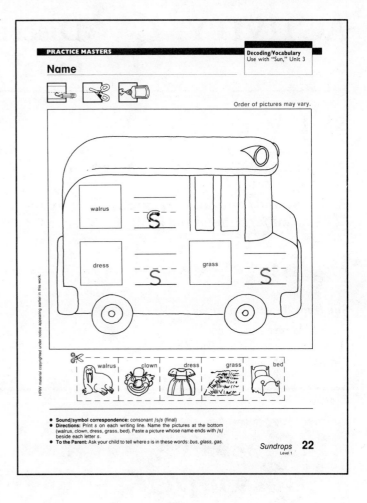

Extending Selection Concepts

MUSIC

SINGING: SONGS Remind pupils that the word *bus* has the /s/ sound at the end of the word. Invite pupils to sing "The People on the Bus" with you. If you do not know the tune, read the words as a poem.

The people on the bus go
  Up and down, up and down, up and down.
The people on the bus go
  Up and down,
All through the town.

The wheels on the bus go
  Round and round, round and round, round and round.
The wheels on the bus go
  Round and round,
All through the town.

Jane Hart

ACTIVITY 6 Discriminating Initial and Final /s/s page 32 (T120–T122)

Skill Strands

DECODING/VOCABULARY

R, T **Sound/symbol correspondence:** consonant /s/s (initial and final)

Materials

Sundrops, Level 1: page 32

Practice Masters: page 23
Word Builder and *Word Builder Card s*
Teacher's Idea Book

Special Populations

See *Teacher's Idea Book* for additional suggestions to help pupils with limited English proficiency.

1 Preparing for the page

R, T **Sound/symbol correspondence:** consonant /s/s (initial, final)

Print letter *s* on the chalkboard and remind pupils that this letter stands for the /s/ sound at the beginning of words such as *sun* and *sad.* Then remind pupils that the /s/ sound can also be heard at the end of words such as *bus* and *glass.*

Display a *Word Builder* and *Word Builder Card s.*

SAY I will say a word that has the /s/ sound at the beginning or at the end. After I say the word, I will call on one of you to place the *s* card in the *Word Builder* to show where the /s/ sound is heard in the word.

Use the following words: *miss, mess, solid, side, sink, press, glass.*

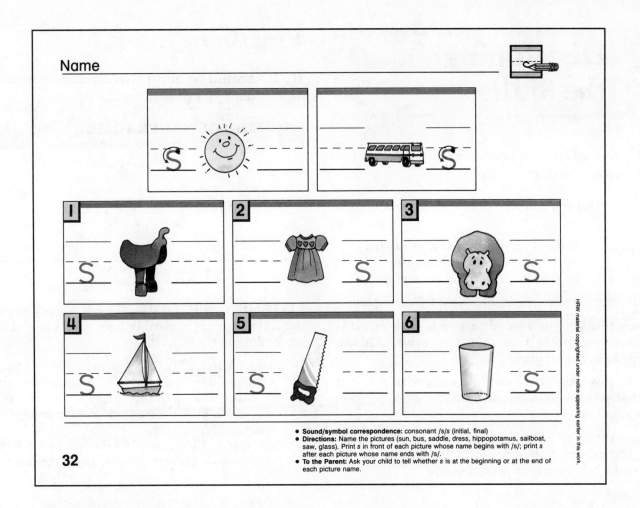

Name _____

1. saddle — S
2. dress — S
3. hippopotamus — S
4. sailboat — S
5. saw — S
6. glass — S

- **Sound/symbol correspondence:** consonant /s/s (initial, final)
- **Directions:** Name the pictures (sun, bus, saddle, dress, hippopotamus, sailboat, saw, glass). Print *s* in front of each picture whose name begins with /s/; print *s* after each picture whose name ends with /s/.
- **To the Parent:** Ask your child to tell whether *s* is at the beginning or at the end of each picture name.

32

HRW material copyrighted under notice appearing earlier in this work.

2 Using the page

R, T Sound/symbol correspondence: consonant /s/s (initial, final)

Help pupils find page 32 in their books and ask them to name the picture in the first example box at the top of the page. (sun) Point out that there is a writing line in front of the sun and one after the sun.

ASK **Where do you hear the /s/ sound in** *sun?* (at the beginning) **Trace letter** *s* **on the line in front of the picture of the sun to show that the /s/ sound is at the beginning of the word** *sun.*

Then have pupils name the picture in the next example box. (bus) Ask where the /s/ sound is heard in the word *bus.* (at the end) Have pupils trace letter *s* after the picture of a bus to show that the /s/ sound is at the end of the word. Explain that pupils should print *s* in front of each picture that has /s/ at the beginning of its name, and print *s* after each picture that has /s/ at the end of its name. Help pupils identify the remaining pictures as saddle, dress, hippopotamus, sailboat, saw, glass.

3 Developing the Skills

R, T **Sound/symbol correspondence:** consonant /s/s (initial, final)

Tell pupils that you will play a game that uses words that begin or end with /s/.

| SAY | **I am thinking of a word that begins with /s/. It names a girl in your** |

family. Is the word *sister, mother,* or *son*? (*sister*)

Continue in the same manner with the following hints:

1. **I am thinking of a word that ends with /s/. It is what you might ride to get to school. Is the word *car, bus,* or *glass*?** (bus)

2. **I am thinking of a word that ends with /s/. It is what you use to drink milk. Is the word *yes, cup,* or *glass*?** (glass)

3. **I am thinking of a word that begins with /s/. It is something you might eat for lunch. Is the word *cracker, soup,* or *potato*?** (soup)

✳ Practicing and Extending

The activities that follow provide practice and extension of skills developed in this lesson. Not every pupil needs to complete these activities. Choose only the activities that are needed to provide for the individual differences in your classroom.

Practicing Skills

R, T **Sound/symbol correspondence:** consonant /s/s (initial, final)

PM 23 **ADDITIONAL PRACTICE** *Practice Masters* page 23 may be used as an optional practice for identifying sound/symbol correspondence /s/s.

Extending Selection Concepts

| LITERATURE |

LISTENING: FICTION Choose a story about the sun and read it to the class. Discuss what kinds of things can be done in the sunshine.

Ginsburg, Mirra. *The Sun's Asleep Behind the Hill.* Greenwillow Books, 1982. After a busy day of working and playing, the sun, the breeze, the leaves, the bird, the squirrel, and the child all go to sleep.

Greene, Carol. *Shine, Sun!* Childrens Press, 1983. A child spends a happy day playing in the sun.

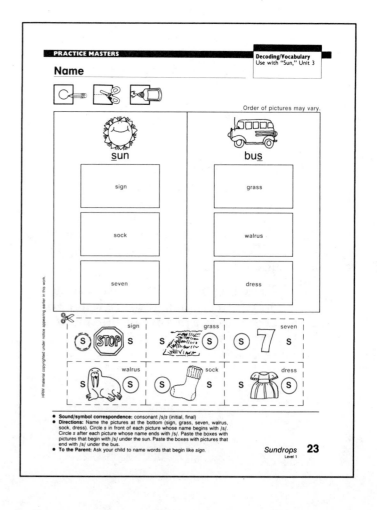

ACTIVITY 7 Building Words

page 33 (T123–T126)

Skill Strands

DECODING/VOCABULARY

I Vocabulary: word building

LANGUAGE

R Speaking: telling stories from pictures

Materials

Sundrops, Level 1: page 33

Practice Masters: page 24
Resource Box: Letter Cards a, m, S
Word Builder and *Word Builder Cards a, m, S*
Pocket Chart
Teacher's Idea Book

Special Populations

See *Teacher's Idea Book* for additional suggestions to help pupils with limited English proficiency.

Key to Symbols
I Introduced in this lesson
R Reinforced from an earlier lesson in this level
M Maintained from previous levels
T Tested in this level

1 Preparing for the page

I Vocabulary: word building

Note: In this lesson, pupils will be introduced to the skill of blending phonic elements to produce a word. You will model the blending technique by sliding your hand under each letter and making the sound of the letter until your hand reaches the next letter. (/Ssaamm/) As the sounds are pronounced slowly, a distorted pronunciation of the word is produced. Subsequent blendings should proceed more quickly, enabling pupils to refine this approximate pronunciation into a word.

Place *Letter Cards m, a,* and *S* in the *Pocket Chart* so that they are each separated from the others. Point to each letter and call on a pupil to name the letter and the sound it stands for. Remind pupils of the game you have played in which you touch a letter and they make the sound the

letter stands for, holding the sound as long as you are touching the letter. Play this game with all three letters, touching each letter several times.

SAY **We can put these letters together to make a word.**

Place the cards together in the *Pocket Chart* to make the word *Sam*. Make sure there is no space between the cards.

Note: Some pupils will be able to read the word. If a pupil does this before you model blending, compliment the pupil and say **Good, you can read the word. When you can read a word, you don't need to blend it. We learn to blend so we can figure out new words.**

Indicate the word in the *Pocket Chart*.

SAY **This is a word. Listen as I blend the sound of each letter together.** (Blend the sounds as you slowly move your hand under the letters: /Ssaamm/.) **Now you say the sounds with me as I slide my hand under the letters.**

Move your hand more quickly this time. Call on a volunteer to identify the word. (*Sam*)

Name _____

1 2 3

Sam   Sam   Sam

• **Vocabulary:** word building
• **Directions:** Print the missing letter to complete the dog's name, *Sam.*
• **To the Parent:** Ask your child to read the dog's name and to explain what is happening in each picture.

33

| SAY | Yes, the word is *Sam.* There is a capital letter at the beginning of *Sam* |

because it is a name.

Make sure each pupil has a *Word Builder* and *Word Builder Cards m, a,* and *S.*

| SAY | You can make this word in your *Word Builders.* Place capital *S* at the begin- |

ning. Then place *a* after the *S* and place *m* after the *a.* Make sure that there is no space between the letters. Blend the sounds to yourself and raise your hand when you can tell what this word is.

Call on volunteers to read the word. (*Sam*) Explain that blending the sounds of the letters is a way to read a new word.

2 Using the page

1 Vocabulary: word building

Tell pupils to open their books to page 33. Call attention to the pictures of a dog on the page and explain that this dog's name is Sam. Indicate the first picture and ask what Sam is doing in this picture. (Sam is watching Dad cook on a barbecue grill.)

| SAY | The word under this picture is sup- posed to be Sam's name. What sound |

is at the beginning of the word *Sam?* (/s/) I can see the letters for /a/ and /m/, but the letter for the /s/ sound is missing from the beginning of the word. What letter stands for the /s/ sound? (*s*) Yes, and because this is the dog's name, print a capital *S* in the space in front of the letters *a* and *m.* (Allow pupils to complete the word.) **Now let's read the word together: *Sam.***

Direct attention to the picture of Sam in the middle of the page and ask what Sam is doing in this picture. (Sam is carrying an umbrella to Dad.)

| SAY | I see the letter for the /s/ sound at the beginning of *Sam*, and I see the letter for the /m/ sound at the end of *Sam*. What sound is missing from the middle of *Sam*? (/a/) What letter stands for the /a/ sound? (a) Print letter *a* in the space in the middle to finish the word Sam. |

Continue in the same manner with the last picture of Sam, asking pupils to tell what is happening in this picture. (Dad is patting Sam on the head.) Ask pupils to print the letter that stands for the sound at the end of *Sam*.

R Speaking: telling stories from pictures

Ask pupils to look at the pictures of Sam on page 33.

| SAY | We can use these pictures to tell a story about Sam. Look at the first picture while I begin the story. |

| READ | One bright sunny day, Dad said he would like to cook dinner outside. |

| ASK | Who can tell some more of the story by looking at the first picture? |

Call on a volunteer to tell another sentence or two. Then have pupils look at the second picture. Ask volunteers to tell what is happening in the story. Follow a similar procedure for the third picture. Have volunteers retell parts of the story. You may want to print the story on chart paper as pupils dictate it. Place the story where pupils may read it on their own.

✳ Practicing and Extending

The activities that follow provide practice and extension of skills developed in this lesson. Not every pupil needs to complete these activities. Choose only the activities that are needed to provide for the individual differences in your classroom.

Practicing Skills

I Vocabulary: word building

PM 24 ADDITIONAL PRACTICE *Practice Masters* page 24 may be used as optional practice for building words.

Extending Selection Concepts

LANGUAGE ARTS

SPEAKING: TELLING A STORY   Invite pupils to pretend that Sam is their dog. Encourage them to dictate a story about something they would do together with Sam. Write the story on chart paper.

LITERATURE

LISTENING: FICTION   Choose a book about a playful dog and read it to the class. Call on volunteers to retell their favorite part of the story and to tell if they would like to own a dog such as the dog in the story.

Kellogg, Steven. *Pinkerton, Behave.* Dial, 1979. Pinkerton is a puppy who is as big as a pony. He's also the worst student at obedience school, but his training helps when a burglar comes.

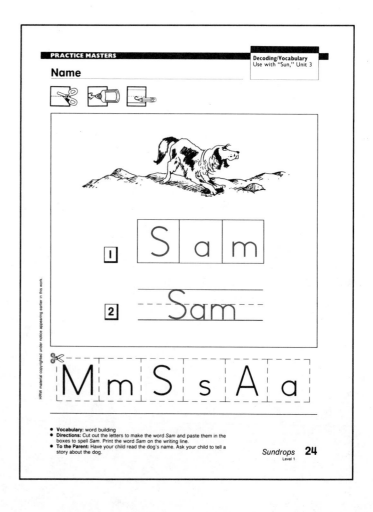

ACTIVITY 8

Reading the Words *I* and *am*
page 34 (T127–T130)

Skill Strands

DECODING/VOCABULARY

I, T Vocabulary: word meaning

Materials

Sundrops, Level 1: page 34
Practice Masters: page 24
Resource Box: Word Cards am, I, Sam
Pocket Chart
Teacher's Idea Book

Special Populations

See *Teacher's Idea Book* for additional suggestions to help pupils with limited English proficiency.

Key to Symbols
I Introduced in this lesson
R Reinforced from an earlier lesson in this level
M Maintained from previous levels
T Tested in this level

1 Preparing for the page

I, T Vocabulary: word meaning

Introduce the words *I am* orally.

> **SAY** **I am** (add your name). **Who are you?** (Call on a pupil to answer, "I am [name].")

Invite the pupil to point to another pupil and ask, "Who are you?" Encourage them to continue the game by alternately asking "Who are you?" and answering "I am (name)."

> **SAY** **If the dog in our books could talk, he might say, "I am Sam."**

Place *Word Cards I, am, Sam* in the *Pocket Chart.* Tell pupils that the words in the *Pocket Chart* say *I am Sam.* Point to each word as you read it aloud. Then point to the word *I.*

> **SAY** **This word is *I.*** (Point to the word *am.*) **This word is *am.* We often use the words *I am* when we talk about ourselves.** (Point to the word *Sam.*) **This is a word you already know. What is this word?** (*Sam*) Call on volunteers to read the words in the *Pocket Chart.*

Remove the word *Sam* from the *Pocket Chart* and ask a volunteer to come to the chart and to read the words *I am.* Have the volunteer complete the sentence by saying his or her own name.

Name

1. I am

2. I am

3. I am (pupil's name).

- **Vocabulary:** word meaning
- **Directions:** Trace *I am*. Complete the first sentence by filling in the circle under the picture that shows who brought an umbrella. Complete the second sentence by filling in the circle under the picture that shows who was cooking dinner. Complete the third sentence by printing your name. Read the completed sentences.
- **To the Parent:** Ask your child to read the sentences to you.

34

2 Using the page

I, T Vocabulary: word meaning

Have pupils open their books to page 34. Call attention to the words *I* and *am* printed in each row on this page, and tell pupils that they are to trace the words *I* and *am* in each row.

Then direct attention to the words in the first box. Have the sentence part read aloud. Have the three pictures following the sentence part identified. (Dad, Sam, sun)

SAY **Finish the sentence by filling in the circle under the picture that shows who brought Dad an umbrella.** (Sam) **Now read the whole sentence.** (I am Sam.) **Look at the second sentence part. Finish the sentence by filling in the circle under the picture that shows who was barbecuing dinner.** (Dad) **Now read the whole sentence.** (I am Dad.)

Have pupils finish the third sentence by printing their own names on the line after the words. Call on volunteers to read the completed sentence to the class. Then have pupils draw pictures showing something they can do. Invite them to make up sentences about the pictures. Pupils might work in pairs and read the completed sentences to each other.

3 Developing the Skills

I, T **Vocabulary:** word meaning

Display *Word Cards I am* in the *Pocket Chart.*

SAY Let's play a riddle game called "Guess What I Am." I will give you some clues. Then I will say "Guess What I Am." I will call on someone to come to the *Pocket Chart* to read the words *I am,* and to give the answer. Let's begin.

Read the following riddles:

1. I like cheese.
   I am small.
   I have a long tail.
   Guess what I am. (I am a mouse.)

2. I am in the sky.
   I keep you warm.
   I give you light.
   Guess what I am. (I am the sun.)

3. I have two wheels.
   I have a handlebar.
   I am something you ride.
   Guess what I am. (I am a bicycle.)

✳ Practicing and Extending

The activities that follow provide practice and extension of skills developed in this lesson. Not every pupil needs to complete these activities. Choose only the activities that are needed to provide for the individual differences in your classroom.

Practicing Skills

I, T **Vocabulary:** word meaning

PM 25 **ADDITIONAL PRACTICE** *Practice Masters* page 25 may be used as optional practice for reading the words *I* and *am.*

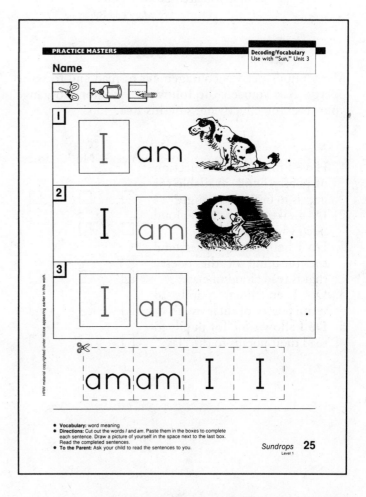

Extending Selection Concepts

LISTENING: POETRY Read the poem "Imagine." Ask pupils to tell what things it might be fun to imagine. Then ask pupils to listen to the poem again and to raise their hands each time the words *I am* are used.

Imagine

I am a king on a golden throne,
    Eating cake and ham.
I'm really not a king, you know,
    But I imagine that I am.

I imagine I am on a kite,
    Zooming over trees.
I am a bright red flower,
    Talking to the bees.

I am on a rocket ship
    Flying through the air.
I am a race car driver
    And I haven't left my chair.

I am just imagining
    All the things that I can be.
But my favorite thing to imagine,
    Is that you are here with me.

Mary Lou Byrne

HOW AM I DOING?

Many pupils need encouragement to read and to write poetry. Ask yourself the following questions to gauge your teaching effectiveness in this area.

	Yes	No	Some-times
1. Have I made a wide selection of poetry books available for pupils to browse through?	☐	☐	☐
2. Do I take time to read aloud poetry to pupils?	☐	☐	☐
3. Do I help pupils understand the meaning of the poetry that is read aloud in class?	☐	☐	☐
4. Do I encourage pupils to write poetry of their own?	☐	☐	☐
5. Do I allow time for pupils to read their poems to the class?	☐	☐	☐

ACTIVITY 9 Reading a Story
page 35 (T131–T133)

Skill Strands

DECODING/VOCABULARY

I **Vocabulary:** words in context

LANGUAGE

I **Conventions of language:** end punctuation (period)

Materials

Sundrops, Level 1: page 35
Big Book: page 35
Resource Box: Word Cards am, I, Sam
                        Punctuation Card period
Pocket Chart
Teacher's Idea Book

Special Populations

See *Teacher's Idea Book* for additional suggestions to help pupils with limited English proficiency.

Key to Symbols
I Introduced in this lesson
R Reinforced from an earlier lesson in this level
M Maintained from previous levels
T Tested in this level

1 Preparing for the page

I **Vocabulary:** words in context

Display *Word Card I* and have the word read. Display *Word Card am* and ask pupils to read the word. Place *Word Cards I* and *am* in the *Pocket Chart* and have the words read together. Place *Word Card Sam* after *I* and *am* and have the three words read.

ASK **Who might say, "I am Sam"?** (someone whose name is Sam) **When I put the words *I*, *am*, and *Sam* together, they make a sentence. A sentence tells an idea. When we talk to each other, we speak in sentences. Listen as I say some more sentences:**

> **Today is a school day.**
> **I like to read.**
> **My birthday is coming soon.**

SAY **When we read, the words are put together in sentences. We need to know when a sentence begins and when the** sentence ends. The first word in every sentence begins with a capital letter. (Point to the *Pocket Chart*.) *I am Sam* is a sentence. Does the first word in *I am Sam* begin with a capital letter? (yes) Yes, the word *I* is written with a capital letter.

When we read a sentence, we need to know when the sentence ends. A sentence ends with a period. (Display *Punctuation Card period*.) This is a period. A period is a little dot at the end of a sentence. Since *I am Sam* is a sentence, it needs a period at the end. (Place the period in the proper position on the *Pocket Chart*.)

When I read a sentence, I stop at the period: *I am Sam*. Now read the sentence with me: *I am Sam*. A period is like a stop sign when we read. We stop when we get to the period and then we go on reading.

Name _____

1. Sam. Sam. Sam.

2. I am Sam.

3. I am Sam.

4. Sam.

● **Vocabulary:** words in context
● **Directions:** Read the story.
● **To the Parent:** Read and discuss the story with your child.

35

2 Using the page

I Vocabulary: words in context

Help pupils find page 35 in their books and tell them that this is a story about Sam. Explain that you are going to tell part of the story and that they will read the part of the story that is printed in their books.

SAY Look at the first picture as I read the beginning of the story.

READ My dog Sam and I had just gone outside for a long walk. All of a sudden, Sam ran away from me. Before I knew it, he disappeared around a corner.

SAY Look at the words at the bottom of the picture. The words tell what the boy said when his dog ran away.

Call on a volunteer to read the line. (Sam. Sam. Sam.)

SAY Now look at the second picture while I read.

READ My dog ran across the street, but I had to wait until the cars stopped. A police officer was telling the drivers when to stop and when to go. I kept calling for Sam.

SAY The words at the bottom of the picture tell what the police officer said to the boy.

Call on a volunteer to read the line. (I am Sam.)

ASK Why did the police officer say, "I am Sam"? (That was his name.)

SAY The dog and the police officer have the same name. Look at the third picture as I read more of the story.

READ When the cars stopped, I quickly crossed the street and ran into the park. I could see my Sam barking at a squirrel in a tree. A girl heard me calling for Sam and came to help me.

SAY Read what the girl said.

Call on a volunteer to read the line. (I am Sam.)

ASK **Why did the girl say, "I am Sam"?** (That was her name, a nickname for Samantha.)

SAY **Now we have a dog, a police officer, and a girl—all named Sam. Look at the last picture.**

READ **Finally I caught up with Sam. He stopped barking and came right to me. I was so glad to have him back that I gave him a big hug.**

SAY **Read what the boy said to his dog.**

Call on a volunteer to read the line. (Sam.) Call on volunteers to read the story in their books. Ask how many Sam's were in the story and who they were. (There were three Sam's: the dog, the police officer, and the girl.)

3 Developing the Skills

I Conventions of language: end punctuation (period)

Distribute *Word Cards* I, am, Sam, and *Punctuation Card* period to several pupils. Ask pupils holding the cards to come to the *Pocket Chart* and to put the cards together to make the sentence *I am Sam.* Redistribute the cards and have pupils take turns making the sentence.

✳ Practicing and Extending

The activities that follow provide practice and extension of skills developed in this lesson. Not every pupil needs to complete these activities. Choose only the activities that are needed to provide for the individual differences in your classroom.

Practicing Skills

I Vocabulary: words in context

CHALLENGE ACTIVITY Tell pupils you will play a game called "Which Sam Am I?"

SAY **I will say a sentence about Sam the dog, Sam the police officer, or Sam the girl. Then I will ask "Which Sam am I?" and you can guess the answer. Sometimes I direct traffic. Which Sam am I?** (Sam the police officer)

Continue with the following sentences:

1. **I like to bury my bones. Which Sam am I?** (Sam the dog)
2. **I like to fly my kite. Which Sam am I?** (Sam the girl)

Encourage pupils to make up their own statements and invite classmates to guess which Sam is speaking.

Extending Selection Concepts

LITERATURE

LISTENING: FICTION   Choose a book that has the word *Sam* in the title and read it aloud. Discuss with pupils who Sam is and what he or she does in the story.

Fujikawa, Gyo. *Sam's All Wrong Day.* Putnam Publishing Group, 1982. One day everything goes wrong for Sam. Just as he is ready to call it an all-wrong day, things take a turn for the better.

Scott, Ann Herbert. *Sam.* McGraw-Hill, 1967. Everyone in Sam's family is too busy to play with him until he starts to cry.

ACTIVITY 10 Reviewing /s/s
page 36 (T134–T136)

Skill Strands

DECODING/VOCABULARY

R, T **Sound/symbol correspondence:** consonant /s/s (initial, final)

LANGUAGE

R **Writing:** language–experience stories

Materials

Sundrops, Level 1: page 36
Practice Masters: page 26
Resource Box: Letter Card s
Teacher's Idea Book
Sound/Symbol Folder (See page T43 for instructions.)

Special Populations

See *Teacher's Idea Book* for additional suggestions to help pupils with limited English proficiency.

Key to Symbols
I Introduced in this lesson
R Reinforced from an earlier lesson in this level
M Maintained from previous levels
T Tested in this level

1 Preparing for the page

R, T **Sound/symbol correspondence:** consonant /s/s (initial, final)

Display *Letter Card s* and ask what sound the letter stands for.

SAY I will say three words. You name the two words that begin with the /s/ sound: *soft, sit, music; box, sand, side.*

Remind pupils that the /s/ sound is sometimes at the end of a word.

SAY Where is the /s/ sound in the word *bus?* (at the end) I will say some more words. Tell me which two words end with the /s/ sound: *across, yes, money; less, grass, card.*

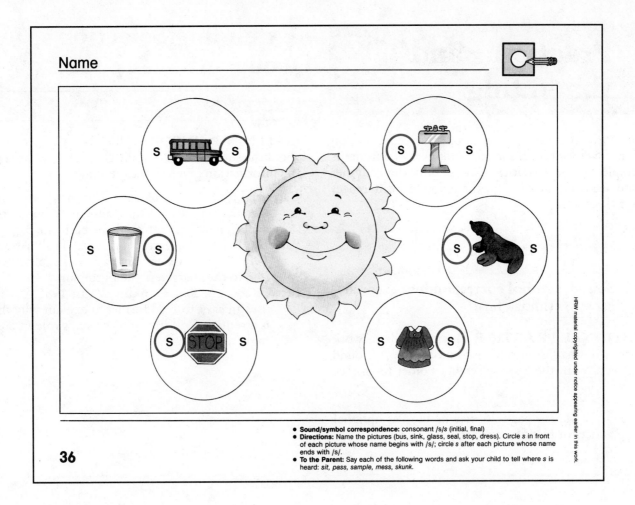

Name _____

HRW material copyrighted under notice appearing earlier in this work.

- **Sound/symbol correspondence:** consonant /s/s (initial, final)
- **Directions:** Name the pictures (bus, sink, glass, seal, stop, dress). Circle *s* in front of each picture whose name begins with /s/; circle *s* after each picture whose name ends with /s/.
- **To the Parent:** Say each of the following words and ask your child to tell where *s* is heard: *sit, pass, sample, mess, skunk.*

36

2 Using the page

3 Developing the Skills

R, T   Sound/symbol correspondence: consonant /s/s (initial, final)

Help pupils find page 36 in their books and ask what is in the center of the page. (the sun) Ask what sound is heard at the beginning of the word *sun.* (/s/)

> **SAY**   Each picture around the sun has the /s/ sound at the beginning or at the end of its name. Look at the picture of a bus. Where do you hear the /s/ sound in the word *bus?* (at the end) Since the /s/ sound is at the end of the word *bus,* circle the letter *s* that is after the picture.

Explain that pupils are to complete the page by circling the letter *s* in front of each picture whose name begins with the /s/ sound and by circling the letter *s* after each picture whose name ends with the /s/ sound. Identify the remaining pictures as sink, glass, seal, stop, dress.

R   Writing: language–experience stories

Display chart paper and tell pupils that they can work together to write a story. Explain that you will write their story on the chart paper for them.

> **SAY**   Let's write about the sun. Before we begin, tell me about some of the things we learned about the sun in "Sun Up, Sun Down." (Possible answers are: The sun gives us light; it keeps us warm; it is very far away; it makes plants grow; it helps make rain; it makes rainbows; it makes day and night.)

After you have discussed the sun, invite pupils to dictate sentences that tell about the sun. Write the sentences on the chart paper. Read back each sentence, running your hand under the words. Encourage pupils to read back parts of the story. Invite pupils to illustrate parts of the story and display the illustrations near the chart paper.

✳ Practicing and Extending

The activities that follow provide practice and extension of skills developed in this lesson. Not every pupil needs to complete these activities. Choose only the activities that are needed to provide for the individual differences in your classroom.

Practicing Skills

R, T   Sound/symbol correspondence: consonant /s/*s* (initial, final)

ADDITIONAL PRACTICE   Invite pupils to work in pairs or in small groups to discriminate the /s/ sound in the pictures in the Sound/Symbol Folder for *s*. (See T43.)

 Practice Masters page 26 may be used as optional practice for identifying /s/*s*, /m/*m*, and /a/*a*.

Extending Selection Concepts

> ### SCIENCE

LISTENING: INFORMATION   Choose a book about the sun and read it to the class. Discuss with pupils the information given about the sun.

Cartwright, Sally. *Sunlight.* Coward, McCann & Geoghagan, 1974. This read-and-do book presents experiments that can easily be performed.

Palazzo, Janet. *Our Friend the Sun.* Troll Associates, 1982. This book presents a very simple introduction to the characteristics of the sun.

Petty, Kate. *The Sun.* Franklin Watts, 1985. This book uses an easy-to-read format to explain why the sun is essential to all life, and the sun's role in creating night and day.

Mid-Book Review
pages 37–40   (T137–T141)

Note: Your own daily observations provide the best information about each pupil's understanding and mastery of skills. The program provides materials to assist in your ongoing evaluation. Pages 37–40 of *Sundrops* are designed to assess pupils' progress. You may tear out these pages after they are completed and send them home to inform parents of their child's progress.

Skill Strands

DECODING/VOCABULARY

R, T   **Sound/symbol correspondence:** consonants /m/*m*, /s/*s;* vowel /a/*a* (initial)

R, T   **Sound/symbol correspondence:** consonants /m/*m*, /s/*s* (final)

R, T   **Sound/symbol correspondence:** vowel /a/*a* (medial)

R, T   **Vocabulary:** word meaning

COMPREHENSION/THINKING

R, T   **Literal:** sequence

Materials

Sundrops, Level 1: pages 37–40
Reteach Masters: pages 1–4
Teacher's Idea Book

Special Populations

See *Teacher's Idea Book* for additional suggestions to help pupils with limited English proficiency.

Key to Symbols
I   Introduced in this lesson
R   Reinforced from an earlier lesson in this level
M   Maintained from previous levels
T   Tested in this level

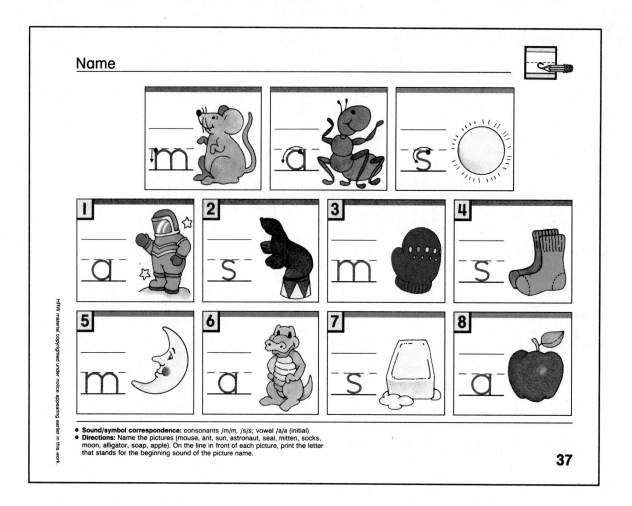

- **Sound/symbol correspondence:** consonants /m/*m*, /s/*s*; vowel /a/*a* (initial)
- **Directions:** Name the pictures (mouse, ant, sun, astronaut, seal, mitten, socks, moon, alligator, soap, apple). On the line in front of each picture, print the letter that stands for the beginning sound of the picture name.

37

Using Page 37

R, T Sound/symbol correspondence: consonants /m/*m*, /s/*s*; vowel /a/*a* (initial)

GUIDED PRACTICE Print letters *m, a,* and *s* on the chalkboard. Point to each letter and have pupils say the sound the letter stands for. Then have pupils find page 37 in their books. Direct pupils' attention to the three example boxes at the top of the page. Point out that there is a writing line and a picture in each box. Ask pupils to name the letters that stand for the beginning sound in *mouse, ant,* and *sun.* (m, a, s) Have pupils trace the letters on the writing line in each example box. Explain that they are to print the letter that stands for the beginning sound of each picture name on the writing line in each box. Identify the pictures as astronaut, seal, mitten, socks, moon, alligator, soap, and apple.

RM 1 Distribute *Reteach Masters* page 1 for further practice of this skill.

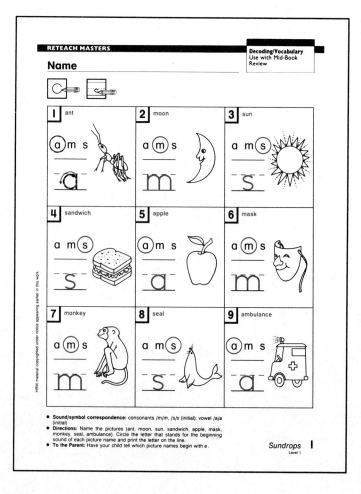

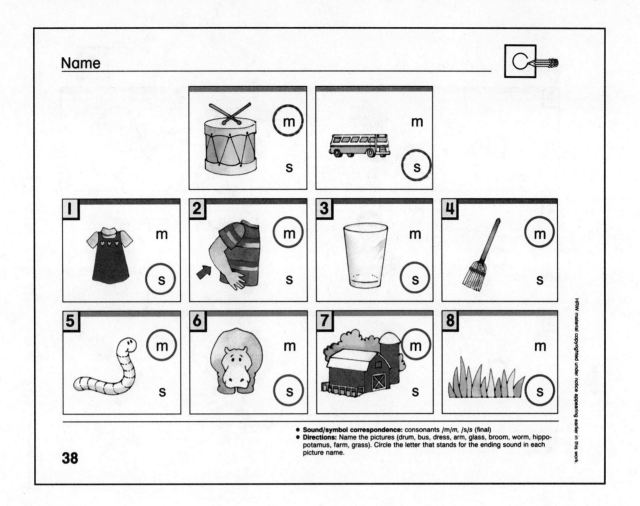

Name _____

• **Sound/symbol correspondence:** consonants /m/m, /s/s (final)
• **Directions:** Name the pictures (drum, bus, dress, arm, glass, broom, worm, hippopotamus, farm, grass). Circle the letter that stands for the ending sound in each picture name.

38

Using Page 38

R, T Sound/symbol correspondence: consonants /m/m, /s/s (final)

GUIDED PRACTICE Say the word *team* and ask pupils to tell where they hear the /m/ sound. (at the end) Then say *class* and ask where they hear the /s/ sound. (at the end) Have pupils find page 38 in their books. Point out the example boxes at the top of the page. Ask what letter stands for the sound at the end of *drum*. (m) Have pupils trace the circle around letter *m*. Ask what letter stands for the sound at the end of *bus*. (s) Have pupils trace the circle around letter *s*. Explain that pupils are to circle letter *m* or letter *s* in each box to show what sound they hear at the end of each picture name. Identify the pictures as dress, arm, glass, broom, worm, hippopotamus, farm, and grass.

 Distribute *Reteach Masters* page 2 for further practice of this skill.

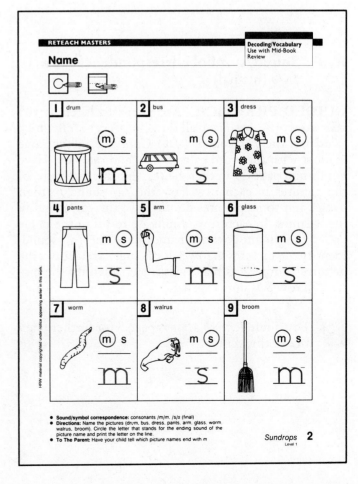

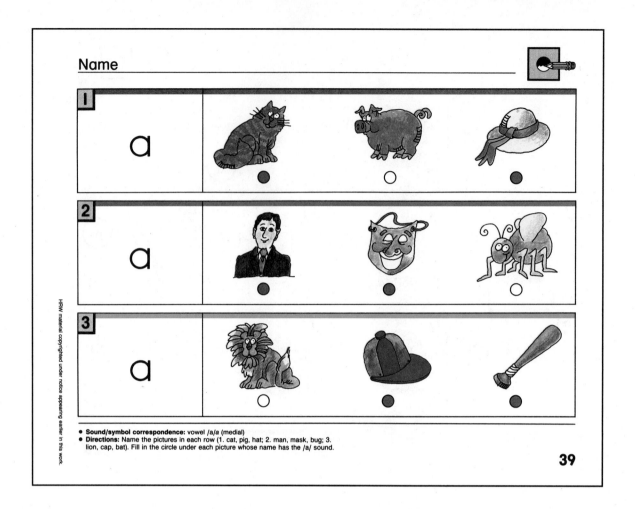

- **Sound/symbol correspondence:** vowel /a/a (medial)
- **Directions:** Name the pictures in each row (1. cat, pig, hat; 2. man, mask, bug; 3. lion, cap, bat). Fill in the circle under each picture whose name has the /a/ sound.

39

HRW material copyrighted under notice appearing earlier in this work.

Using page 39

R, T   Sound/symbol correspondence: vowel /a/a (medial)

GUIDED PRACTICE   Ask pupils to listen as you say two words: *fan, big.* Call on volunteers to tell which word has the /a/ sound. (*fan*) Continue in the same manner with the word pairs *fish, cat* and *cub, sack.* Have pupils find page 39 in their books. Explain that some of the pictures in each row have the /a/ sound in their names and some pictures do not have the /a/ sound in their names. In each row, pupils are to fill in the circle under the pictures whose names have the /a/ sound. Identify the pictures in row 1 as cat, pig, hat. Identify the pictures in row 2 as man, mask, bug. Identify the pictures in row 3 as lion, cap, bat.

RM 3   Distribute *Reteach Masters* page 3 for further practice of this skill.

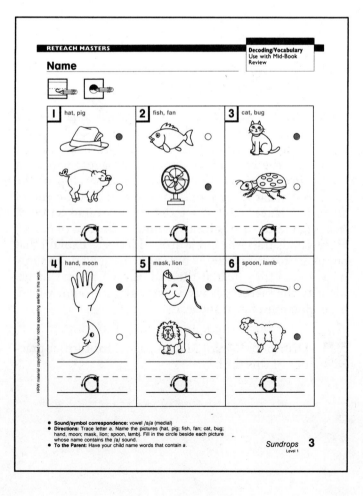

Name

• **Literal:** sequence
• **Directions:** Number the pictures to show what happened first, next and last. Fill in the missing letters to complete the sentence *I am Sam.* Fill in the circle under the picture that goes with the sentence.

40

Using Page 40

R, T Literal: sequence
R, T Vocabulary: word meaning

GUIDED PRACTICE Have pupils turn to page 40 in their books. Tell pupils to look at the pictures across the top of the page. Explain that these pictures tell a story, but that they are not in the correct order. Ask pupils to number the pictures in the correct order to tell a story.

Ask pupils to trace the dashed letters to complete the sentence at the bottom of the page. Have pupils read the completed sentence to themselves. Then ask them to draw a line from the sentence to the picture at the top that goes with the sentence.

RM 4 Distribute *Reteach Masters* page 4 for further practice of this skill.

UNIT 4 "Dogs"
pages 41–50 (T142–T177)

Skill Strands

DECODING/VOCABULARY

I, T **Sound/symbol correspondence:** consonant /d/*d* (initial, final)

R, T **Sound/symbol correspondence:** consonants /d/*d* /s/*s*; vowel /a/*a* (initial)

I   **Vocabulary:** word building

I, T **Vocabulary:** word meaning

I   **Vocabulary:** words in context

STUDY SKILLS

R **Organizing information:** classification

COMPREHENSION/THINKING

I   **Critical thinking:** using prior knowledge

R, T **Literal:** sequence

R, T **Literal:** cause and effect

LANGUAGE

R **Listening:** story comprehension

R **Speaking:** retelling stories

I   **Conventions of language:** end punctuation (question mark)

Materials

Sundrops, Level 1: pages 41–50

Big Book: pages 41, 50
Practice Masters: pages 27–33
Resource Box: Picture Cards *Chihuaha, Great Dane, Pekingese, Scottish terrier, sheep dog, St. Bernard*
    Letter Cards *a, D, d, m, S, s*
    Word Cards *am, Dad, I, is, Is, mad, sad, Sam*
    Punctuation Cards *period, question mark*
Word Builder and *Word Builder Cards a, D, d, m, S, s,*
Pocket Chart
Teacher's Idea Book

Language Applications

EXTENDING SELECTION CONCEPTS

Speaking: telling about a picture
Listening: fiction
Listening: poetry
Listening: information

Special Populations

See *Teacher's Idea Book* for additional suggestions to help pupils with limited English proficiency.

Key to Symbols
I Introduced in this lesson
R Reinforced from an earlier lesson in this level
M Maintained from previous levels
T Tested in this level

Idea Center

SOUND/SYMBOL FOLDER

For Activity 10, make a sound/symbol folder for letter *d*. See page T43 for directions.

FINGER PUPPETS

For Activity 1, see the *Teacher's Idea Book* for patterns to use to make finger puppets. Cut along the outline for each puppet. Use tape to connect the long ends of the puppets. The ends can be adjusted to fit pupils' fingers. Pupils will use the puppets to tell the feelings of story characters in "Angus and the Ducks." You may wish to have pupils make their own sets of finger puppets.

BIBLIOGRAPHY

The book below is the literary selection that has been reprinted for use in Activity 1. You may wish to have this book on display for pupils to enjoy after you have read the story.

Flack, Marjorie. *Angus and the Ducks.* Doubleday, 1930.

Add other books about dogs or books that have /d/ in the title to the reading corner or reading table. Encourage pupils to look at the books on their own. Suggestions for reading books aloud appear throughout this lesson. Listed below is a bibliography to choose from. Annotations for the books appear in the activities.

Aardema, Verna. *Why Mosquitoes Buzz in People's Ears.* Dial, 1975.

Caines, Jeanette. *Daddy.* Harper & Row, 1977.

Flack, Marjorie. *Angus and the Cat.* Doubleday, 1931.

Gackenbach, Dick. *Do You Love Me?* The Seabury Press, 1975.

Hinds, P. Mignon. *Puppies Need Someone to Love.* Golden Press, 1981.

Hoban, Russell. *Dinner at Alberta's.* Thomas Y. Crowell, 1975.

Hughes, Shirley. *David and Dog.* Prentice-Hall, 1977.

Kroll, Steven. *Is Milton Missing?* Holiday House, 1975.

Raskin, Ellen. *Who, Said Sue, Said Whoo?* Atheneum, 1973.

Selsam, Millicent, and Joyce Hunt. *A First Look at Dogs.* Walker and Co., 1981.

Skorpen, Liesel Moak. *His Mother's Dog.* Harper & Row, 1978.

ACTIVITY 1 Listening to "Angus and the Ducks" page 41 (T144–T147)

Skill Strands

| COMPREHENSION/THINKING |

I **Critical thinking:** using prior knowledge

| LANGUAGE |

R **Listening:** story comprehension
R **Speaking:** retelling stories

Materials

Sundrops, Level 1: page 41
Big Book: page 41
Teacher's Idea Book
Finger puppets (See page T143 for instructions.)

Special Populations

See *Teacher's Idea Book* for additional suggestions to help pupils with limited English proficiency.

Key to Symbols
I Introduced in this lesson
R Reinforced from an earlier lesson in this level
M Maintained from previous levels
T Tested in this level

1 Preparing for the page

SUMMARY Angus, a young Scottish terrier, is very curious about the places and things that surround him. He is most curious, however, about the noise he hears coming from the other side of a large green hedge. When the door of the house where he lives is left open, Angus is free to satisfy his curiosity. He confronts two ducks and frightens them with his loud barking. When the ducks have had enough of Angus, they hiss at him and chase him home.

I **Critical thinking:** using prior knowledge

Ask pupils to tell what they know about dogs. Guide the discussion by asking who takes care of a dog and what kinds of things dogs like to do. (Possible answers include: The owners of a dog take care of feeding it and giving it a warm place to sleep; dogs like to run and play, chase balls, chew socks, and explore anything that is new to them.)

Print the title "Angus and the Ducks" on the chalkboard and read it. Tell pupils that this is the title of a story that you are going to read. Explain that the story is about Angus, a young dog who is curious.

| ASK | **Who knows what *curious* means?**

Call on volunteers. You may need to explain that *curious* means "wanting to know about things." Tell pupils that in this story, Angus hears some strange noises and is curious about them.

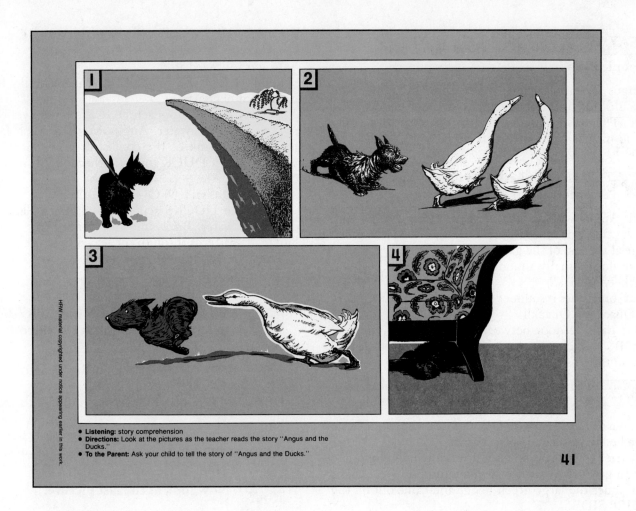

- **Listening:** story comprehension
- **Directions:** Look at the pictures as the teacher reads the story "Angus and the Ducks."
- **To the Parent:** Ask your child to tell the story of "Angus and the Ducks."

41

2 Using the page

R Listening: story comprehension

Help pupils find page 41 in their books. Explain that the pictures on this page are from the story "Angus and the Ducks" and that pupils can look at these pictures as you read the story. Ask pupils to listen to find out how Angus, the dog in the story, finds out what is making the noises he hears. The words in boldface type are possible aside comments to be read or stated by you as if you were thinking aloud.

Angus and the Ducks
by Marjorie Flack

SAY | **Look at the first picture while I read part of the story.**

Once there was a very young little dog whose name was Angus, because his mother and his father came from Scotland.

Although the rest of Angus was quite small, his head was very large and so were his feet.

Angus was curious about many places and many things.

Hé was curious about **WHAT** lived under the sofa and in dark corners and **WHO** was the little dog in the mirror.

He was curious about Things-Which-Come-Apart and those Things-Which-Don't-Come-Apart; such as **SLIPPERS** and gentlemen's **SUSPENDERS** and things like that.

SAY **Suspenders are what some people wear to hold up their pants. Many people use a belt instead of suspenders.**

Angus was also curious about Things-Outdoors but he could not find out much about them because of a leash. The leash was fastened at one end to a collar around his neck and at the other end to SOMEBODY ELSE.

SAY **Can you guess who is holding the other end of the leash?**

But Angus was most curious of all about a NOISE which came from the OTHER SIDE of the large green hedge at the end of the garden.

The noise usually sounded like this: Quack! Quack! Quackety! Quack!!

But sometimes it sounded like this: Quackety! Quackety! Quackety! Quack!!

One day the door between OUTDOORS and IN-DOORS was left open by mistake; and out went Angus without the leash or SOMEBODY ELSE.

SAY **I think I know what Angus is going to do. What do you think he will do?**

Down the little path he ran until he came to the large green hedge at the end of the garden.

He tried to go around it but it was much too long. He tried to go over it but it was much too high. So Angus went under the large green hedge and came out on the OTHER SIDE.

There, directly in front of him were two white DUCKS. They were marching forward, one-foot-up and one-foot-down.

Quack! Quack! Quackety! Quack!!

SAY **I wonder if Angus knows what he found? Do you think Angus ever saw ducks before? Look at the second picture.**

Angus said. WOO-OO-OOF!!!
Away went the DUCKS all of a flutter.

Quackety! Quackety! Quackety! Quackety! Quackety!!

Angus followed after.

Soon the DUCKS stopped by a stone watering trough under a mulberry tree.

Angus stopped, too. Each DUCK dipped a yellow bill in the clear cool water. Angus watched. Each DUCK took a long drink of the cool clear water. Still Angus watched. Each DUCK took another long drink of cool clear water.

Then Angus said: WOO-OO-OOF!!!

Away the DUCKS scuttled, and Angus lapped the cool clear water. Birds sang in the mulberry tree. The Sun made patterns through the leaves over the grass.

The DUCKS talked together:
Quack! Quack! Quack! Then:
HISS-S-S-S-S-S!!! HISS-S-S-S-S-S!!!

SAY **What are the ducks doing? Why did the ducks hiss? Look at the third picture.**

The first DUCK nipped Angus's tail! HISS-S-S-S-S-S!!!

HISS-S-S-S-S-S!!! The second DUCK flapped his wings!

Angus scrambled under the large green hedge, scurried up the little path, scampered into the house and crawled under the sofa.

SAY **Now look at the last picture.**

For exactly THREE minutes by the clock, Angus was NOT curious about anything at all.

SAY **What was making the noises that Angus heard?** (two ducks) **How did Angus find out that the ducks were making the noises?** (When the door was left open, Angus ran out and sneaked under the hedge.)

3 Developing the Skills

R Speaking: retelling stories

The questions that follow have been designed to help pupils reconstruct the story "Angus and the Ducks." Call attention to the pictures on page 41 or display *Big Book* page 41 as you ask the questions.

Picture 1: **What was the noise that Angus heard from the other side of the hedge?** (Quack! Quack! Quackety! Quack!!)
Did Angus know what was making the noise? (no) **Why?** (He had never seen a duck before; he didn't know the noise came from ducks.)

Picture 2: **Why do you think Angus barked at the ducks?** (Possible answers include: He was curious about the ducks; he wanted to talk to them, and barking was the way he talked; Angus was trying to frighten the ducks by barking loudly.)

Picture 3: **Why did the ducks nip at Angus's tail and chase him?** (The ducks had been frightened and chased away from their drinking water by Angus; so they decided to fight back.)

Picture 4: **Why did Angus run into the house and hide under the sofa?** (He had been frightened by the ducks; he thought hiding under the sofa would keep him safe from the ducks.)

Encourage pupils to retell the parts of the story that they enjoyed most.

✳ Practicing and Extending

The activities that follow provide practice and extension of skills developed in this lesson. Not every pupil needs to complete these activities. Choose only the activities that are needed to provide for the individual differences in your classroom.

Practicing Skills

R Speaking: retelling stories

CHALLENGE ACTIVITY To discuss story character's feelings, make the finger puppets shown in the *Teacher's Idea Book.* (See T143.) Use them to help pupils tell how they think a character from "Angus and the Ducks" feels. For example, give the dog puppet to a volunteer and say **Pretend you are Angus and you can talk. Tell how you felt when you were kept on a leash.** Then give the duck puppets to two volunteers and say **Pretend you are the ducks and you can talk. Tell how you felt when Angus barked at you while you were drinking.** If you wish, have pupils make their own finger puppets.

Extending Selection Concepts

> ### LITERATURE

LISTENING: FICTION Choose another book about the adventures of Angus the Scottish terrier and read it aloud to the class. Discuss the problem Angus has in the new story.

Flack, Marjorie. *Angus and the Cat.* Doubleday, 1931. Angus chases the cat around the house but is suddenly lonely when the cat disappears for a long time.

ACTIVITY 2 Recognizing Cause and Effect
page 42 (T148–T150)

Skill Strands

> COMPREHENSION/THINKING

R, T **Literal:** cause and effect

Materials

Sundrops, Level 1: page 42
Teacher's Idea Book

Special Populations

See *Teacher's Idea Book* for additional suggestions to help pupils with limited English proficiency.

Key to Symbols
I Introduced in this lesson
R Reinforced from an earlier lesson in this level
M Maintained from previous levels
T Tested in this level

1 Preparing for the page

R, T **Literal:** cause and effect

Ask pupils to think about "Angus and the Ducks."

ASK **Why did Angus go outside?** (He wanted to find out what was making a strange noise.) **Yes, Angus went outside because he wanted to find out what was making the noise. Why did Angus hide under the sofa?** (because the ducks chased him) **Yes, Angus hid under the sofa because the ducks chased him.**

Remind pupils that in a story one thing *causes,* or makes, another thing happen. Tell pupils they can understand a story better when they know what makes things happen.

SAY **You are going to look at some pictures to decide what happened and what made it happen.**

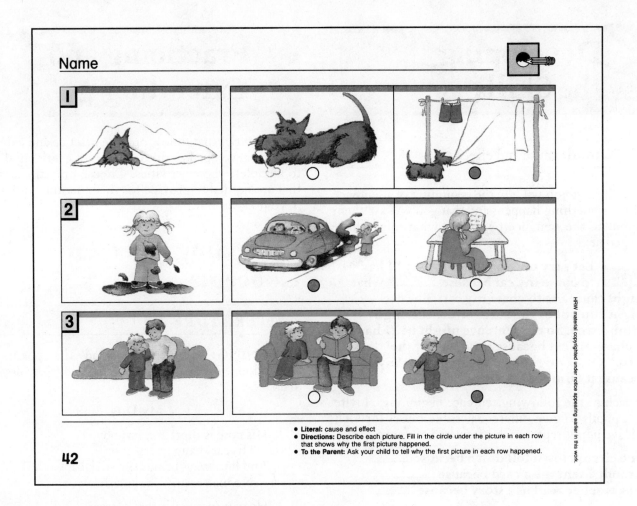

Name

1

2

3

• **Literal:** cause and effect
• **Directions:** Describe each picture. Fill in the circle under the picture in each row that shows why the first picture happened.
• **To the Parent:** Ask your child to tell why the first picture in each row happened.

42

2 Using the page

R, T   Literal: cause and effect

Help pupils find page 42 in their books. Call attention to the first picture in the first row and ask pupils to describe what happened in this picture. (A clothesline has fallen on a dog.) Tell pupils to look at the other pictures in the same row.

ASK   **What does the second picture show?** (A dog is chewing on a bone.) **What does the third picture show?** (A dog is tugging on a clothesline.) **Which picture shows why the clothesline fell on the dog?** (the third picture)

Tell pupils the circle under the third picture is to be filled in to show that the clothesline fell because the dog pulled on the sheet. Ask pupils to darken the circle with their pencils. Then have pupils look at the other rows of pictures. Explain that they are to tell what happened in the first picture and then color in the circle under the picture in the row that shows why it happened.

Call on pupils to look at each row of pictures again and to complete each of the following sentences:

1. **The clothesline fell down because, _____.** (the dog pulled on the sheet)
2. **The girl had to take a bath because, _____.** (she played in the mud)
3. **The boy started to cry because, _____.** (the balloon flew away)

3 Developing the Skills

R, T   Literal: cause and effect

Tell pupils that you will say the beginning of a sentence in which something happens and that you will ask them to complete the sentence by telling what might have happened next.

SAY Let's try one together. If I say "I had to chase my cat because _____." what might cause me to chase my cat? The cat might run out of the yard, or the cat might climb a tree. So the sentence might be "I had to chase my cat because it ran out of the yard." Or, it might be, "I had to chase my cat because it climbed up a tree."

Give each of the following sentence beginnings. Invite several pupils to give different possible causes for each one. Have pupils repeat each completed sentence.

1. The circus clown fell down because _____.
2. Grandpa sent me a card because _____.
3. Our teacher read us a story because _____.

* Practicing and Extending

The activities that follow provide practice and extension of skills developed in this lesson. Not every pupil needs to complete these activities. Choose only the activities that are needed to provide for the individual differences in your classroom.

Extending Selection Concepts

LITERATURE

LISTENING: POETRY: Read the poem "My Dog" aloud. Then ask some of the things the dog likes to do.

My Dog

His nose is short and scrubby;
   His ears hang rather low;
And he always brings the stick back.
   No matter how far you throw.

He gets spanked rather often
   For things he shouldn't do,
Like lying-on-beds, and barking,
   And eating up shoes when they're new.

He always wants to be going
   Where he isn't supposed to go,
He tracks up the house when it's snowing—
   Oh, puppy, I love you so!

Marchette Chute

LISTENING: FICTION   Read aloud a book that has a clear cause and effect. Discuss with pupils what happens and why it happens.

Aardema, Verna. *Why Mosquitoes Buzz in People's Ears.* Dial, 1975. Because the iguana doesn't want to listen to the mosquito's nonsense, he puts two sticks in his ears. This leads to a series of misunderstandings and misinterpreted actions.

Hoban, Russell. *Dinner at Alberta's.* Thomas Y. Crowell, 1975. Arthur Crocodile learns some quick table manners when he is invited to Alberta Saurian's house for dinner.

ACTIVITY 3 Relating Initial /d/ to *d*

page 43 (T151–T153)

Skill Strands

DECODING/VOCABULARY

I, T **Sound/symbol correspondence:** consonant /d/ *d* (initial)

Materials

Sundrops, Level 1: page 43
Practice Masters: page 27
Resource Box: Letter Cards D, d
Word Builder Card d
Pocket Chart
Teacher's Idea Book

Special Populations

See *Teacher's Idea Book* for additional suggestions to help pupils with limited English proficiency.

Key to Symbols
I Introduced in this lesson
R Reinforced from an earlier lesson in this level
M Maintained from previous levels
T Tested in this level

1 Preparing for the page

I, T **Sound/symbol correspondence:** consonant /d/ *d* (initial)

Tell pupils you are going to read a nursery rhyme.

READ **Diddle diddle dumpling, my son John,**
Went to bed with his stockings on.
One shoe off, one shoe on.
Diddle diddle dumpling, my son John.

SAY **You might have heard this nursery rhyme when you were younger. It is** a little story that a mother tells about how her son went to bed still partly dressed. The rhyme starts with three words that begin with /d/. The words are *diddle, diddle, dumpling.* Say *diddle, diddle, dumpling* with me: *diddle, diddle, dumpling.*

Place *Letter Card d* in the *Pocket Chart.*

SAY **The name of this letter is *d.* The letter** *d* **stands for the /d/ sound in words.** When we see the letter *d,* we make the /d/

sound. Watch my finger and only make the /d/ sound when I touch the *d.*

Hold your finger above the letter and touch the letter quickly. Then lift your finger.

SAY **The letter *d* stands for the /d/ sound** **at the beginning of the word *dog.* Say** *dog* **with me: *dog.* Now say *doll* with me: *doll.*** **What sound do you hear at the beginning of** *doll?* (/d/) **Yes, *doll* begins with the /d/ sound.** **I'll say some other words that begin with the** /d/ **sound, and you say each word after me.**

Use the following words: *dance, danger, dinner.*

Make sure each pupil has *Word Builder* Card *d.* Have pupils name the letter.

SAY **I am going to say some words that** **begin with /d/ and some words that** do not begin with /d/. Each time you hear a word that begins with the /d/ sound, hold up your letter *d.* Do not hold up your card if a word does not begin with /d/.

Use the following words: *dig, daffodil, nose, dinner, dollar, mouse, daughter.* Call on pupils to name other words that begin with the /d/ sound.

Name

dog

dog

1

2

3

4

5

6

7

8

- **Sound/symbol correspondence:** consonant /d/ *d* (initial)
- **Directions:** Trace *d* in *dog*. Name the pictures (doll, chair, duck, cat, door, deer, clown, desk). Print *d* in front of each picture whose name begins with /d/.
- **To the Parent:** Ask your child to name each picture that begins with *d*.

43

Place *Letter Card D* in the *Pocket Chart* beside letter *d*.

SAY **The name of this letter is capital *D*. Capital *D* stands for the same sound as small *d*. What sound is that? (/d/) We use capital *D* at the beginning of names such as Dawn, David, and Donald.**

Have pupils whose first or last names begin with *D* stand up and say their names. Have pupils whose names begin with *D* say the /d/ sound when you point to the capital *D* and have the rest of the pupils make the /d/ sound when you point to the small *d*. Point to each letter several times.

2 Using the page

I, T   Sound/symbol correspondence: consonant /d/ *d* (initial)

Call attention to the picture of the dog at the top of page 43 and tell pupils that the word beside the picture is *dog*.

Have pupils point to the first letter in the word *dog*. Then call on volunteers to name the letter. (*d*) Ask what sound this letter stands for. (/d/) Have pupils trace the *d* at the beginning of the second word *dog*. Then have pupils identify the picture in the first box with writing lines. (doll)

ASK **Does *doll* begin with the /d/ sound? (yes) Since *doll* begins with the /d/ sound, trace a *d* on the writing line in front of the picture.**

Have pupils name the second picture. (chair)

ASK **Does *chair* begin with the /d/ sound? (no) Since *chair* does not have the /d/ sound at the beginning, do not print *d* on the line.**

Tell pupils that they are to print the letter *d* on the line in front of each picture whose name begins with the /d/ sound. Identify the pictures as duck, cat, door, deer, clown, desk.

3 Developing the Skills

I, T   Sound/symbol correspondence: consonant /d/ *d* (initial)

Tell pupils that you will say some riddles and that each answer begins with the /d/ sound. Read each of the riddles and have pupils guess the answer.

1. **I am an animal that likes to swim.**
   I say "Quack, quack."
   What am I? (duck)

2. **I am something that opens and closes.**
   I have a doorknob.
   What am I? (door)

3. **I am an animal that some people keep as a pet.**
   When I was little, I was called a puppy.
   What am I? (dog)

4. **I am a kind of paper money.**
   I have the number one printed on me.
   What am I? (dollar)

✳ Practicing and Extending

The activities that follow provide practice and extension of skills developed in this lesson. Not every pupil needs to complete these activities. Choose only the activities that are needed to provide for the individual differences in your classroom.

Practicing Skills

I, T   Sound/symbol correspondence: consonant /d/ *d* (initial)

PM 27   ADDITIONAL PRACTICE *Practice Masters* may be used as optional practice for associating the letter *d* with the /d/ sound in words.

ACTIVITY 4 Discriminating Initial /d/ *d*, /s/ *s*, and /a/ *a* page 44 (T154–T156)

Skill Strands

DECODING/VOCABULARY

R, T **Sound/symbol correspondence:** consonants /d/ *d*, /s/ *s*, vowel /a/ *a* (initial)

Materials

Sundrops, Level 1: page 44

Practice Masters: page 28
Resource Box: Letter Cards a, d, s
Word Builder Cards a, d, s
Pocket Chart
Teacher's Idea Book

Special Populations

See *Teacher's Idea Book* for additional suggestions to help pupils with limited English proficiency.

Key to Symbols
I Introduced in this lesson
R Reinforced from an earlier lesson in this level
M Maintained from previous levels
T Tested in this level

---

1 Preparing for the page

R, T **Sound/symbol correspondence:** consonants /d/ *d*, /s/ *s*; vowel /a/ *a* (initial)

Display *Letter Cards d, s,* and *a* in the *Pocket Chart.* Remind pupils that they have learned the sound that each letter stands for. Point to each letter and call on pupils to say the sound the letter stands for.

> **SAY** **I am going to say some words. Each word begins with one of these letters. After I say each word, I will ask one of you to point to the letter that stands for the sound at the beginning of the word.**

Use the following words: *dinner, sun, apple, door, danger, sail, animal, seven, dinosaur.*

Make sure each pupil has *Word Builder Cards d, a,* and *s.*

> **SAY** **I am going to say some words that begin with /d/, /s/, or /a/. When you hear a word that begins with /d/, hold up your letter d. When you hear a word that begins with /s/, hold up your letter s. When you hear a word that begins with /a/, hold up your letter a.**

Use the following words: *decorate, sandwich, apple, sad, dentist, ambulance.*

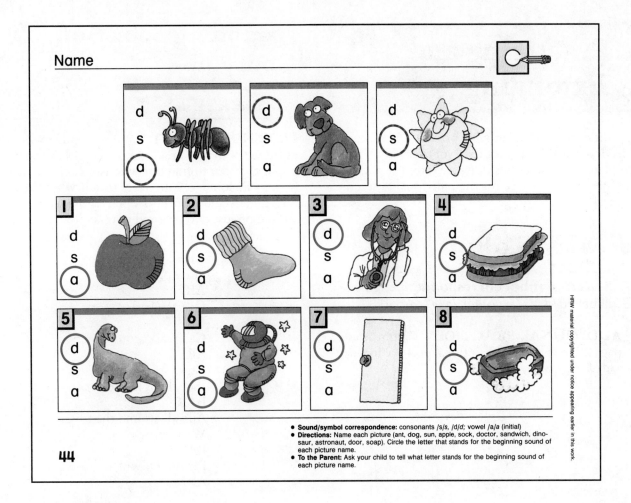

- **Sound/symbol correspondence:** consonants /s/s, /d/d; vowel /a/a (initial)
- **Directions:** Name each picture (ant, dog, sun, apple, sock, doctor, sandwich, dinosaur, astronaut, door, soap). Circle the letter that stands for the beginning sound of each picture name.
- **To the Parent:** Ask your child to tell what letter stands for the beginning sound of each picture name.

44

2 Using the page

R, T   **Sound/symbol correspondence:** consonants /d/*d*, /s/*s*; vowel /a/*a* (initial)

Help pupils locate page 44 in their books and identify the picture in the first box at the top. (ant)

SAY   **What sound do you hear at the beginning of the word *ant*?** (/a/) **What letter stands for that sound?** (a) **Find the letter *a* in the box with the picture. Trace the circle around the *a* to show that the word *ant* begins with the /a/ sound.**

Have pupils identify the picture of a dog and trace the circle around letter *d*. Have pupils identify the picture of the sun and trace the circle around letter *s*.

Tell pupils to complete the page by circling the letter in each box that stands for the beginning sound of the picture name. Identify the pictures as apple, sock, doctor, sandwich, dinosaur, astronaut, door, soap.

3 Developing the Skills

R, T   **Sound/symbol correspondence:** consonants /d/*d*, /s/*s*; vowel /a/*a* (initial)

SAY   **I'm going to read a sentence that has some words that begin with /d/.** **After I read the sentence, I'll ask you to tell me all the words that begin with /d/. Listen to this sentence: *Dennis dances with Denise.* What words begin with /d/?** (Dennis, dances, Denise)

Follow a similar procedure with the following sentences:

1. (/s/) **Sarah sells sunflowers.**

2. (/s/) **Annie and Andy were astronauts.**

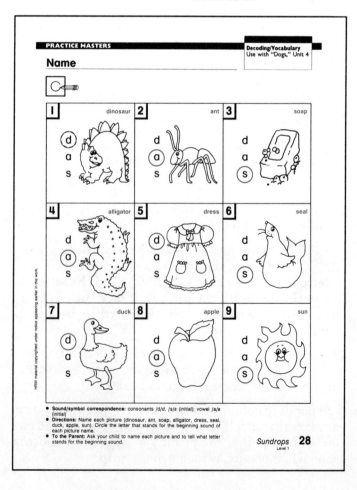

*Practicing and Extending

The activities that follow provide practice and extension of skills developed in this lesson. Not every pupil needs to complete these activities. Choose only the activities that are needed to provide for the individual differences in your classroom.

Practicing Skills

R, T   Sound/symbol correspondence: consonants /d/*d*, /s/*s*; vowel /a/*a* (initial)

PM 28   ADDITIONAL PRACTICE   *Practice Masters* page 28 may be used as optional practice for identifying /d/*d*, /s/*s*, and /a/*a*.

Extending Selection Concepts

LISTENING: POETRY   Ask pupils to listen to an untitled poem by Karla Kuskin. Reread the poem asking pupils to listen to find out who is speaking in the poem. (a dog) Encourage volunteers to tell what the dog does not understand about people. (how they can walk around on just two legs and not fall down)

> I do not understand
> ARF
> How people
> ARF
> GROWL
> BARK
> Can walk around on two
> ARF
> Legs.
> I see them in the park
> BARK
> And all around the town
> Without
> BARK
> Falling Down!
> ARF
>
> *Karla Kuskin*

ACTIVITY 5 Relating Final /d/ to *d*

Skill Strands

DECODING/VOCABULARY

I, T **Sound/symbol correspondence:** consonant /d/*d* (final)

Materials

Sundrops, Level 1: page 45
Practice Masters: page 29
Resource Box: Letter Card d
Word Builder and *Word Builder Card d*
Pocket Chart
Teacher's Idea Book

Special Populations

See *Teacher's Idea Book* for additional suggestions to help pupils with limited English proficiency.

Key to Symbols
I Introduced in this lesson
R Reinforced from an earlier lesson in this level
M Maintained from previous levels
T Tested in this level

---

1 Preparing for the page

I, T **Sound/symbol correspondence:** consonant /d/*d* (final)

Place *Letter Card d* in the *Pocket Chart.* Ask volunteers to name the letter and to tell what sound the letter stands for. (/d/) Ask them to name words that begin with the /d/ sound.

> **SAY** **I am going to say a word that has the /d/ sound at the end: *sled*. Say the word *sled* after me: *sled*. I will say some other words that have /d/ at the end, and you say them after me.**

Use the following words: *sad, glad, thread, mud.*

Make sure each pupil has *Word Builder Card d.*

> **SAY** **I am going to say some words that have /d/ at the end and some words that do not have /d/ at the end. When you hear a word that has /d/ at the end, hold up letter *d*. Do not hold up your card if you do not hear /d/ at the end of a word.**

Use the following words: *red, clock, food, mud, skid, ship, hood.*

Make sure each pupil has a *Word Builder.* Point to the left side of the *Word Builder* and remind pupils that the left side is the beginning of the *Word Builder.* Remind pupils that the right side is the end of the *Word Builder.*

> **SAY** ***Dog* has the /d/ sound at the beginning, so I put *d* in the beginning of the *Word Builder* for the word *dog*.** (Demonstrate.) ***Sled* has the /d/ sound at the end, so I put *d* at the end of the *Word Builder* for the word *sled*.** (Demonstrate.)

Explain that you will say some words that have the /d/ sound at the beginning and some words that have the /d/ sound at the end. Pupils should place their *d* card at the beginning of the *Word Builder* if they hear /d/ at the beginning of the word and they should place their *d* card at the end of the *Word Builder* if they hear /d/ at the end of the word. Use these words: *donkey, down, glad, kid, delicious, read, mad, sand.*

Unit 4 "Dogs" (pages 41–50)   T157

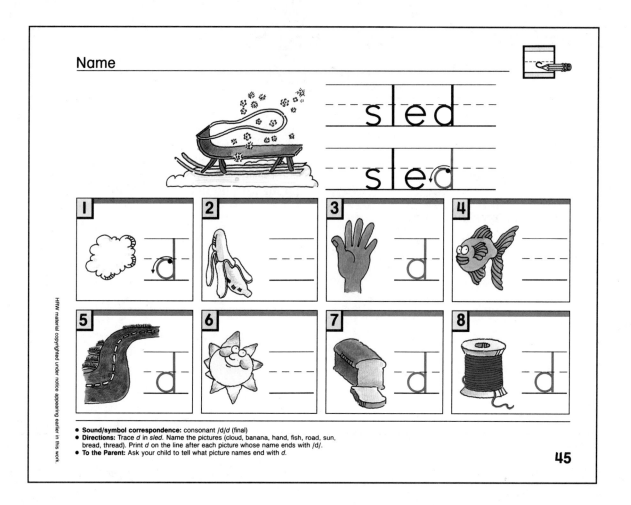

Name _____

sled
sled

1 [cloud] d↻	2 [banana] ____	3 [hand] d	4 [fish] d
5 [road] d	6 [sun] ____	7 [bread] d	8 [thread] d

- **Sound/symbol correspondence:** consonant /d/ *d* (final)
- **Directions:** Trace *d* in *sled.* Name the pictures (cloud, banana, hand, fish, road, sun, bread, thread). Print *d* on the line after each picture whose name ends with /d/.
- **To the Parent:** Ask your child to tell what picture names end with *d.*

45

2 Using the page

I, T   Sound/symbol correspondence: consonant /d/ *d* (final)

Help pupils find page 45 in their books and identify the picture at the top of the page. (sled) Ask pupils to tell where they hear the /d/ sound in *sled.* (at the end) Have them point to the letter *d* in the word *sled* and tell where it appears. (at the end) Have pupils trace the letter *d* at the end of the second word *sled.*

Call on a volunteer to identify the picture in the first box. (cloud)

SAY Do you hear the /d/ sound at the end of the word *cloud?* (yes) Trace the letter *d* on the line after the picture to show that *cloud* has the /d/ sound at the end.

Have the next picture identified. (banana)

SAY Do you hear the /d/ sound at the end of *banana?* (no) Because *banana* does not have the /d/ sound at the end, do not print letter *d* on the line.

Help pupils identify the remaining pictures as hand, fish, road, sun, bread, thread. Tell pupils to finish the page by printing *d* on the line after each picture whose name ends with the /d/ sound.

3 Developing the Skills

I, T   Sound/symbol correspondence: consonant /d/ *d* (final)

Tell pupils that you will say some rhymes that have the last word missing and that each of the missing words ends with the /d/ sound. Read each rhyme and invite pupils to guess the missing word. Encourage them to repeat the completed rhymes and to name the rhyming words.

1. **Be careful how you get out of bed.**
   I wouldn't want you to bump your _____. (head)

2. **If you grab dry sand,**
   It will slip through your _____. (hand)

3. **My grandmother said,**
   "Please buy some _____." (bread)

4. **We found a toad**
   Sitting in the _____. (road)

✳ Practicing and Extending

The activities that follow provide practice and extension of skills developed in this lesson. Not every pupil needs to complete these activities. Choose only the activities that are needed to provide for the individual differences in your classroom.

Practicing Skills

I, T   Sound/symbol correspondence: consonant /d/ *d* (final)

PM 29   ADDITIONAL PRACTICE   *Practice Masters* page 29 may be used as optional practice for identifying sound/symbol correspondence /d/ *d*.

Extending Selection Concepts

> ART

SPEAKING: TELLING ABOUT A PICTURE
Have pupils print letter *d* on the bottom of a piece of drawing paper. Ask each pupil to draw a picture of a dog. Invite volunteers to tell about the dog they have drawn. Display the pictures. Have a "dog show" by inviting pupils to select the biggest dog, the funniest dog, the dog with the longest tail, etc. Try to give a construction-paper ribbon to each dog picture.

PRACTICE MASTERS

Decoding/Vocabulary
Use with "Dogs," Unit 4

Name

- **Sound/symbol correspondence:** consonant /d/ *d* (final)
- **Directions:** Name the pictures (cloud, tree, road, car, sled, rock). Print *d* after each picture whose name ends with /d/.
- **To the Parent:** Ask your child to name the words that end with *d*.

Sundrops **29**
Level 1

ACTIVITY 6 Discriminating Initial and Final /d/ *d* page 46 (T160–T162)

Skill Strands

| DECODING/VOCABULARY |

R, T **Sound/symbol correspondence:** consonant /d/*d* (initial, final)

Materials

Sundrops, Level 1: page 46

Practice Masters: page 30
Word Builder and *Word Builder Card d*
Teacher's Idea Book

Special Populations

See *Teacher's Idea Book* for additional suggestions to help pupils with limited English proficiency.

Key to Symbols
I Introduced in this lesson
R Reinforced from an earlier lesson in this level
M Maintained from previous levels
T Tested in this level

---

1 Preparing for the page

R, T **Sound/symbol correspondence:** consonant /d/*d* (initial, final)

Print letter *d* on the chalkboard and remind pupils that this letter stands for the /d/ sound at the beginning of words such as *dog.* Then remind pupils that the /d/ sound can also be found at the end of words, such as *sled.*

Display a *Word Builder* and *Word Builder Card d.*

> **SAY** I will say a word that has the /d/ sound at the beginning or at the end. After I say the word, I will call on someone to take the *d* Card and place it in the *Word Builder* to show where the /d/ sound is heard in the word.

Use the following words: *doll, had, found, dessert, daisy, sand, pond, dumpling.*

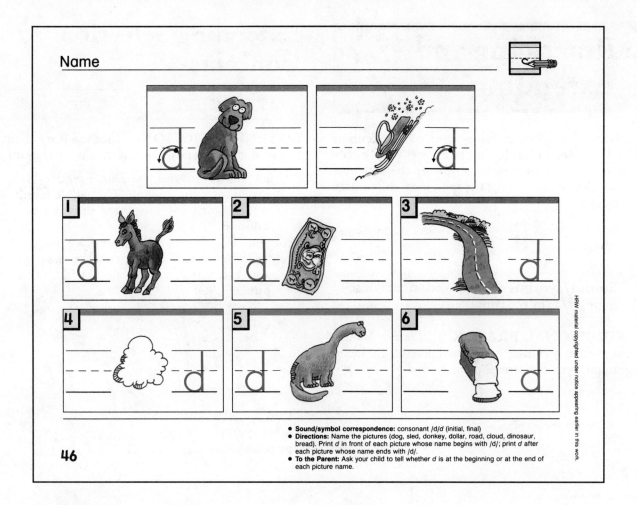

Name _____

- **Sound/symbol correspondence:** consonant /d/d (initial, final)
- **Directions:** Name the pictures (dog, sled, donkey, dollar, road, cloud, dinosaur, bread). Print *d* in front of each picture whose name begins with /d/; print *d* after each picture whose name ends with /d/.
- **To the Parent:** Ask your child to tell whether *d* is at the beginning or at the end of each picture name.

46

2 Using the page

3 Developing the Skills

R, T **Sound/symbol correspondence:** consonant /d/*d* (initial, final)

R, T **Sound/symbol correspondence:** consonant /d/*d* (initial, final)

Help pupils find page 46 in their books and call on a volunteer to identify the first picture at the top. (dog)

ASK **Does the /d/ sound come at the beginning of the word *dog* or at the end of the word?** (at the beginning) **Trace the letter *d* on the writing line in front of the picture of the dog to show that the /d/ sound is heard at the beginning of the word.**

Have pupils identify the picture in the next box. (sled) Ask where the /d/ sound is heard in *sled.* (at the end) Have pupils trace the *d* after the picture of a sled to show that the /d/ sound is at the end of the word. Have pupils complete the page by printing *d* in front of pictures whose names begin with /d/ and printing *d* after pictures whose names end with /d/. Identify the pictures as donkey, dollar, road, cloud, dinosaur, bread.

Tell pupils that you will read some sentences that have words that begin or end with the /d/ sound. Ask pupils to repeat the sentence after you say it. Then say each underlined word in the sentence and have pupils tell if they hear /d/ at the beginning of the word or at the end of the word. Use the following sentences:

1. The <u>dog</u> ran out the <u>door.</u>
2. The <u>dentist</u> said, "<u>Don't</u> chew gum."
3. A cat and a <u>duck</u> <u>tried</u> to get the <u>bread.</u>
4. The <u>dog</u> left its <u>yard</u> to <u>dig</u> for bones.
5. I put my <u>hand</u> in my <u>desk.</u>
6. <u>David</u> <u>discovered</u> <u>sand</u> in the <u>pond.</u>

✳ Practicing and Extending

The activities that follow provide practice and extension of skills developed in this lesson. Not every pupil needs to complete these activities. Choose only the activities that are needed to provide for the individual differences in your classroom.

Practicing Skills

R, T   Sound/symbol correspondence: consonant /d/ *d* (initial, final)

PM 30   ADDITIONAL PRACTICE   *Practice Masters* page 30 may be used as optional practice for identifying sound/symbol correspondence /d/ *d*.

HOW AM I DOING?

Many pupils need to establish or improve their self-confidence in reading. To help improve children's self-confidence, ask yourself the following questions to gauge your teaching effectiveness in this area.

	Yes	No	Some-times
1. Have I made a wide selection of picture books available?	☐	☐	☐
2. Have I encouraged pupils to look through books even if they may be unable to read the words?	☐	☐	☐
3. Have I provided time to permit individuals to tell about the books they have read and enjoyed?	☐	☐	☐
4. Have I praised pupils for reading?	☐	☐	☐

Extending Selection Concepts

LITERATURE

LISTENING: FICTION   Choose a story about a dog and read it to the class. Discuss the dog in the story.

Hughes, Shirley, *David and Dog*. Prentice-Hall, 1977. David loses his toy dog. The whole family is concerned until his big sister provides a touching solution.

Skorpen, Liesel Moak, *His Mother's Dog*. Harper & Row, 1978. A boy is disappointed when the puppy he has always wanted likes his mother more than it likes him.

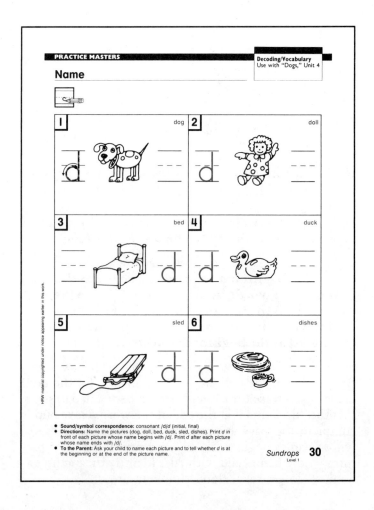

PRACTICE MASTERS

Decoding/Vocabulary
Use with "Dogs," Unit 4

Name

1 dog
2 doll
3 bed
4 duck
5 sled
6 dishes

• Sound/symbol correspondence: consonant /d/ *d* (initial, final)
• **Directions:** Name the pictures (dog, doll, bed, duck, sled, dishes). Print *d* in front of each picture whose name begins with /d/. Print *d* after each picture whose name ends with /d/.
• **To the Parent:** Ask your child to name each picture and to tell whether *d* is at the beginning or at the end of the picture name.

Sundrops
Level 1   **30**

ACTIVITY 7 Building Words
page 47 (T163–T165)

Skill Strands

DECODING/VOCABULARY

I **Vocabulary:** word building

COMPREHENSION/THINKING

R, T **Literal:** sequence

Materials

Sundrops, Level 1: page 47
Resource Box: Letter Cards a, d, D, m, s, S
Word Builder and *Word Builder Cards a, d, D, m, s, S*
Pocket Chart
Teacher's Idea Book

Special Populations

See *Teacher's Idea Book* for additional suggestions to help pupils with limited English proficiency.

Key to Symbols
I Introduced in this lesson
R Reinforced from an earlier lesson in this level
M Maintained from previous levels
T Tested in this level

1 Preparing for the page

I **Vocabulary:** word building

Place *Letter Cards m, a, s, S, d,* and *D* in random order in the *Pocket Chart.* Point to each letter and call on a volunteer to name the letter and the sound it stands for. Remind pupils that letters can be put together to make words. Place *Letter Cards S, a,* and *m* together to make the word *Sam* and have the word read. (*Sam*) Remind pupils that the word *Sam* has a capital letter at the beginning because it is a name. Now place *Letter Cards s, a,* and *d* in the *Pocket Chart* to make the word *sad.*

SAY **This is a word. Listen as I blend the sounds together.** (Move your hand under the letters as you blend the sounds: *ssaad.*) **Now you blend the sounds together with me: *ssaad.***

Now read the word. (sad) **Yes, the word is *sad.* I can change the word *sad* by changing the first letter.**

Replace the *s* in the *Pocket Chart* with *Letter Card d,* making the word *dad.*

SAY **Now blend the sounds with me.** (Move your hand under the letters as you blend the sounds with pupils: *daad.* **What is this word?** (*dad*)

Ask volunteers to use the word *dad* in a sentence.

Make sure each pupil has a *Word Builder* and *Word Builder Cards a, m, s,* and *d.*

SAY **You can use the letters you know to make words that you can read. I will tell you what letters to put in your *Word Builder.* Then I will ask you to read the word you made. First, place *s* at the beginning, then place *a* after *s,* and *d* after *a.***

Check to see that pupils have placed the cards in the correct order. Make sure that the cards touch each other so that there is no space between the letters of the word. Call on volunteers to read the word. (*sad*)

SAY **Now let's make the word *mad.* Take letter *s* out of the *Word Builder* and place letter *m* in front of letter *a.* What is the word?** (*mad*)

Name _____

- **Vocabulary:** word building
- **Directions:** Print the missing letters to complete the words *Dad*, *mad*, and *sad*.
- **To the Parent:** Ask your child to read the word under each picture and to tell a story from the pictures.

47

Repeat this procedure with the word *dad*. Ask pupils to take letter *m* out of the *Word Builder* and to place letter *d* at the beginning of the word. Call on volunteers to read the word. (*dad*) Remind pupils that blending the sounds of letters together is a way to figure out what a word is when they read.

2 Using the page

I Vocabulary: word building

Help pupils find page 47 in their books and call attention to the first picture. Ask what is happening in this picture. (A man is reading the newspaper.) Explain that this man is a girl's father and that his daughter calls him "Dad."

> **SAY** Since his daughter calls him "Dad," *Dad* is a name. That is why it begins with a capital letter. I see the letters that stand for /da/ in the word *dad*. What sound is missing from the end of the word *Dad*? (/d/) What letter do you need to finish the word *Dad*? (*d*) Print *d* after *Da*. Now let's read the word together: *Dad*.

Direct attention to the second picture and ask what is happening. (The dog Sam has torn up the paper.) Ask how the girl in the picture feels. (She is mad at Sam.)

> **SAY** The word under this picture should say *mad*. I see the letters that stand for /m/ and /d/. What sound is missing from the middle of the word? (/a/) What letter stands for the /a/ sound? (*a*) Print letter *a* between the *m* and the *d*. Now let's read the word together: *mad*.

Ask pupils to tell what is happening in the third picture. (The girl is picking up the papers.)

> **SAY** Look at Sam. How does Sam feel? (*sad*) This word should say *sad*. What letter is missing from the beginning of *sad*? (*s*) Print letter *s* in front of *ad* to finish the word. Let's read the word together: *sad*.

3 Developing the Skills

R, T Literal: sequence

Tell pupils to look at the pictures on page 47 and to listen as you will read a story about the pictures.

READ Sam liked to rest behind Dad's chair when Dad read the paper. Sam liked to hear the rustle of the paper as Dad turned the pages. Sam closed his eyes and listened to the friendly rustling sound.

Suddenly Dad got up and left the chair. The rustling sound stopped. Sam looked at the paper. Could he make the rustling sound? Sam picked up the paper and began to shake it. The lovely rustling started again. The more he shook, the better the sound was. Sam was having a wonderful time. Then Tam came in. She saw Sam shaking the papers. She was not happy with the rustling sound. She scolded Sam and made him stop.

Then Tam began to pick up the papers. Sam did not mean to make anyone mad. He only wanted to play. Now Sam was sad.

Tell pupils to look at the first picture and to tell what happened first in the story. (Sam listened to Dad rustle the newspaper as he read.)

SAY What happened next? (Sam shook the papers to make them rustle; Tam scolded him.) What happened last? (Tam picked up the papers; Sam was sad.)

* Practicing and Extending

The activities that follow provide practice and extension of skills developed in this lesson. Not every pupil needs to complete these activities. Choose only the activities that are needed to provide for the individual differences in your classroom.

Practicing Skills

I Vocabulary: word building

ADDITIONAL PRACTICE To review reading words by blending the sounds, display *Letter Cards a, m, s, S, d,* and *D.* Say a word and ask pupils to place the *Letter Cards* in the *Pocket Chart* to make the word. Possible words are: *am, Dad, mad, sad, Sam.*

ACTIVITY 8

Reading the Word *is*
page 48 (T166–T169)

Skill Strands

DECODING/VOCABULARY

I, T Vocabulary: word meaning

Materials

Sundrops, Level 1: page 48
Practice Masters: page 31
Resource Box: Word Cards *is, mad, sad, Sam*
              Punctuation Card *Period*
Pocket Chart
Teacher's Idea Book

Special Populations

See *Teacher's Idea Book* for additional suggestions to help pupils with limited English proficiency.

Key to Symbols
I Introduced in this lesson
R Reinforced from an earlier lesson in this level
M Maintained from previous levels
T Tested in this level

---

1 Preparing for the page

I, T Vocabulary: word meaning

SAY We have seen the dog Sam in several pictures in our books. Let's play a game to see how many things we can tell about Sam. You can make up something about Sam if you like. I will begin: Sam is furry. Sam is big. Who would like to tell me a sentence about Sam?

Call on volunteers to tell about Sam, using the words *Sam is _____.*

Place the sentence *Sam is sad.* in the *Pocket Chart.*

SAY Here is a sentence about Sam. Listen as I read the sentence. (Point to each word as you read *Sam is sad.* Point to the word *is.*) This is the word *is.* Say this word with me: *is.* Say *is* again. (*is*) Sometimes, when letter *s* is at the end of a word, it has the sound /z/. Read this word with me again. (*is*)

Then have pupils join you in reading the complete sentence. (*Sam is sad.*) Call on several pupils to point to the words as they read the sentence. Remove the word *sad* and replace it with the word *mad.* Have pupils read the new sentence. (*Sam is mad.*) Remove the word *mad* and call on pupils to point to and read the words *Sam is* and then to finish the sentence by telling something about Sam. (Possible answers are: Sam is noisy; Sam is shaggy.)

Hold up the *Word Card*s *Is* and *is* and have the words read. Then ask how the words are different. (One word begins with a capital letter.) Call on a volunteer to tell which word would be at the beginning of a sentence and why. (*Is*, because it begins with a capital letter)

Name _____

1. Sam

2. sad

3. Sam is mad.

4. Sam is sad.

• **Vocabulary:** word meaning
• **Directions:** Trace and read the word or sentence in each box. Fill in the circle under the picture that goes with the word or sentence.
• **To the Parent:** Ask your child to read the word or sentence and to explain which picture goes with that word or sentence.

48

2 Using the page

___

I, T Vocabulary: word meaning

Help pupils find page 48 in their books and ask them to look at box number 1 at the top of the page. Have pupils trace the word *Sam* and read it. Then have them look at the pictures in the box.

SAY **Which picture shows the dog Sam?** (the first picture) **Fill in the circle under the picture of Sam to show that this picture goes with the word *Sam*.**

Continue in the same manner with the next box. Then have pupils look at box number 3 and trace the words.

SAY **I can tell that these words are a sentence. How can I tell?** (There is a capital letter at the beginning and a period at the end.)

Have pupils read the sentence. Tell pupils to fill in the circle under the picture that goes with the sentence.

Continue in the same manner with the last box.

3 Developing the Skills

___

I, T   Vocabulary: word meaning

Tell pupils that you will play a guessing game called "What Is It?"

> **SAY** I will give you some clues. Every clue has the word *is* in it. After I give you all the clues, I will say, "What is it?" When you answer be sure to say "It is _____."

Give the following sets of clues:

1. **It is small and cuddly.**
   It is a baby dog.
   What is it? (It is a puppy.)

2. **It is a fruit.**
   It is long.
   It is yellow.
   What is it? (It is a banana.)

3. **It is a toy.**
   It is round.
   It is something you can bounce.
   What is it? (It is a ball.)

✳ Practicing and Extending

The activities that follow provide practice and extension of skills developed in this lesson. Not every pupil needs to complete these activities. Choose only the activities that are needed to provide for the individual differences in your classroom.

Practicing Skills

___

I, T   Vocabulary: word meaning

PM 31   ADDITIONAL PRACTICE *Practice Masters* page 31 may be used as optional practice for reading the word *is*.

Extending Selection
Concepts

LISTENING: INFORMATION Choose an informational book about dogs and read it aloud to the class. Ask volunteers to tell what they learned about dogs.

Hinds, P. Mignon. *Puppies Need Someone to Love.* Golden Press, 1981. This straightforward text tells just what puppies need to grow up healthy and happy.

Selsam, Millicent and Joyce Hunt. *A First Look at Dogs.* Walker and Co., 1981. This informative book explains that wolves, coyotes, foxes, and jackals are members of the dog family.

Skill Strands

DECODING/VOCABULARY

I Vocabulary: words in context

LANGUAGE

I Conventions of language: end punctuation (question mark)

Materials

Sundrops, Level 1: page 49
Practice Masters: page 32
Resource Box: Word Cards *am, Dad, I, Is, is, mad, sad, Sam,* Punctuation Cards *period, question mark*
Pocket Chart
Teacher's Idea Book

Special Populations

See *Teacher's Idea Book* for additional suggestions to help pupils with limited English proficiency.

Key to Symbols
I   Introduced in this lesson
R Reinforced from an earlier lesson in this level
M Maintained from previous levels
T Tested in this level

1 Preparing for the page

I Conventions of language: end punctuation (question mark)

Place *Word Cards I, am,* and *Sam* in the *Pocket Chart.* Tell pupils that this is a sentence and have it read. (*I am Sam*) Remind pupils that every sentence begins with a capital letter. Call on a volunteer to tell what capital letter begins the sentence *I am Sam.* (*I*)

SAY We learned that a sentence ends with a period. (Show *Punctuation Card period.*) This is a period. Who can place this period where it belongs in the sentence *I am Sam?*

Call on a volunteer. Then ask pupils to read the sentence.

Place the sentence *Dad is sad* in the *Pocket Chart.*

SAY Read this sentence with me: *Dad is sad.* This sentence tells something about Dad. Now watch as I change this sentence.

Rearrange the cards to make *Is Dad sad.* Point to each word as you read the question *Is Dad sad?*

SAY This sentence asks a question. If I ask, "Is Dad sad?" you could answer "yes" or "no." A sentence that asks something is called a question. We use a different kind of mark at the end of a question.

(Hold up *Punctuation Card question mark.*) This is a question mark. It looks like a hook that has a period under it. (Point to the question in the *Pocket Chart.*) Since *Is Dad sad* is a question, it needs a question mark at the end.

Place the question mark in the proper position on the *Pocket Chart.*

SAY Now read the question with me: *Is Dad sad?*

Place the question *Is Sam sad* in the *Pocket Chart.*

SAY This is also a question. What should we place after the word *sad* to show that this is a question? (a question mark)

Call on pupils to read the question. (*Is Sam sad?*) Encourage volunteers to tell why Sam might be sad.

Name _____

1	2
I am Sam.	Is Dad mad?
3	4
Is Sam sad?	Sam is mad.

- **Vocabulary:** words in context
- **Directions:** Read the story.
- **To the Parent:** Read and discuss the story with your child.

49

HRW material copyrighted under notice appearing earlier in this work.

2 Using the page

I Vocabulary: words in context

Have pupils open their books to page 49. Explain that you are going to tell part of a story about Sam and Dad and that they are going to read the part of the story that is printed in their books.

SAY Look at the first picture while I read part of the story.

READ Sam had a bone that he could hardly wait to bury. He began to dig a hole just the right size for his bone. Sam was so busy digging that he didn't see Dad looking out the window at him.

SAY Look at the words at the bottom of the first picture. They tell you what Sam might say if he could introduce himself to you.

Call on a volunteer to read the sentence. (*I am Sam.*)

SAY Now look at the second picture while I read the next story part.

READ Dad came out of the house and watched Sam make a big hole in the yard. Sam stopped digging and looked up at Dad.

SAY Look at the question at the bottom of the picture. The question asks how Dad might feel as he watches Sam dig a hole in the yard.

Call on a volunteer to read the question. (*Is Dad mad?*)

SAY Look at the third picture while I read more of the story.

READ Sam thought Dad was mad at him for digging in the yard. Sam hung his head in shame. Then Dad came out of the garage with a shovel and a rosebush.

SAY Look at the question at the bottom of the picture. The question asks how Sam might feel as Dad comes toward him.

Call on a volunteer to read the question. (*Is Sam sad?*)

SAY Now look at the last picture while I read.

READ Dad thought Sam's hole was just right, but not for a bone. Dad decided to plant a rosebush in the hole. Sam had helped Dad without knowing it. Now Dad didn't have to dig a hole for the rosebush. Now Sam had no hole for his bone after all his hard work!

SAY Look at the sentence at the bottom of the picture. The sentence tells how Sam feels about giving up his hole to a rosebush.

Call on a volunteer to read the sentence. (*Sam is mad.*)

Ask pupils to tell if they think Dad was mad when he saw Sam digging in the yard and to tell why they think that way. (Answers will vary. Possible answers include: yes, but then he had an idea or no, he knew what to do with the hole.) Ask if Sam was sad when Dad caught him digging a hole and why. (Yes, because the story said he hung his head in shame.)

3 Developing the Skills

I Vocabulary: words in context

Display *Word Cards I, am, Sam, Is, Dad, mad, sad, is,* and *Punctuation Cards period* and *question mark* in random order. Tell pupils that you will say a sentence and then you will ask them to use the cards to make the sentence in the *Pocket Chart.*

Say the sentence *I am Sam* and have volunteers place the words in the *Pocket Chart.* Remind pupils to place the correct mark at the end of the sentence. Continue in the same manner with these sentences:

1. Sam is mad.
2. Is Dad mad?
3. Is Sam sad?
4. I am Sam.

* Practicing and Extending

The activities that follow provide practice and extension of skills developed in this lesson. Not every pupil needs to complete these activities. Choose only the activities that are needed to provide for the individual differences in your classroom.

Practicing Skills

I, T   Vocabulary: words in context

PM 32   ADDITIONAL PRACTICE   *Practice Masters* page 32 may be used as optional practice for reading sentences and questions.

Extending Selection Concepts

LISTENING: FICTION   Choose a book with a question mark in the title and read it aloud. After the reading, have pupils answer the question in the title as the story character would have answered it.

Gackenbach, Dick. *Do You Love Me?* The Seabury Press, 1975. After the accidental death of a humming-bird, Walter learns that not all creatures want to be pets. To help Walter, his sister gives him a puppy that wants to be Walter's pet.

Raskin, Ellen. *Who, Said Sue, Said Whoo?* Atheneum, 1973. In this nonsense book, animals speak and jump into Sue's car, all looking for the one who said "chitter-chitter chatter."

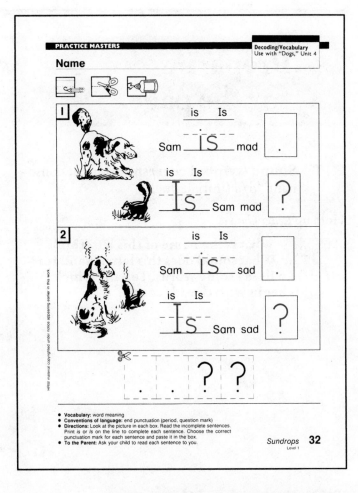

ACTIVITY 10 Reviewing /d/*d*

Skill Strands

DECODING/VOCABULARY

R, T **Sound/symbol correspondence:** consonant /d/*d* (initial, final)

STUDY SKILLS

R **Organizing information:** classification

Materials

Sundrops, Level 1: page 50
Practice Masters: page 33
Resource Box: Letter Card d
Picture Cards *Chihuahua, Great Dane, Pekingese, sheep dog, St. Bernard, toy poodle*
Pocket Chart
Teacher's Idea Book
Sound/Symbol Folder (See page T43 for instructions.)

Special Populations

See *Teacher's Idea Book* for additional suggestions to help pupils with limited English proficiency.

Key to Symbols
I Introduced in this lesson
R Reinforced from an earlier lesson in this level
M Maintained from previous levels
T Tested in this level

1 Preparing for the page

R, T **Sound/symbol correspondence:** consonant /d/*d* (initial, final)

Hold up *Letter Card d.*

ASK **What is the name of this letter?** (d) **What sound does this letter stand for?** (/d/) **I will say some words. Tell me which words begin with the /d/ sound.**

Use the words *do, kite, dim, dog, flower, dance, dug.*

Remind pupils that in some words the /d/ sound comes at the end of the word.

SAY **In the word *bed,* where do you hear the /d/ sound?** (at the end) **Now I will say some more words. Tell me which words end with the /d/ sound.**

Use the words *hid, puppy, sound, sand, carrot, show*

T174 *Sundrops,* Level 1

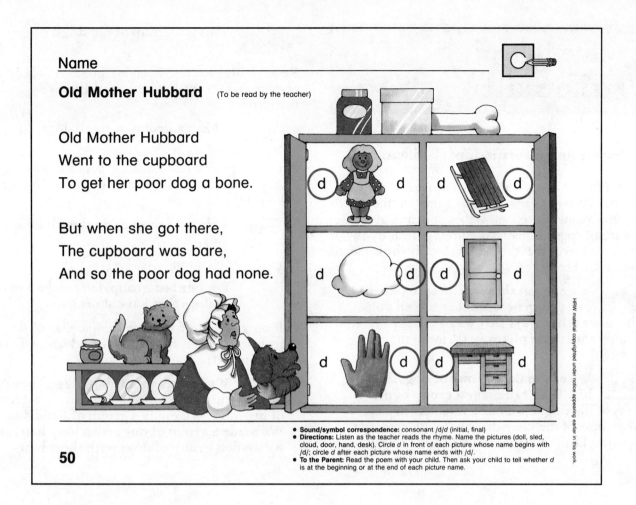

Name _____

Old Mother Hubbard (To be read by the teacher)

Old Mother Hubbard
Went to the cupboard
To get her poor dog a bone.

But when she got there,
The cupboard was bare,
And so the poor dog had none.

- **Sound/symbol correspondence:** consonant /d/d (initial, final)
- **Directions:** Listen as the teacher reads the rhyme. Name the pictures (doll, sled, cloud, door, hand, desk). Circle d in front of each picture whose name begins with /d/; circle d after each picture whose name ends with /d/.
- **To the Parent:** Read the poem with your child. Then ask your child to tell whether d is at the beginning or at the end of each picture name.

50

2 Using the page

R, T Sound/symbol correspondence: consonant /d/d (initial, final)

Display *Big Book* page 50. Point to the nursery rhyme and ask pupils to guess what nursery rhyme this is. If necessary, explain that this nursery rhyme is called "Old Mother Hubbard." Have pupils listen as you read the rhyme. Reread the rhyme and ask pupils to say the words with you. Then have pupils find page 50 in their books. Point out the cupboard shelves.

SAY **Mother Hubbard didn't find a bone in the cupboard, but this cupboard has some other things in it. What is the first thing on the top shelf?** (a doll) **Where do you hear the /d/ sound in the word *doll*?** (at the beginning) **Circle the *d* in front of the doll to show that the /d/ sound is at the beginning of the word.**

Help pupils identify the remaining pictures as sled, cloud, door, hand, and desk. Tell pupils to circle *d* in front of each picture whose name begins with /d/ and to circle *d* after each picture whose name ends with /d/.

When pupils have completed the page ask them to draw a bone for Mother Hubbard's dog.

3 Developing the Skills

R   Organizing information: classification

Display *Picture Cards sheep dog, St. Bernard, Great Dane, Chihuaha, Pekingese,* and *Scottish terrier* in the *Pocket Chart.* Ask pupils to tell how these pictures are alike. (They are all dogs.) Call on volunteers to identify any of the pictured breeds that they know. Supply the names of the unknown breeds.

| SAY | We can put these pictures together in one group because they are all dogs. There are other ways that we can make groups with these pictures. (Remove the pictures.) |

| SAY | We can make a group of dogs that are big. Who can make a group of pictures of big dogs? (Call on a volunteer to place the pictures of the sheep dog, the St. Bernard, and the Great Dane in the *Pocket Chart.*) |

| SAY | This is a group of big dogs. |

Remove the pictures. Then ask pupils to make a group of dogs that are small. (Chihuaha, Pekingese, and Scottish terrier)

| SAY | This is a group of small dogs. |

Remove the pictures. Then ask pupils to make a group of dogs that have long hair. (sheep dog, St. Bernard, Pekingese)

| SAY | This is a group of dogs with long hair. |

Remove the pictures.

| SAY | For our last group, let's make a group of dogs that have short hair. |

Call on a volunteer to place the pictures of dogs with short hair in the *Pocket Chart.* (Great Dane, Chihauaha, Scottish terrier)

| SAY | We had six pictures of dogs. From that group of dogs, we made a group of big dogs. We made a group of little dogs. We made a group of dogs with long hair, and we made a group of dogs with short hair. |

✳ Practicing and Extending

The activities that follow provide practice and extension of skills developed in this lesson. Not every pupil needs to complete these activities. Choose only the activities that are needed to provide for the individual differences in your classroom.

Practicing Skills

R, T   Sound/symbol correspondence: consonant /d/*d* (initial, final)

PM 33   ADDITIONAL PRACTICE   *Practice Masters* page 33 may be used as optional practice for identifying sound/symbol correspondence /d/*d*.

ADDITIONAL PRACTICE   Invite pupils to work in pairs or small groups to discriminate the /d/ sound in the pictures in the Sound/Symbol Folder for *d*. (See page T43.)

Extending Selection Concepts

LITERATURE

LISTENING: POETRY   Read aloud the nursery rhyme "Hey, Diddle, Diddle."

> Hey, diddle diddle,
> The cat and the fiddle,
> The cow jumped over the moon;
> The little dog laughed
> To see such sport,
> And the dish ran away with the spoon.

Reread the rhyme several times and ask pupils to join you. Ask pupils to tell what each animal in the rhyme did. Then have pupils tell whether the animals could be real.

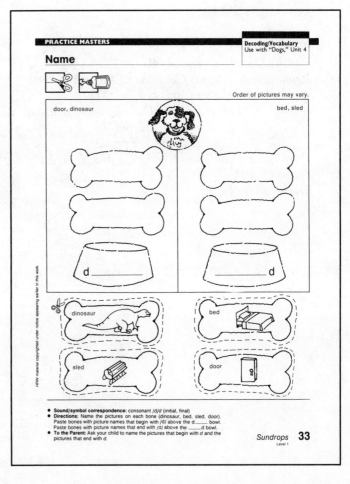

Unit 5 "Turtles"
pages 51–60 (T178–T213)

Skill Strands

DECODING/VOCABULARY

I, T   **Sound/symbol correspondence:** consonant /t/*t* (initial, final)

R, T   **Sound/symbol correspondence:** consonants /m/*m,* /s/*s,* /d/ (initial)

I   **Vocabulary:** word building

I, T   **Vocabulary:** word meaning

I   **Vocabulary:** words in context

STUDY SKILLS

R   **Graphic aids:** illustrations

COMPREHENSION/THINKING

I   **Critical thinking:** using prior knowledge

R, T   **Inferential:** main idea

R, T   **Literal:** sequence

LANGUAGE

R   **Listening:** specific information

R   **Writing:** language–experience stories

Materials

Sundrops, Level 1: pages 51–60

Practice Masters: pages 34–40

Resource Box: Picture Cards ducks, fire engine, turtle
     Letter Cards a, d, m, s, T, t
     Word Cards Dad, is, mad, mat, on, sad, Sam, sat, Tad, the, The
     Punctuation Card period

Word Builder and Word Builder Cards a, d, m, s, t

Pocket Chart

Teacher's Idea Book

Language Applications

EXTENDING SELECTION CONCEPTS

Listening: fiction
Listening: tongue twisters
Listening: poetry
Speaking: retelling stories
Listening: information

Special Populations

See *Teacher's Idea Book* for additional suggestions to help pupils with limited English proficiency.

Key to Symbols
I   Introduced in this lesson
R   Reinforced from an earlier lesson in this level
M   Maintained from previous levels
T   Tested in this level

Idea Center

EGG-CARTON TURTLES

For Activity 1, gather materials for pupils to make egg-carton turtles: egg-carton, green or brown construction paper, paste. Follow the directions in the *Teacher's Idea Book* to complete the turtles.

"TORTOISE AND HARE RACE"

For Activity 8, make the "Tortoise and Hare Race" game. On the inside of a manila folder, duplicate the gameboard found in the *Teacher's Idea Book*. Use *Word Cards* from the *Resource Box*, or make a set of word cards with the words *am, dad, I, is, mad, mat, on, sad, Sam, sat, Tad, the*. Buttons or beans may be used as game markers.

SOUND/SYMBOL FOLDER

For Activity 10, make a Sound/Symbol Folder for letter *t*. See page T43 for instructions.

BIBLIOGRAPHY

The book below is the literary selection that has been reprinted in Activity 1. You may wish to have this book on display for pupils to enjoy after you have read the story.

Freschet, Berniece. *Turtle Pond.* Charles Scribner's Sons, 1971.

Add other books about turtles or books that have turtles as characters to the reading table. Encourage pupils to look at the books on their own. Suggestions for reading books aloud appear throughout this lesson. Listed below is a bibliography to choose from. Annotations for the books appear in the activities.

Asch, Frank. *Turtle Tale.* Dial, 1978.
Balian, Lorna. *The Aminal.* Abingdon Press, 1972.
Castle, Caroline. *The Hare and the Tortoise.* Dial Press, 1985.
Craig, Janet. *Turtles.* Troll Associates, 1982.
Roche, A. K. *The Clever Turtle.* Prentice Hall, 1969.
Rosenbloom, Joseph. *Twist These on Your Tongue.* Thomas Nelson, 1978.
Van Woerkom, Dorothy. *Harry and Shellburt.* Macmillan, 1977.
Waters, John F. *Hatchlings: The Lives of Baby Turtles.* Walker and Company, 1979.
Williams, Barbara. *Albert's Toothache.* Dutton, 1974.

ACTIVITY 1 Listening to "Turtle Pond"
page 51 (T180–T184)

Skill Strands

COMPREHENSION/THINKING

I Critical thinking: using prior knowledge

LANGUAGE

R Listening: specific information

STUDY SKILLS

R Graphic aids: illustrations

Materials

Sundrops, Level 1: page 51
Egg-carton Turtles (See page T179 for instructions.)

Special Populations

See *Idea Book* for additional suggestions to help pupils with limited English proficiency.

Key to Symbols
I Introduced in this lesson
R Reinforced from an earlier lesson in this level
M Maintained from previous levels
T Tested in this level

1 Preparing for the page

SUMMARY A female turtle lumbers along to a dry, sandy place and lays eleven eggs in a hole. Within two months, the eggs hatch, and the baby turtles begin their treacherous journey to the safety of the pond.

I Critical thinking: using prior knowledge

Ask pupils to tell what they know about turtles. Guide the discussion by asking pupils to describe a turtle. (It is a small animal with a shell.) Ask how turtles protect themselves. (Most turtles can pull their head, legs, and tail into the shell to protect themselves.)

Print the title "Turtle Pond" on the chalkboard and read it. Tell pupils that this is the title of a story that you are going to read. Explain that this is a true story. Tell pupils that the person who wrote this book wanted us to learn about turtles.

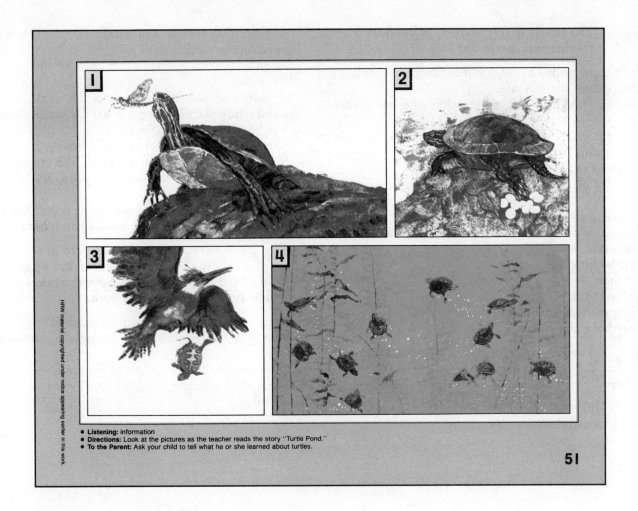

- **Listening:** information
- **Directions:** Look at the pictures as the teacher reads the story "Turtle Pond."
- **To the Parent:** Ask your child to tell what he or she learned about turtles.

51

2 Using the page

R Listening: specific information

Help pupils find page 51 in their books. Explain that the pictures on this page are from the story "Turtle Pond" and that pupils can look at these pictures as you read. Ask pupils to listen to find out how mother turtles care for their babies. The words in boldface type are possible aside comments to be read or stated by you as if you were thinking aloud.

Turtle Pond
by Berniece Freschet

SAY | **Look at the first picture as I read.**

It was a warm June day at the pond.

White lilies opened wide. Bees buzzed near. A red-headed woodpecker drummed on a maple tree.

A turtle lay on a rock.

Because of the color of her shell she looked very much like the rock.

She lay in the sun and waited for a mayfly.

A mayfly flew down.

The turtle stretched her long neck out. With a quick snap of her jaws—the mayfly was gone.

The turtle laid her head on one foot and waited for another fly to come close.

Two young otters slid down a mudbank and into the water.

The otters liked to play, and this was one of their favorite games. The noisy, splashing otters frightened the turtle.

SAY **The turtle is frightened. What does a frightened turtle do?**

Quickly she pulled her legs and neck into her shell. In her shell-house she was safe.

She was very still. For a long time she hid in her house.

Not far from the turtle's rock, two green frogs sat side by side on a lily pad.

A big bass swam near.

A family of ducks went by, making ripples on the water.

"Quack, quack!" they called.

After a while—slowly—very slowly—the turtle peeked out of her shell.

Little by little, her neck stretched out farther.

And then, one by one, out came her feet.

She looked around.

When she was sure it was safe, she moved off the rock and crawled along the shore.

SAY **The turtle is moving. I wonder where she's going. Let's look at the next picture.**

Slowly, she pushed up the bank, moving first one chunky foot and then the other.

A butterfly, yellow and black, fluttered down and lighted on the turtle's shell.

High in a tree, a sparrow sang. The butterfly flew away.

A short distance from the water the turtle came to a dry and sandy place. This was what she was looking for.

She began to dig in the sand.

She dug a hole, and there she laid her eggs.

She laid eleven eggs in the hole. She covered them with sand. And over the sand she piled dry leaves and twigs.

Soon she crawled away, back to the pond. She would not return. She knew the sun would hatch her eggs.

SAY **A turtle buries her eggs to protect them. She doesn't sit on her eggs the way a bird does. I wonder how she takes care of her babies when they hatch.**

In two months, the baby turtles hatched.

The little turtles pushed up through the sun-warmed earth.

They poked their heads out of the sand.

From that moment they knew how to take care of themselves.

SAY So, a mother turtle doesn't take care of her babies at all. The baby turtles take care of themselves. Look at the third picture and listen while I read what the babies have to do.

They hurried toward the pond.

This was a very dangerous time for the little turtles. In the water they could swim and hide in the thick weeds, but on land they were clumsy and easy to catch.

They must get into the water before an enemy found them.

The eleven little turtles fell over each other as they made their way to the pond.

From the alder bushes a catbird watched.

The turtles crawled close to a log where a water snake dozed.

They passed a parade of ants.

Now they were halfway to the pond.

In the blue sky above, a fishing bird dove downward. Newly hatched turtles were good to eat.

SAY Uh, oh! Look out little turtles!

The little turtles were almost to the pond.

Down, down dove the fishing bird.

Plop—plop—plop, three turtles pushed into the water.

Plop—plop—plop—plop, now seven turtles swam in the pond.

Soon all the turtles pushed into the water except one. The last turtle struggled over a mound of sand.

SAY Hurry up, little turtle!

The kingfisher swooped low. His beak opened. SNAP!

The fishing bird's beak shut over the tip of the last little turtle's tail.

The baby turtle was lifted up into the air. But the turtle's tail was so small that it slipped out of the fishing bird's beak.

Down fell the last little turtle—right into the middle of the pond.

SAY Whew! Our turtles were lucky. They all made it to the pond. Let's look at the last picture.

The turtles swam quickly away to hide.

They hid from the kingfisher.

They hid from the big bass.

They hid from the green heron.

They hid from the old bullfrog—and the water snake.

Now, deep in the pond, ten little turtles, and one with a crook in his tail, were safe, hidden among the waterweeds.

The mother turtle lay on her rock.

She lay in the warm sun and waited for a mayfly.

SAY How did the mother turtle take care of her babies? (She did not take care of them; they knew how to take care of themselves.) Why did the turtles want to get to the pond? (In the pond they would be able to hide from their enemies.)

3 Developing the Skills

R   Graphic aids: illustrations

SAY **Pictures in a book are called illustrations. Illustrations help us to understand a book. Let's look at the illustrations for "Turtle Pond" to see what they help us learn about turtles.**

Call attention to the pictures on page 51 as you ask these questions:

Picture 1: **What is happening in this picture?** (A turtle is catching a mayfly.) **Why?** (Some turtles eat flies and other insects.)

Picture 2: **What is the mother turtle doing in the second picture?** (laying her eggs in a sandy hole) **Will the mother sit on her eggs?** (No, the sun will warm the eggs until they hatch.)

Picture 3: **What is happening in this picture?** (A turtle is falling after being dropped by a fishing bird.) **Why is the turtle unlucky?** (He was caught by the bird; his tail has a crook in it from being in the bird's beak.) **Why is the turtle lucky?** (He fell into the pond, where he was safe.)

Picture 4: **Where are the turtles?** (swimming in the pond) **How do you think the turtles feel now that they are in the pond?** (Possible answers are: happy to be hiding in the waterweeds, safer than on the sand.) **Can you find the turtle with the crook in its tail?**

Encourage pupils to tell the parts of the story they thought were most exciting.

✳ Practicing and Extending

The activities that follow provide practice and extension of skills developed in this lesson. Not every pupil needs to complete these activities. Choose only the activities that are needed to provide for the individual differences in your classroom.

Extending Selection Concepts

ART

SPEAKING: RETELLING STORIES   Provide the materials for pupils to make egg-carton turtles. (See page T179.) The completed turtles can be used to help tell the adventures of the baby turtles in "Turtle Pond." Encourage volunteers to tell how the turtles hatched from their eggs and dodged their enemies to reach the safety of the pond.

HOW AM I DOING?

Most pupils are filled with creative ideas. Ask yourself the following questions to gauge your teaching effectiveness in this area.

	Yes	No	Some-times
1. Have I encouraged pupils to share their ideas with others?	☐	☐	☐
2. Have I provided a time for pupils to respond to one another's ideas?	☐	☐	☐
3. Have I provided an opportunity to let pupils organize their ideas before asking them to speak before a group?	☐	☐	☐

ACTIVITY 2 Recognizing Main Idea
page 52 (T185–T187)

Skill Strands

COMPREHENSION/THINKING

R, T Inferential: main idea

Materials

Sundrops, Level 1: page 52

Resource Box: Picture Cards ducks, fire engine, turtle
Pocket Chart

Special Populations

See *Teacher's Idea Book* for additional suggestions to help
pupils with limited English proficiency.

Key to Symbols
I Introduced in this lesson
R Reinforced from an earlier lesson in this level
M Maintained from previous levels
T Tested in this level

1 Preparing for the page

R, T Inferential: main idea

SAY In the last activity, I read you a story.
What was the story about? (turtles)
The title of the story was "Turtle Pond." The
person who wrote the story gave it that title.

Remind pupils that they can learn a lot from a title.

SAY Remember that the title of a story
often tells what the story is about.
Why is "Turtle Pond" a good name for this
story? (The story was about turtles and the pond
they lived in.)

I will show you some pictures. Then I will tell
you a story. After I finish telling the story, I
will ask you to tell me which picture the story
is about. Then tell me a title for the story.

Place *Picture Cards fire engine, turtle,* and *ducks*
in the *Pocket Chart.*

READ Tad wanted to go to the garden
where he could find some delicious
bugs. On his way across the yard, he saw a cat.
Tad stopped and pulled his head and his legs
inside his shell until the cat went away. After
the cat was gone, Tad crawled to the garden.

ASK Which picture goes with this story?
(turtle) **Why?** (The story is about a turtle
in a garden.) **What is a good title for this story?**
(Possible answers are: "The Turtle Crawls," "Tad
Turtle Goes to the Garden")

READ Everything was quiet in the apart-
ment. I was reading a book when I
heard the noise of a siren. It got louder and
louder. I ran to the window and saw a huge,
red fire engine race by our building. Before
long it was out of sight. I never found out
where it was going.

ASK Which picture goes with this story?
(fire engine) **Why?** (The story is about a
fire engine racing by.) **What is a good title for
this story?** (Possible answers are: "Fire Engine on
My Street" or "Seeing a Fire Engine Race By")

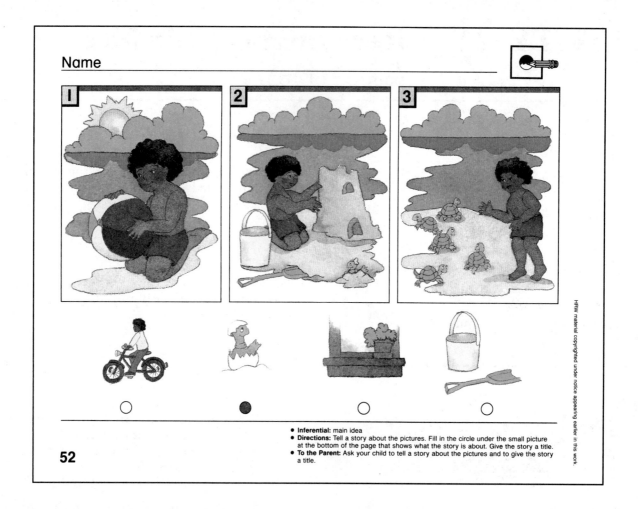

- **Inferential:** main idea
- **Directions:** Tell a story about the pictures. Fill in the circle under the small picture at the bottom of the page that shows what the story is about. Give the story a title.
- **To the Parent:** Ask your child to tell a story about the pictures and to give the story a title.

52

HRW material copyrighted under notice appearing earlier in this work.

2 Using the page

R, T   Inferential: main idea

Help pupils find page 52 in their books and call attention to the three large pictures on the page.

SAY These pictures tell a story. Look at the first picture. What is happening in the first picture? (A boy is playing in the sand, and water is nearby.) **Now look at the second picture. What is happening in this picture?** (A baby turtle is poking its head through the sand near the boy's feet.) **Now look at the last picture. Tell me what is happening in this picture.** (The boy is watching baby turtles walk toward the pond.)

Ask pupils to think about the story they just read in pictures. Then have them look at the little pictures at the bottom of the page. Have the pictures identified as a child riding a bicycle, a baby turtle hatching from an egg, a plant on a windowsill, and a sand pail and shovel.

ASK Which picture shows what the story on this page is about? (the baby turtle hatching from its egg) **Fill in the circle under the picture of the baby turtle to show that this story was about baby turtles.**

SAY We might call this story "A Sandy Surprise." Why is this a good title? (Possible answers include: The boy was surprised by the baby turtle on the beach.) **Can you think of other titles for this story?** (Answers will vary.)

3 Developing the Skills

R, T Inferential: main idea

Explain that you will tell a story and then you will ask what the story is about. Tell pupils that you will ask them to choose a title for the story.

READ **Today I learned to ride a bicycle. I had been practicing for a long time, but I always fell off. Today, though, I was able to keep the front wheel straight and steer the bike the way I wanted it to go. Wait until I tell my friend, Pablo.**

ASK **What is this story about?** (learning to ride a bicycle) **Is the best title for this story "Pablo," or "Riding My Bicycle"?** ("Riding My Bicycle")

READ **A puppy followed me to school. I hope my mom and dad will let me keep it. It picked me out of all the kids going to school. I think it likes me. I will take care of it, feed it, and teach it tricks.**

ASK **What is this story about?** (a puppy that followed me to school) **Is the best title for this story "A Day at School," or "My Puppy"?** ("My Puppy")

READ **My family is going to the circus. Dad bought the tickets on his way home from work. My brother wants to see the lion tamer, but I like the clowns the best.**

ASK **What is this story about?** (going to the circus) **Is the best title for this story "A Trip to the Circus," or "Dad Bought Tickets"?** ("A Trip to the Circus")

✳ Practicing and Extending

The activities that follow provide practice and extension of skills developed in this lesson. Not every pupil needs to complete these activities. Choose only the activities that are needed to provide for the individual differences in your classroom.

Extending Selection Concepts

LANGUAGE ARTS

WRITING: STORIES Tell pupils to pretend that they are on the beach and that they have just found a baby turtle. Suggest that they can make up a story. Have pupils dictate parts of the story. Print the story on chart paper. Help pupils organize the story by making these suggestions:

1. **Tell where you were.**
2. **Tell what you were doing in the sand.**
3. **Tell how you discovered the baby turtle.**
4. **Tell what you did with the baby turtle.**

Read the completed story and ask pupils to suggest a title for it. (Possible titles are: "The Day I Found a Baby Turtle at the Beach" or "The Turtle Who Found Me") When the story is completed, read it aloud several times, running your hand under the words. Encourage volunteers to join in the reading. Interested pupils might like to illustrate the story. Display the story and the illustrations in the classroom.

LITERATURE

LISTENING: FICTION Choose a story about a turtle and read it aloud to the class. Have pupils discuss what the story is about.

Asch, Frank. *Turtle Tale.* Dial 1978. A young turtle learns to be wise—the hard way.

Roche, A. K. *The Clever Turtle.* Prentice Hall, 1969. This traditional African tale tells how a turtle tricked a whole village.

ACTIVITY 3

Relating Initial /t/ to *t*
page 53 (T188–T190)

Skill Strands

> DECODING/VOCABULARY

I, T **Sound/symbol correspondence:** consonant /t/*t* (initial)

Materials

Sundrops, Level 1: page 53
Practice Masters: page 34
Resource Box: Letter Cards T, t
Word Builder Card t
Pocket Chart
Teacher's Idea Book

Special Populations

See *Teacher's Idea Book* for additional suggestions to help pupils with limited English proficiency.

Key to Symbols
I Introduced in this lesson
R Reinforced from an earlier lesson in this level
M Maintained from previous levels
T Tested in this level

1 Preparing for the page

I, T **Sound/symbol correspondence:** consonant /t/*t* (initial)

> **SAY** In the story "Turtle Pond," the baby turtles crawled to the pond. The word *turtle* begins with the sound /t/. Say *turtle* with me: *turtle.*

Place *Letter Card t* in the *Pocket Chart.*

> **SAY** The name of this letter is *t.* The letter *t* stands for the /t/ sound in words. When we see the letter *t,* we make the /t/ sound. When I point to the letter *t,* you make the /t/ sound. (Point to the letter several times.)

Make sure each pupil has *Word Builder Card t.*

> **SAY** I will say some words that have the /t/ sound at the beginning and some words that do not have the /t/ sound at the beginning. Hold up your *t* card each time you hear a word that begins with /t/.

Use the following words: *tickle, towel, soap, tangerine, taxi, balloon, tulip.*

Place *Letter Card T* in the *Pocket Chart* beside letter *t.*

> **SAY** The name of this letter is capital *T.* Capital *T* stands for the same sound as small *t.* What sound is that? (/t/) We use capital *T* at the beginning of names such as Tim, Tina, and Terry.

Point to small *t* and capital *T* several times, asking pupils to make the sound.

Name _____

turtle

turtle

| 1 | 2 | 3 | 4 |
| 5 | 6 | 7 | 8 |

- **Sound/symbol correspondence:** consonant /t/*t* (initial)
- **Directions:** Trace *t* in *turtle*. Print *t* in each box and name the pictures (girl, table; bed, toothbrush; tiger, alligator; bee, tent; pumpkin, turkey; toes, grapes; hand, toaster; tape, cup). Circle each picture whose name begins with /t/.
- **To the Parent:** Ask your child to tell which picture names begin with *t*.

53

2 Using the page

I, T Sound/symbol correspondence: consonant /t/*t* (initial)

Call attention to the picture of the turtle at the top of page 53 and tell pupils that the word beside the picture is *turtle.* Have them point to and name the first letter in the word *turtle.* (*t*) Ask what sound letter *t* stands for. (/t/) Tell pupils to trace letter *t* at the beginning of the second word *turtle.* Call attention to the first box with writing lines. Tell pupils to trace letter *t* on the lines. Then have pupils name the two pictures in the box. (girl, table) Ask which picture begins with /t/. (table) Tell pupils to trace the circle around the picture of a table to show that *table* begins with /t/.

Tell pupils to complete the page by printing *t* on each writing line and by circling the picture in each box whose name begins with /t/. Identify the pictures as bed, toothbrush; tiger, alligator; bee, tent; pumpkin, turkey; toes, grapes; hand, toaster; tape, cup.

3 Developing the Skills

I, T Sound/symbol correspondence: consonant /t/*t* (initial)

Tell pupils that they are going to pretend that two friends, Tina and Tom, are taking a trip. On this trip, Tina and Tom can only take things whose names begin with the /t/ sound.

> **SAY** **Tina and Tom are taking a trip. Can Tina and Tom take a towel?** (yes) **Why?** (*Towel* begins with the /t/ sound.) **Can Tina and Tom take a bed?** (no) **Why not?** (*Bed* does not begin with the /t/ sound.)

Follow a similar procedure by asking the questions that follow.

1. **Can Tina and Tom take tomatoes?** (yes)
2. **Can Tina and Tom take bananas?** (no)
3. **Can Tina and Tom take a toad?** (yes)
4. **Can Tina and Tom take a telephone?** (yes)

Encourage volunteers to ask about other things that Tina and Tom might take on their trip.

✳ Practicing and Extending

The activities that follow provide practice and extension of skills developed in this lesson. Not every pupil needs to complete these activities. Choose only the activities that are needed to provide for the individual differences in your classroom.

Practicing Skills

I, T **Sound/symbol correspondence:** consonant /t/t (initial)

PM 34 **ADDITIONAL PRACTICE** *Practice Masters* page 34 may be used as optional practice for identifying sound/symbol correspondence /t/t.

CHALLENGE ACTIVITY Show pupils how to make a *T* with their hands by holding one hand with the fingers pointing straight up, and holding the palm of the other hand across the fingers of the first hand. Tell pupils you will say some words and that they should make a *T* with their hands each time they hear a word that begins with /t/. Use the following words: *tank, ten, ruler, cheese, top, tall, sun, mouse, tiptoe, tack.* Encourage volunteers to suggest other words that begin with the /t/ sound.

Extending Selection Concepts

LITERATURE

LISTENING: FICTION Read a story about turtles. Discuss with pupils what characteristics of real turtles were important to the story.

Castle, Caroline. *The Hare and the Tortoise.* Dial Press, 1985. The fable has been embellished with a jogging hare, a literate tortoise, and other delightful characters.

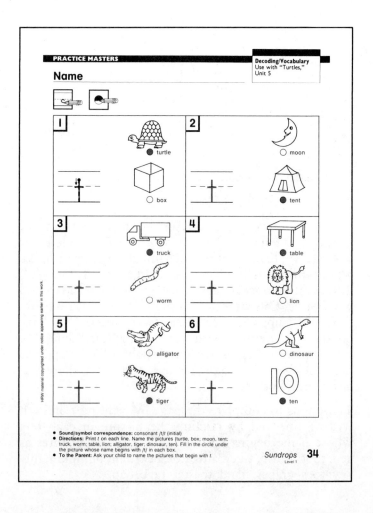

ACTIVITY 4 Discriminating Initial /d/d, /m/m, /s/s, /t/t page 54 (T191–T193)

Skill Strands

DECODING/VOCABULARY

R, T **Sound/symbol correspondence:** consonants /d/d, /m/m, /s/s, /t/t (initial)

Materials

Sundrops, Level 1: page 54
Practice Masters: page 35
Resource Box: *Letter Cards d, m, s, t*
Word Builder Cards d, m, s, t
Pocket Chart
Teacher's Idea Book

Special Populations

See *Teacher's Idea Book* for additional suggestions to help pupils with limited English proficiency.

1 Preparing for the page

R, T **Sound/symbol correspondence:** consonants /d/d, /m/m, /s/s, /t/t, (initial)

Place *Letter Card t* in the *Pocket Chart.*

> **ASK**   **What sound does this letter stand for?** (/t/) **The letter *t* stands for the sound at the beginning of words like *turtle* and *top*.**

Now place *Letter Card m* in the *Pocket Chart.*

> **ASK**   **What sound does this letter stand for?** (/m/) **The letter *m* stands for the sound at the beginning of words such as *mailbox* and *milk*.**

Place *Letter Card d* in the *Pocket Chart* and call on pupils to say the sound that this letter stands for (/d/). Tell pupils that the letter *d* stands for the sound at the beginning of words such as *dog* and *down*.

Place *Letter Card s* in the *Pocket Chart* and ask pupils to say the sound that this letter stands for. (/s/) Tell pupils that the letter *s* stands for the sound at the beginning of words such as *sister* and *sorry*.

> **SAY**   **I will say some words. I will ask one of you to point to the letter that stands for the beginning sound in each word.**

Use these words: *six, tickle, door, money, dinosaur, socks, mulberry, tangerine.*

Make sure each pupil has *Word Builder Cards t, m, d, s.*

> **SAY**   **I am going to say some words that begin with /t/, /m/, /d/, or /s/. When I say a word, hold up the letter that stands for the sound you hear at the beginning of the word.**

Use the following words: *tooth, many, soft, delicious, tank, super, dent, money.* Call on volunteers to name other words that begin with /t/, /m/, /d/, or /s/.

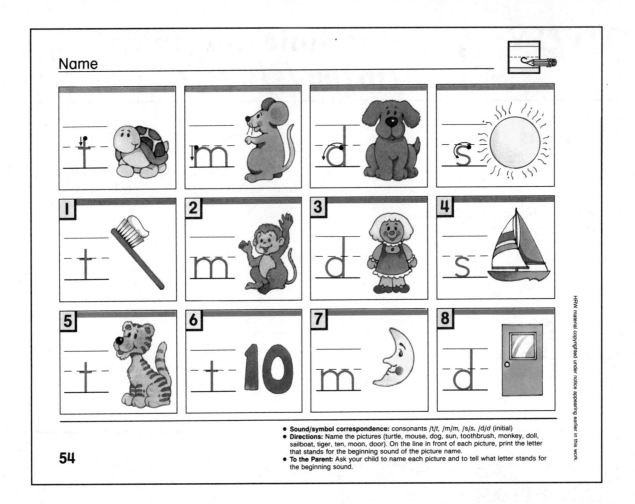

Name _____

- **Sound/symbol correspondence:** consonants /t/t, /m/m, /s/s, /d/d (initial)
- **Directions:** Name the pictures (turtle, mouse, dog, sun, toothbrush, monkey, doll, sailboat, tiger, ten, moon, door). On the line in front of each picture, print the letter that stands for the beginning sound of the picture name.
- **To the Parent:** Ask your child to name each picture and to tell what letter stands for the beginning sound.

54

2 Using the page

R, T   Sound/symbol correspondence: consonants /d/*d*, /m/*m*, /s/*s*, /t/*t* (initial)

Help pupils locate page 54 in their books. Call attention to the first picture and ask pupils to name the picture. (turtle)

ASK **What sound do you hear at the beginning of the word *turtle*?** (/t/) **What letter stands for that sound?** (*t*) **Trace the letter *t* on the writing line to show that *turtle* begins with the /t/ sound.**

Have pupils identify each of the remaining example pictures and tell what letter stands for the beginning sound of the picture name. (mouse, *m;* dog, *d;* sun, *s*) Tell pupils to trace the letter that stands for the beginning sound of each picture name. Have pupils complete the page by printing the letter that stands for the beginning sound of each picture name on the writing line in each box. Identify the pictures as toothbrush, monkey, doll, sailboat, tiger, ten, moon, door.

3 Developing the Skills

R, T Sound/symbol correspondence: consonants /d/*d*, /m/*m*, /s/*s*, /t/*t* (initial)

Print letter *t* on the chalkboard.

SAY I am going to say a sentence that has some words that begin with /t/. You tell me what those words are.

A turtle has no teeth. (*turtle, teeth*)

Follow a similar procedure with the letters *m*, *d*, and *s*.

1. **A mouse was in the mailbox.** (*mouse, mailbox*)
2. **My dog can dance.** (*dog, dance*)
3. **A turtle can tiptoe.** (*turtle, tiptoe*)
4. **My sister sits in the sun.** (*sister, sits, sun*)

Point to each letter on the chalkboard and invite pupils to suggest the words that begin with each letter. Then have pupils make up a sentence using the suggested words. The sentences may be silly.

* Practicing and Extending

The activities that follow provide practice and extension of skills developed in this lesson. Not every pupil needs to complete these activities. Choose only the activities that are needed to provide for the individual differences in your classroom.

Practicing Skills

R, T Sound/symbol correspondence: consonants /d/*d*, /m/*m*, /s/*s*, /t/*t* (initial)

PM 35 ADDITIONAL PRACTICE *Practice Masters* page 35 may be used as optional practice for associating the sounds /t/, /m/, /d/, and /s/ with the letters *t*, *m*, *d*, and *s*.

CHALLENGE ACTIVITY Place *Letter Cards t, m, d,* and *s* in a container. Have pupils choose a letter from the container and name a word that begins with the sound represented by the letter.

Extending Selection Concepts

LISTENING: TONGUE TWISTERS Ask pupils to listen as you read some tongue twisters using the letters *t, m, d,* or *s*. Encourage volunteers to try the tongue twisters themselves.

1. **Ten tan tents toppled.**
2. **Max the moose munched many marshmallows.**
3. **How much dew could a dewdrop drop if a dewdrop did drop dew?**
4. **Sam sold six sacks.**

Additional tongue twisters may be found in the following book:

Rosenbloom, Joseph. *Twist These On Your Tongue.* Thomas Nelson, 1978. The tongue twisters in this collection are arranged in alphabetical order.

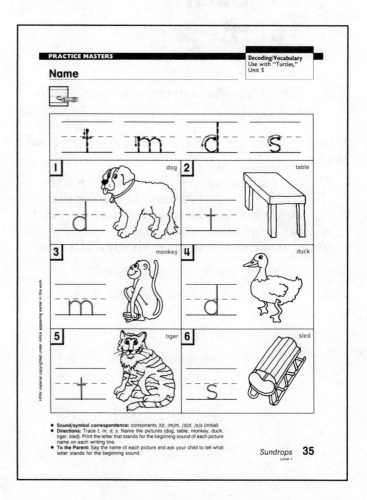

Relating Final /t/ to *t*

page 55 (T194–T196)

Skill Strands

DECODING/VOCABULARY

I, T **Sound/symbol correspondence:** consonant /t/*t* (final)

Materials

Sundrops, Level 1: page 55
Practice Masters: page 36
Resource Box: Letter Card t
Word Builder and *Builder Card t*
Pocket Chart
Teacher's Idea Book

Special Populations

See *Teacher's Idea Book* for additional suggestions to help pupils with limited English proficiency.

Key to Symbols
I Introduced in this lesson
R Reinforced from an earlier lesson in this level
M Maintained from previous levels
T Tested in this level

---

1 Preparing for the page

I, T **Sound/symbol correspondence:** consonant /t/*t* (final)

Place *Letter Card t* in the *Pocket Chart* and ask what sound the letter stands for. (/t/)

SAY **I am going to say a word that has the /t/ sound at the end. Listen for the /t/ sound: *bat.* Say the word *bat* after me: *bat.* I will say some other words that have the /t/ sound at the end. You say each word after me.**

Use the following words: *hot, spot, mat, meat.*

Make sure each pupil has *Word Builder Card t.*

SAY **I am going to say some words that have /t/ at the end and some words that do not have /t/ at the end. When you hear a word that has /t/ at the end, hold up your *t* card.**

Use the following words: *seat, pet, shoe, flat, sit, bowl, night, fat.*

Then make sure each pupil has a *Word Builder.*

SAY ***Turtle* has the /t/ sound at the beginning, so I put the *t* card at the beginning of the *Word Builder* for the word *turtle.* (Demonstrate.) *Bat* has the /t/ sound at the end, so I put the *t* card at the end of the *Word Builder* for the word *bat.* (Demonstrate.)**

Tell pupils that you will say some words that have the /t/ sound at the beginning and some words that have the /t/ sound at the end. Pupils should place their *t* card at the beginning or at the end of their *Word Builders* to show where they hear the /t/ sound in each word. Use the following words: *fat, sat, toes, great, tap, tail, greet, toad.*

Name _____

hat

hat

| 1 | 2 | 3 | 4 |
| 5 | 6 | 7 | 8 |

- **Sound/symbol correspondence:** consonant /t/*t* (final)
- **Directions:** Trace *t* in *hat*. Name the pictures (cat, pig, boat, brush, goat, desk, net, foot). Print *t* on the line after each picture whose name ends with /t/.
- **To the Parent:** Ask your child to tell which picture names end with *t*.

55

2 Using the page

I, T   **Sound/symbol correspondence:** consonant /t/*t* (final)

Ask pupils to open their books to page 55 and point to the picture of a hat at the top of the page. Ask pupils to tell where they hear the /t/ sound in the word *hat*. (at the end) Have pupils point to the letter *t* in the word *hat* and tell where they see the *t* in *hat*. (at the end) Have pupils trace the letter *t* in the second word *hat*.

Have the first picture with a writing line identified. (cat)

SAY **Do you hear the /t/ sound at the end of the word cat?** (yes) **Trace the letter t on the line after the picture to show that cat has the /t/ sound at the end.**

Help pupils identify the remaining pictures as pig, boat, brush, goat, desk, net, foot.

SAY **Finish the page by printing t on the line after each picture that has the /t/ sound at the end of its name.**

3 Developing the Skills

I, T Sound/symbol correspondence: consonant /t/t (final)

Ask pupils to pretend to put an imaginary hat on their heads.

SAY **Where do you hear the /t/ sound in the word hat?** (at the end)

Then ask pupils to pat their imaginary hats.

SAY **Where do you hear the /t/ sound in the word pat?** (at the end) **Let's play "Pat Your Hat." I will say some words. Some of the words have the /t/ sound at the end. Each time you hear a word that has the /t/ sound at the end, pat your hat. When you hear a word that does not end with /t/, keep your hands in your lap.**

Use the following words: *wheat, neat, rain, sweet, board, bit, fit, about, fish.* Ask pupils to suggest other words for the game.

✱ Practicing and Extending

The activities that follow provide practice and extension of skills developed in this lesson. Not every pupil needs to complete these activities. Choose only the activities that are needed to provide for the individual differences in your classroom.

Practicing Skills

I, T Sound/symbol correspondence: consonant /t/t (final)

PM 36 **ADDITIONAL PRACTICE** *Practice Masters* page 36 may be used as optional practice for reviewing final /t/t.

Extending Selection Concepts

LITERATURE

LISTENING: POETRY Ask pupils to listen to the poem "Slow Pokes." Read the poem a second time and ask why turtles do not have to hurry. (because they always have their homes on their backs) Encourage volunteers to tell if they would like to travel with their homes on their backs.

Slow Pokes

Turtles are slow,
As we all know,
But
To them
It is no worry,
For
Wherever they roam,
They are always at home,
So
They do not
HAVE
To hurry.

Laura Arlon

PRACTICE MASTERS
Name

Decoding/Vocabulary
Use with "Turtles,"
Unit 5

1. nut, goat, hand
2. cat, lamb, foot
3. doll, hat, boat
4. bat, dress, coat
5. cot, mat, clock

● Sound/symbol correspondence: consonant /t/t (final)
● Directions: Print *t* on the writing line. Name the pictures in each row (nut, goat, hand; cat, lamb, foot; doll, hat, boat; bat, dress, coat; cot, mat, clock). Circle the pictures in each row whose names end with /t/.
● To the Parent: Ask your child to name the pictures that end with *t*.

Sundrops Level 1 **36**

ACTIVITY 6 Discriminating Initial and Final /t/t page 56 (T197–T199)

Skill Strands

DECODING/VOCABULARY

R, T **Sound/symbol correspondence:** consonant /t/t (initial, final)

Materials

Sundrops, Level 1: page 56
Practice Masters: page 37
Word Builder and *Builder Card t*
Teacher's Idea Book

Special Populations

See *Teacher's Idea Book* for additional suggestions to help pupils with limited English proficiency.

Key to Symbols
I Introduced in this lesson
R Reinforced from an earlier lesson in this level
M Maintained from previous levels
T Tested in this level

1 Preparing for the page

R, T **Sound/symbol correspondence:** consonant /t/t (initial, final)

Print letter *t* on the chalkboard and remind pupils that this letter stands for the /t/ sound at the beginning of words such as *turtle* and *tickle*. Then remind pupils that the /t/ sound can also be found at the end of some words such as *bat* and *hat*.

Display a *Word Builder* and *Word Builder Card t.*

SAY I will say a word that has the /t/ sound at the beginning or at the end. After I say the word, I will ask one of you to place the *t* card in the *Word Builder* to show where the /t/ sound is heard in the word.

Use the following words: *table, rat, basket, tin, tiger, goat, lost, ten.*

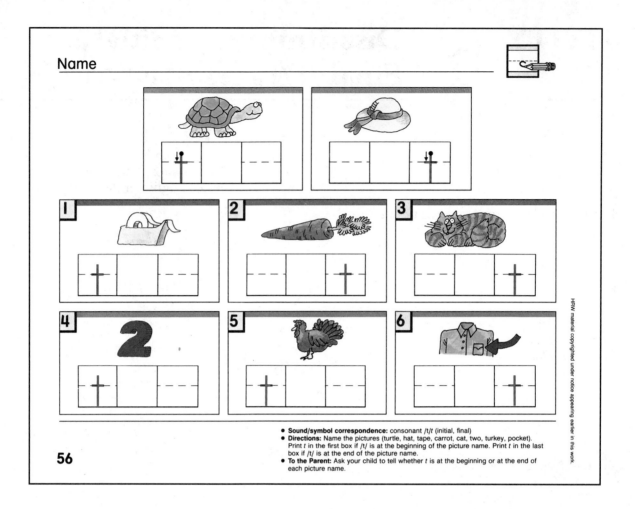

- **Sound/symbol correspondence:** consonant /t/t (initial, final)
- **Directions:** Name the pictures (turtle, hat, tape, carrot, cat, two, turkey, pocket). Print *t* in the first box if /t/ is at the beginning of the picture name. Print *t* in the last box if /t/ is at the end of the picture name.
- **To the Parent:** Ask your child to tell whether *t* is at the beginning or at the end of each picture name.

56

2 Using the page

R, T **Sound/symbol correspondence:** consonant /t/t (initial, final)

Help pupils find page 56 in their books and call on a volunteer to identify the first picture. (turtle)

ASK **Where do you hear the /t/ sound in the word** *turtle?* (at the beginning) **Trace the letter** *t* **in the first box under the picture to show that the /t/ sound is heard at the beginning of the word.**

Have a pupil identify the second picture. (hat)

ASK **Where do you hear the /t/ sound in the word** *hat?* (at the end) **Trace letter** *t* **in the last box under the picture to show that the /t/ sound is heard at the end of the word** *hat.*

Help pupils identify the remaining pictures as tape, carrot, cat, two, turkey, and pocket. Explain that pupils should print *t* in the first box under the picture if they hear /t/ at the beginning of the picture name, and that they should print *t* in the last box under the picture if they hear /t/ at the end of the picture name.

3 Developing the Skills

R, T Sound/symbol correspondence: consonant /t/t (initial, final)

Tell pupils that you will read some sentences and that each sentence has a word missing. The missing word begins or ends with the /t/ sound.

| SAY | **I play baseball with a ball and a _____.** |

Call on volunteers to name the missing word. (bat) Then have pupils tell where they hear the /t/ sound in the word *bat*. (at the end) Continue in the same manner with the following sentences:

1. **When the _____ rang, I answered it.** (telephone)
2. **It's so cold I need to wear a _____.** (coat, hat)
3. **Use a _____ to brush your teeth.** (toothbrush)
4. **I put the dishes on the _____.** (table)
5. **The sun is very _____ today.** (hot)

✳ Practicing and Extending

The activities that follow provide practice and extension of skills developed in this lesson. Not every pupil needs to complete these activities. Choose only the activities that are needed to provide for the individual differences in your classroom.

Practicing Skills

R, T Sound/symbol correspondence: consonant /t/t (initial, final)

PM 37 **ADDITIONAL PRACTICE** *Practice Masters* page 37 may be used as optional practice for identifying sound/symbol correspondence /t/t.

CHALLENGE ACTIVITY Read the nursery rhyme "Star Light." Ask pupils to listen as you read the rhyme again to find words that begin or end with /t/. Then ask which word has the /t/ sound at the beginning and at the end. (*tonight*)

Star Light

Star light, star bright,
First star I see tonight,
I wish I may, I wish I might,
Have the wish I wish tonight.

Extending Selection Concepts

| SCIENCE |

LISTENING: INFORMATION Read an informational book about turtles and ask pupils to tell interesting facts they learned.

Craig, Janet. *Turtles.* Troll Associates, 1982. Beautiful drawings and simple text introduce turtles and their habits.

Waters, John F. *The Lives of Baby Turtles.* Walker and Company, 1979. The first dangerous days in the lives of several species of turtles are explained in this book. The illustrations are photographs.

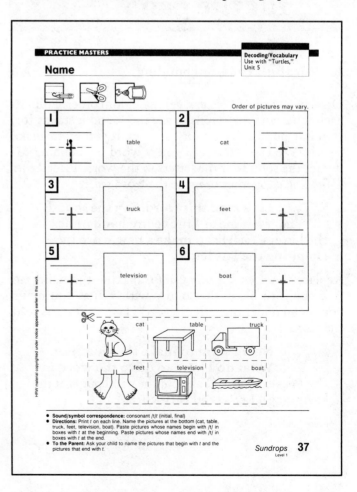

ACTIVITY 7 Building Words
page 57 (T200–T202)

Skill Strands

DECODING/VOCABULARY

I Vocabulary: word building

Materials

Sundrops, Level 1: page 57
Practice Masters: page 38
Resource Box: Letter Cards a, d, m, s, t, T
Word Builder and *Word Builder Cards a, d, m, s, t*
Pocket Chart
Teacher's Idea Book

Special Populations

See *Teacher's Idea Book* for additional suggestions to help pupils with limited English proficiency.

Key to Symbols
I Introduced in this lesson
R Reinforced from an earlier lesson in this level
M Maintained from previous levels
T Tested in this level

---

1 Preparing for the page

I Vocabulary: word building

Display *Letter Cards m, a, s, d, t* in random order. Point to each letter and ask pupils to say the sound it stands for. Remind pupils that letters are put together to make words. We can often read a new word by blending together the sounds of the letters in the word. Place *Letter Cards s, a, d* together to make the word *sad.*

SAY Let's read this word. Say the sounds with me as I move my hand under the letters. (*sad*) I can make a new word by changing the last letter.

Replace the *d* with *Letter Card t,* making the word *sat.* Ask pupils to blend the sounds with you as you move your hand under the letters. (*ssaat*) Have volunteers read the word. (*sat*)

SAY Now I want to make the word *mat.* What do I have to do to the word in the *Pocket Chart?* (Take out the *s* and put *m* at the beginning.) Let's read this word.

Move your hand under the letters as the pupils read with you. (*mat*)

Now place *Letter Cards T, a, d* in the *Pocket Chart.*

SAY This is another word. You blend the sounds as I move my hand under the letters. Raise your hand when you can tell me what this word is. (*Tad*) There is a capital letter at the beginning of the word *Tad* because Tad is a name. *Tad* is the name of a turtle you will meet in your books.

Make sure each pupil has a *Word Builder* and *Word Builder Cards m, a, s, d, t.*

SAY Make the word *sat* in your *Word Builder.* Place *s* at the beginning, then place *a* after the *s,* then place *t* at the end. Who can read the word? (*sat*)

Now let's make the word *mat.* What letter in *sat* do you have to change to make the word *mat?* (Change *s* to *m.*) Place *m* in front of letters *at.* Who can read the word? (*mat*)

Repeat this procedure with the words *sat* and *sad.*

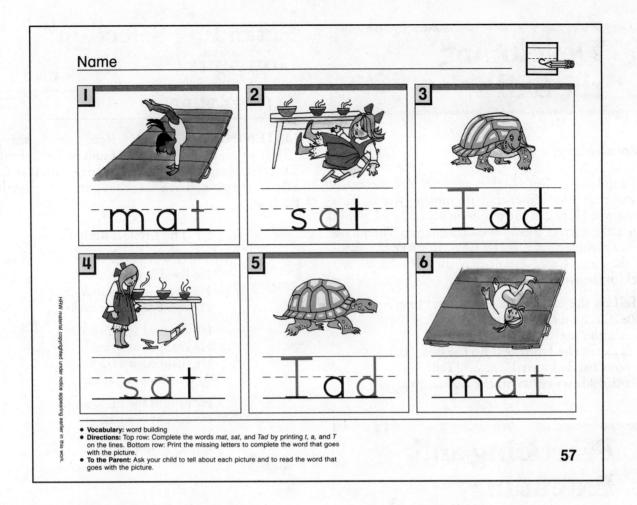

Name

- **Vocabulary:** word building
- **Directions:** Top row: Complete the words *mat*, *sat*, and *Tad* by printing *t*, *a*, and *T* on the lines. Bottom row: Print the missing letters to complete the word that goes with the picture.
- **To the Parent:** Ask your child to tell about each picture and to read the word that goes with the picture.

57

2 Using the page

I Vocabulary: word building

Tell pupils to open their books to page 57 and call attention to the picture of the child in the first picture. Ask what the child is using to keep from being hurt. (a mat)

SAY The word under this picture is supposed to be *mat*. I see the letter that stands for the /m/ sound at the beginning of *mat*, and I see the letter that stands for the /a/ sound in the middle of *mat*. What letter stands for the /t/ sound at the end of *mat*? (*t*) Print letter *t* in the space at the end of the word. (Have pupils read the word.)

Call attention to the second picture.

ASK What happened in this picture? (Goldilocks sat in the chair and broke it.) The word under this picture should say *sat*. I see the letter *s* at the beginning of the word, and I see the letter *t* at the end of the word. What letter stands for the /a/ sound in the middle of *sat*? (*a*) Print letter *a* in the middle to finish the word *sat*. (Have pupils read the finished word.)

Have pupils look at the third picture and tell what they see. (a turtle)

SAY Here is Tad the turtle. The word under the turtle should be the name *Tad*. What sound do you hear at the beginning of the word *Tad*? (/t/) What letter stands for the /t/ sound? (*t*) You need to print letter *t* at the beginning of the word *Tad*. Because *Tad* is a name, what kind of *t* should you make? (capital *T*)

Have pupils look at the remaining three pictures. Tell pupils to complete the word that goes with each picture by using the top three pictures as examples. Have volunteers read the completed words.

3 Developing the Skills

I Vocabulary: word building

Have pupils continue to look at page 57. Tell them that you will read some sentences with missing words. Each missing word is one of the words on page 57. Ask pupils to guess the correct word for each sentence. Then have volunteers come to the *Pocket Chart* to make the word with the *Letter Cards*. Pupils may use their books as a model for the words.

1. **I fell on the _____ and did not get hurt.** (mat)
2. **We _____ on the bench.** (sat)
3. **_____ the turtle ate a fly.** (Tad)
4. **I _____ in the front seat on the bus.** (sat)
5. **Is your turtle named _____?** (Tad)
6. **We did somersaults on the _____.** (mat)

❋ Practicing and Extending

The activities that follow provide practice and extension of skills developed in this lesson. Not every pupil needs to complete these activities. Choose only the activities that are needed to provide for the individual differences in your classroom.

Practicing Skills

I Vocabulary: word building

PM 38 **ADDITIONAL PRACTICE** *Practice Masters* page 38 may be used as optional practice for reading words by blending sounds.

CHALLENGE ACTIVITY Encourage pupils to make up sentences that contain the three words from this lesson: *mat, sat,* and *Tad.* Some possible examples follow:

Tad sat on the mat.
Who sat on the mat with Tad?

Extending Selection Concepts

LITERATURE

LISTENING: POETRY Read aloud the poem "The Little Turtle" by Vachel Lindsay. Read the poem a second time and ask what the turtle caught. (a mosquito, a flea, a minnow) Then ask what got away from the turtle. (me)

The Little Turtle

There was a little turtle.
He lived in a box.
He swam in a puddle.
He climbed on the rocks.

He snapped at a mosquito.
He snapped at a flea.
He snapped at a minnow.
And he snapped at me.

He caught the mosquito.
He caught the flea.
He caught the minnow.
But he didn't catch me.

Vachel Lindsay

PRACTICE MASTERS

Decoding/Vocabulary
Use with "Turtles,"
Unit 5

Name

1. (sat) sad
2. (Tad) Sam
3. mad (mat)
4. sat (sad)

• **Vocabulary:** word building
• **Directions:** Look at each picture and read the words under it. Circle the word that goes with the picture.
• **To the Parent:** Ask your child to read the word that belongs with each picture.

Sundrops **38**
Level 1

ACTIVITY 8 Reading the Words *on* and *the*
page 58 (T203–T206)

Skill Strands

DECODING/VOCABULARY

I, T Vocabulary: word meaning

Materials

Sundrops, Level 1: page 58
Practice Masters: page 39
*Resource Box: Word Cards is, mat, on, Sam, sat, Tad, the
          Punctuation Card period*
Pocket Chart
Teacher's Idea Book
"Tortoise and Hare Race" game (See page T179.)

Special Populations

See *Teacher's Idea Book* for additional suggestions to help pupils with limited English proficiency.

1 Preparing for the page

I, T Vocabulary: word meaning

SAY **Tad is a turtle. Where might we find a turtle?** (Possible answers are: in the woods, by a pond, in the grass.)

Use the *Word Cards* and *Punctuation Card period* to make the sentence *Tad sat on the mat.* in the *Pocket Chart.*

SAY **This sentence tells where Tad is. Listen as I read the sentence.**

Move your hand under the words as you read the sentence. Ask where Tad sat. (on the mat) Read the sentence again and point to the word *on.*

SAY **This is the word *on.* Read the word with me: *on.***

Read the sentence again and point to the word *the.*

SAY **This is the word *the.* Read this word with me: *the.***

Ask pupils to read the last word. (mat) Have pupils join you as you read the sentence several times, pointing to each word. Have pupils come up and point to the words *on* and *the* as you say them.

Remove the word *Tad* and replace it with the word *Sam.* Have pupils read the new sentence. (*Sam sat on the mat.*) Then ask where Sam is. (on the mat) Remove the word *mat* and call on pupils to point to and read the words *Sam sat on the* and then to finish the sentence by saying where Sam sat. (Possible answers include: rug, chair, porch.)

Place the sentence *The mat is on Tad.* in the *Pocket Chart* and read it. Ask pupils how Tad the turtle might feel about having a mat on him. Remind pupils that the first word in a sentence begins with a capital letter. Ask what is the first word of this sentence. (*The*) Have a volunteer point out the capital letter at the beginning of *The.* Then call on volunteers to read the sentence.

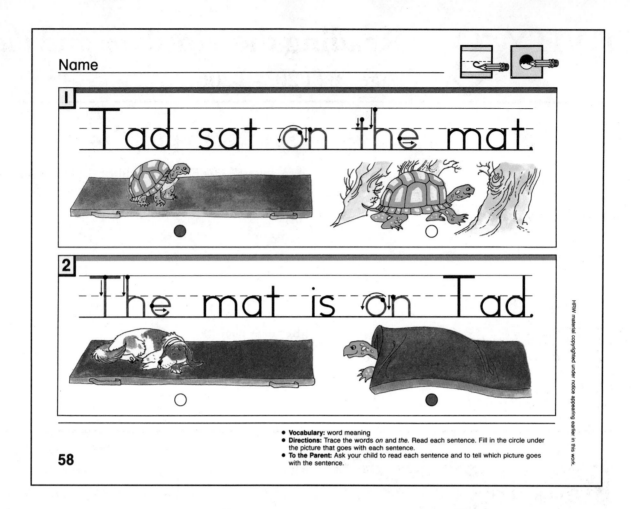

Name

1 Tad sat on the mat.

2 The mat is on Tad.

- **Vocabulary:** word meaning
- **Directions:** Trace the words *on* and *the*. Read each sentence. Fill in the circle under the picture that goes with each sentence.
- **To the Parent:** Ask your child to read each sentence and to tell which picture goes with the sentence.

58

2 Using the page

I, T   Vocabulary: word meaning

Have pupils open their books to page 58 and call attention to the sentence at the top of the page. Tell pupils that they are to trace the words *on* and *the*. Call on pupils to read the sentence. (*Tad sat on the mat.*) Then have pupils look at the pictures under the sentence and tell what is happening in the first picture. (Tad is on the mat.) Have pupils tell what is happening in the second picture. (Tad is crawling in the woods.)

SAY **One of these pictures goes with the sentence *Tad sat on the mat*. Fill in the circle under the picture that goes with the sentence.** (the first picture)

Call attention to the second sentence. Have pupils trace the words *The* and *on*. Call on volunteers to read the sentence. (*The mat is on Tad.*) Have pupils look at the two pictures under the sentence. Ask what is happening in the first picture. (Sam is on the mat.) Then ask what is happening in the second picture. (Tad is crawling out from under the mat.) Have pupils fill in the circle under the picture that goes with the sentence. (the second picture)

3 Developing the Skills

I, T   Vocabulary: word meaning

Tell pupils that you will play a guessing game called "Where Is It?"

SAY **I am thinking of something in this room. You may ask questions about where it is, until you can guess what I am thinking of. You might ask "Is it on the wall?" or "Is it on the bookshelf?" The pupil who correctly guesses the object may choose the next object to be guessed.**

✳ Practicing and Extending

The activities that follow provide practice and extension of skills developed in this lesson. Not every pupil needs to complete these activities. Choose only the activities that are needed to provide for the individual differences in your classroom.

Practicing Skills

I, T   Vocabulary: word meaning

PM 39   ADDITIONAL PRACTICE *Practice Masters* page 39 may be used as optional practice for reading the words *on* and *the.*

CHALLENGE ACTIVITY Invite pairs of pupils to play the "Tortoise and Hare Race" game. (See page T179.) If pupils are not familiar with the fable, begin by telling an abbreviated version. Explain that a hare is a rabbit and that a tortoise is a turtle.

The Tortoise and the Hare

The hare was bragging that he could run faster than any of the other animals. He dared anyone to race him. The tortoise said that he would race the hare. The hare laughed because the tortoise was so slow, but he decided to go ahead and run the race. After the start of the race, the hare was so far ahead of the tortoise that he decided to take a nap and wait for the tortoise to catch up. While the hare was sleeping, the tortoise kept plodding along. Soon the tortoise passed the sleeping hare. When the hare woke up, he saw that the tortoise was almost to the finish line. The hare ran as fast as he could, but it was too late. The steady tortoise won the race.

Display the "Tortoise and Hare Race" game board and explain that one pupil will be the tortoise and one pupil will be the hare. The pupils take turns choosing a *Word Card* and reading the word on the card. If the word is read correctly, the pupil may toss the game cube and move a game marker the indicated number of spaces.

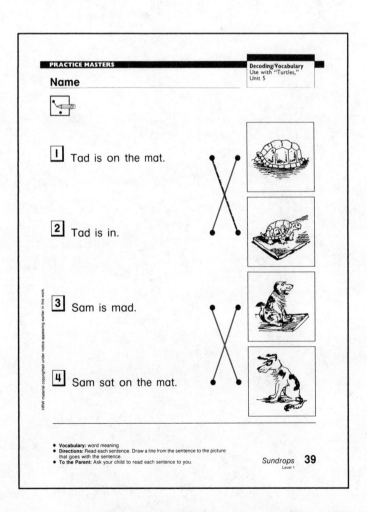

Extending Selection Concepts

LISTENING: FICTION   Choose a humorous book that has a turtle for a character. Discuss with pupils what was funny about the story.

Van Woerkom, Dorothy. *Harry and Shellburt.* Macmillan, 1977. Harry the hare cannot believe that a turtle ever beat a hare in a race, so he and his friend Shellburt have a race of their own.

Williams, Barbara. *Albert's Toothache.* Dutton, 1974. Albert has a toothache, but no one will believe him because turtles don't have teeth! Grandma saves the day.

ACTIVITY 9   Reading a Story
page 59 (T207–T209)

Skill Strands

DECODING/VOCABULARY

I   **Vocabulary:** words in context

Materials

Sundrops, Level 1: page 59
Resource Box: Word Cards *Dad, is, mad, mat, on, sad, Sam, Tad, the*
                 Punctuation Card period
Pocket Chart
Teacher's Idea Book

Special Populations

See *Teacher's Idea Book* for additional suggestions to help pupils with limited English proficiency.

Key to Symbols
I   Introduced in this lesson
R   Reinforced from an earlier lesson in this level
M   Maintained from previous levels
T   Tested in this level

---

1   Preparing for the page

I   **Vocabulary:** words in context

Place *Word Cards Tad, is,* and *sad* in the *Pocket Chart.*

> **SAY**   **This is a sentence. Read the sentence with me:** *Tad is sad.* **Because this is a sentence, it should end with a period.**

Call on a pupil to place *Punctuation Card period* in the proper position after the word *sad* in the *Pocket Chart.*

Place the sentence *Tad is on the mat.* in the *Pocket Chart.*

> **SAY**   **Read this sentence to yourself as I move my hand under the words. When you know what the sentence says, raise your hand.**

Move your hand under the words in the sentence. Call on volunteers to read the sentence. (Tad is on the mat.)

Name _____

1. Tad is sad.

2. Tad is on the mat.

3. Sam is mad.

4. Sam sat on the mat.

- **Vocabulary:** words in context
- **Directions:** Read the story.
- **To the Parent:** Read and discuss the story with your child.

59

2 Using the page

I Vocabulary: words in context

Have pupils open their books to page 59. Explain that you are going to tell part of a story about Tad and Sam and that pupils are going to read the part of the story that is printed in their books.

SAY Look at the first picture.

READ Poor Tad! He is turned over on his back. Once a turtle is on its back, it is very hard for the turtle to turn over on its feet.

SAY Look at the sentence at the bottom of the first picture. It tells how Tad felt about being upside down.

Call on a volunteer to read the sentence. (Tad is sad.)

SAY Now look at the second picture.

READ Tad was stuck. He couldn't crawl away. Then, along came Sam. Sam started to bark at the poor turtle.

SAY Look at the sentence at the bottom of the picture. Read it to yourself to find out why Sam is barking at Tad.

Then have the sentence read aloud. (Tad is on the mat.)

SAY Look at the third picture.

READ Poor Tad! He was not only upside down, but he was stuck on Sam's mat. From the way he sounded, Sam wanted his mat back. While Tad was trying to figure out how to get away, Sam lifted up the mat and shook it. Tad pulled into his shell to protect himself and rolled right off the mat!

| SAY | Look at the sentence at the bottom of the picture. The sentence tells how Sam felt when he saw Tad on his mat. |

Call on a volunteer to read the sentence. (Sam is mad.)

| SAY | Look at the last picture. |

| READ | Tad was very happy to be turned right-side-up again. He started to crawl home. Sam was happy to have his mat back. |

| SAY | Read the sentence at the bottom of the picture. It tells what Sam did. |

Call on a volunteer to read the sentence. (Sam sat on the mat.)

Ask how Tad and Sam felt during the story. (Tad was sad. Sam was mad.) Ask how both characters felt at the end of the story. (Both Tad and Sam were happy.)

3 Developing the Skills

I Vocabulary: words in context

Display *Word Cards Tad* and *Sam* and have the words read.

| SAY | These words are names. |

Then display *Word Cards is, on, the, mat, sad,* and *mad* and have them read.

| SAY | These are words that help tell what happened in the story. |

Display *Punctuation Card period* and tell pupils that they can use these cards to make the sentences from the story. Have pupils find page 59 in their books. Ask a pupil to read the first sentence. Then have a volunteer make the sentence in the *Pocket Chart.* Have pupils compare the sentence in the *Pocket Chart* with the sentence in their books to be sure it is correct. Continue in the same manner with the rest of the sentences on page 59.

❋ Practicing and Extending

The activities that follow provide practice and extension of skills developed in this lesson. Not every pupil needs to complete these activities. Choose only the activities that are needed to provide for the individual differences in your classroom.

Practicing Skills

I, T   Vocabulary: words in context

ADDITIONAL PRACTICE   Place *Word Cards Tad, sad, is* in the *Pocket Chart* and have pupils read the words. Then ask pupils to put the words in order to make a sentence. (Tad is sad) Provide *Punctuation Card period* so pupils can make a complete sentence. Have pupils read the sentence. Then replace the cards with words *is, Sam, mad* and have pupils put the words in order in the same manner. Continue with the following scrambled sentences:

on, the, mat, is, Sam
Dad, on, the, is, mat
sad, is, Dad

ACTIVITY 10 Reviewing /t/t
page 60 (T210–T213)

Skill Strands

DECODING/VOCABULARY

R, T **Sound/symbol correspondence:** consonant /t/t (initial, final)

COMPREHENSION/THINKING

R, T **Literal:** sequence

Materials

Sundrops, Level 1: page 60
Practice Masters: page 40
Resource Box: Letter Card t
Teacher's Idea Book
Sound/Symbol Folder (See page T43 for instructions.)

Special Populations

See *Teacher's Idea Book* for additional suggestions to help pupils with limited English proficiency.

Key to Symbols
I Introduced in this lesson
R Reinforced from an earlier lesson in this level
M Maintained from previous levels
T Tested in this level

1 Preparing for the page

R, T **Sound/symbol correspondence:** consonant /t/t (initial, final)

Display *Letter Card t.* Ask pupils to name the letter and to tell what sound it stands for. (/t/)

> **SAY** I will say three words. Tell me which of the words begins with the /t/ sound.

Use these word groups: *taxi, walk, towel; team, fruit, tap; wind, table, today.*

Remind pupils that the /t/ sound can be at the end of some words.

> **SAY** In the word *bat,* where do you hear the /t/ sound? (at the end) **Now I will say some more words. Tell me which of the words end with the /t/ sound.**

Use these word groups: *meat, pet, girl; about, puppet, face; hat, fan, net.*

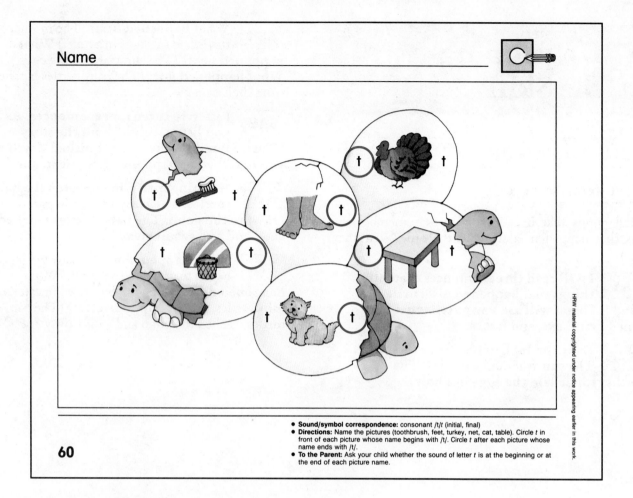

Name _____

- **Sound/symbol correspondence:** consonant /t/t (initial, final)
- **Directions:** Name the pictures (toothbrush, feet, turkey, net, cat, table). Circle *t* in front of each picture whose name begins with /t/. Circle *t* after each picture whose name ends with /t/.
- **To the Parent:** Ask your child whether the sound of letter *t* is at the beginning or at the end of each picture name.

60

2 Using the page

R, T   Sound/symbol correspondence: consonant /t/t (initial, final)

Help pupils find page 60 in their books and ask what is happening on this page. (Baby turtles are hatching out of their eggs.) Tell pupils to look at the picture on each egg.

> **SAY** Each picture name has the /t/ sound at the beginning or at the end.

Have the picture on the first egg identified. (toothbrush)

> **ASK** Where do you hear the /t/ sound in the word *toothbrush?* (at the beginning) Since the /t/ sound is at the beginning of the word *toothbrush,* circle the letter *t* in front of the picture.

Tell pupils to circle the letter *t* after the picture if the /t/ sound is heard at the end of the word. Identify the remaining pictures as feet, turkey, net, cat, and table.

3 Developing the Skills

COMPREHENSION/THINKING

R, T Literal: sequence

Remind pupils that it is important to remember the things that happen in a story in the order that they happen.

SAY I will read three sentences that tell things that happened in "Turtle Pond." Then I will ask you to tell what happened first, next, and last.

READ Baby turtles hatched from their eggs. The sun warmed the eggs. The mother turtle laid the eggs in a hole.

ASK **What happened first?** (The mother turtle laid the eggs in a hole.) **What happened next?** (The sun warmed the eggs.) **What happened last?** (The baby turtles hatched from their eggs.)

SAY Listen to three more sentences. As you listen, think about the story "Turtle Pond." When I am finished, I will ask you to tell what happened first, next, and last.

READ A fishing bird tried to catch the baby turtles. The baby turtles began to crawl to the pond. The baby turtles reached the pond and swam away.

ASK **What happened first?** (Baby turtles began to crawl to the pond.) **What happened next?** (A fishing bird tried to catch the baby turtles.) **What happened last?** (The baby turtles reached the pond and swam away.)

The activities that follow provide practice and extension of skills developed in this lesson. Not every pupil needs to complete these activities. Choose only the activities that are needed to provide for the individual differences in your classroom.

Practicing Skills

DECODING/VOCABULARY

R, T **Sound/symbol correspondence:** consonant /t/*t* (initial and final)

PM 40 **ADDITIONAL PRACTICE** *Practice Masters* page 40 may be used as optional practice for identifying sound/symbol correspondence /t/*t*.

ADDITIONAL PRACTICE Invite pupils to work in pairs or small groups to discriminate /t/ in the pictures in the Sound/Symbol Folder for *t*. (See page T43.)

Extending Selection Concepts

LITERATURE

LISTENING: FICTION Choose a fictional book about turtles and read it aloud to the class. Call on volunteers to share their favorite part of the story.

Balian, Lorna. *The Aminal.* Abingdon Press, 1972. Patrick tells Molly he has an aminal that is "round and green and blinky-eyed with lots of prickly toenails and a waggy tail." As the description is repeated, the aminal becomes more and more frightening—until everyone discovers what the aminal is.

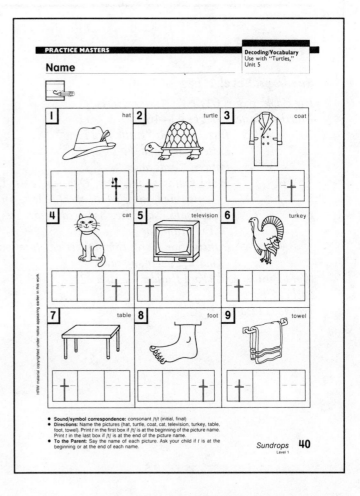

UNIT 6 "Seeds"
pages 61–70 (T214–T248)

Skill Strands

DECODING/VOCABULARY

I, T	**Sound/symbol correspondence:** vowel /ē/ *ea, ee*
R, T	**Sound/symbol correspondence:** vowel /a/ *a*
I, T	**Word structure:** inflectional ending *-s*
I	**Vocabulary:** word building
I, T	**Vocabulary:** word meaning
I	**Vocabulary:** words in context

COMPREHENSION/THINKING

R	**Critical thinking:** using prior knowledge
R, T	**Literal:** sequence
R, T	**Literal:** cause and effect

LANGUAGE

R	**Listening:** story comprehension
R	**Speaking:** retelling stories
R	**Conventions of language:** end punctuation (period, question mark)
I	**Conventions of language:** quotation marks (with comma and *said*)

Materials

Sundrops, Level 1: pages 61–70
Big Book: pages 61, 70
Practice Masters: pages 41–46
Resource Box: Picture Cards *"Little Red Hen"*
        Letter Cards *a, d, m, s (2), t,*
        Pattern Cards *ea, ee*
        Word Cards *a, am, Dee, Dad, eat, eats, I, Is, is, mad, mat, Matt, meat, Meet, on, sad, said, Sam, see, See, seed, seeds, sees, Tad, Tam, the*
        Punctuation Cards *comma, period, question mark, quotation marks*
Word Builder and *Word Builder Cards a (2), e*
Pocket Chart
Teacher's Idea Book

Language Applications

EXTENDING SELECTION CONCEPTS
Speaking: role playing
Speaking: telling about a picture
Speaking: using complete sentences
Listening: fiction
Listening: poetry
Listening: information
Speaking: telling about observations

Special Populations

See *Teacher's Idea Book* for additional suggestions to help pupils with limited English proficiency.

Key to Symbols
I Introduced in this lesson
R Reinforced from a previous lesson in this level
M Maintained from previous levels
T Tested in this level

Idea Center

BEAN-PLANTING MATERIALS

For Activity 1, gather the materials needed for pupils to plant bean seeds: one milk carton per pupil, potting soil, bean seeds. Fill the milk cartons about two-thirds full of soil. Help pupils plant two or three bean seeds and lightly cover the seeds with soil.

BIBLIOGRAPHY

Add to your reading corner or reading table various books about seeds or plants. Encourage pupils to look at the books on their own. Suggestions for reading books aloud appear throughout this lesson. Listed below is a bibliography to choose from. Annotations for the books appear in the lesson plans.

Cauley, Lorinda Bryan. *Jack and the Beanstalk*. Putnam, 1983.

Hamsa, Bobbie. *Your Pet Giraffe*. Childrens Press, 1982.

Krauss, Ruth. *The Carrot Seed*. Harper & Row, 1982.

Kuchalla, Susan. *All About Seeds*. Troll Associates, 1982.

LeTord, Bijou. *Rabbit Seeds*. Four Winds Press, 1984.

Lindsey, Treska. *When Batistine Made Bread*. Macmillan, 1985.

Rockwell, Anne, and Harlow Rockwell. *How My Garden Grows*. Macmillan, 1982.

ACTIVITY 1 Listening to "Little Red Hen"
page 61 (T216–T219)

Skill Strands

COMPREHENSION/THINKING

I **Critical thinking:** using prior knowledge

LANGUAGE

R **Listening:** story comprehension
R **Speaking:** retelling stories

Materials

Sundrops, Level 1: page 61
Big Book: page 61
Teacher's Idea Book
Bean–Planting Materials (See page T215.)

Special Populations

See *Teacher's Idea Book* for additional suggestions to help pupils with limited English proficiency.

Key to Symbols
I Introduced in this lesson
R Reinforced from an earlier lesson in this level
M Maintained from previous levels
T Tested in this level

1 Preparing for the page

SUMMARY Little Red Hen finds a wheat seed and dreams of having bread to eat. As she plants, cuts, and grinds the wheat, she asks for help from her friends. Her "friends" refuse to help with the work, but they eagerly offer to help eat the bread. Little Red Hen eats the bread the same way she did the work—all by herself.

I **Critical thinking:** using prior knowledge

Tell pupils that in the springtime, many people plant seeds in a garden. Ask what might come from the seeds. (Possible answers include: various vegetables and flowers.) Point out that plants grow from seeds.

Ask why someone might want to plant seeds. (Possible answers include: People want to grow pretty flowers; they want to grow some food.)

Print the title "Little Red Hen" on the chalkboard and read it. Explain that this is the title of a story you are going to read. Tell pupils that Little Red Hen found a seed. Little Red Hen knew that she could plant the seed to grow wheat. Wheat is ground into flour to bake bread. Explain that Little Red Hen knew that growing wheat was a lot of work, so, she asked her friends for help.

Tell pupils that the characters in this story are a hen, a dog, a duck, and a pig, but that these animals speak and act just like people. Ask pupils to tell if they think this story will be about real things or about make-believe things and why. (make-believe; because animals do not act like people in real life)

- **Listening:** story comprehension
- **Directions:** Look at the pictures as the teacher reads the story "The Little Red Hen."
- **To the Parent:** Ask your child to tell you the story of "The Little Red Hen."

61

2 Using the page

R Listening: story comprehension

Help pupils find page 61 in their books. Explain that the pictures on this page are from the story "Little Red Hen" and that pupils can look at these pictures as you read the story. Ask pupils to listen to find out what work Little Red Hen had to do, and how she got it done. The words in boldface type are possible aside comments to be read or stated by you, as if you were thinking aloud.

Little Red Hen

SAY **Look at the first picture while I read the first part of the story.**

One fine spring day, Little Red Hen was in the barnyard looking for seeds to eat. She liked to eat nice fat corn seeds. Suddenly, she saw some seeds that were not corn.

"These are wheat seeds," said Little Red Hen.

"Wheat makes flour, and flour makes bread. I can plant this seed, and someday I'll have good bread to eat."

So Little Red Hen picked up the wheat seeds and went to show her friends, the dog, the duck, and the pig.

SAY **Do you think the dog, the duck, and the pig will be excited about the seeds? Look at the second picture while I read more of the story.**

"Look what I found," Little Red Hen said. "These are wheat seeds. We can plant them to grow wheat. Then we can grind the wheat into flour. Then we can bake the flour into bread. Who will help me plant the seeds?"

"Not I," said the dog.

"Not I," said the duck.

"Not I," said the pig.

"Then I will do it myself," said Little Red Hen. And she did.

Soon the seeds grew into tall, golden wheat.

Little Red Hen said, "It's time to cut the wheat to grind into flour to bake into bread. Who will help me cut the wheat?"

"Not I," said the dog.

"Not I," said the duck.

"Not I," said the pig.

"Then I will do it myself," said Little Red Hen. And she did.

SAY **The dog, the duck, and the pig have not helped Little Red Hen. Why do you think they won't help? Look at the third picture.**

When all the wheat was cut, Little Red Hen said, "It's time to take the wheat to the mill to grind it into flour to bake into bread. Who will help me take the wheat to the mill?"

"Not I," said the dog.

"Not I," said the duck.

"Not I," said the pig.

"Then I will do it myself," said Little Red Hen. And she did.

When the wheat was ground into flour, Little Red Hen said, "At last I can bake my bread. Who will help me bake the bread?"

SAY **What do you think the dog, the duck, and the pig will say?**

"Not I," said the dog.

"Not I," said the duck.

"Not I," said the pig.

"Then I will do it myself," said Little Red Hen. And she did.

SAY **Little Red Hen worked hard to plant and cut the wheat all by herself. She took the wheat to the mill, and she baked the bread all by herself. Look at the last picture while I finish the story.**

When the bread was done, Little Red Hen took the warm loaf from the oven. "Now I can finally eat my bread," said Little Red Hen.

"Let me help you!" said the dog.

"Let me help you!" said the duck.

"Let me help you!" said the pig.

"Oh, no," said Little Red Hen. "You wouldn't help me plant the seeds. You wouldn't help me cut the wheat. You wouldn't help me take the wheat to the mill. You wouldn't help me bake the bread, and now you cannot help me eat it. I will eat the bread myself."

And she did!

SAY **What work did Little Red Hen need to do to have bread?** (She had to plant the seeds, cut the wheat, take the wheat to the mill, and bake the bread.) **How did she get the work done?** (She did it all herself.) **I wonder if the dog, the duck, and the pig were sorry that they didn't help. Do you think Little Red Hen did the right thing by not sharing her bread?** (Answers will vary.)

3 Developing the Skills

R   Speaking: retelling stories

The questions that follow have been designed to help pupils reconstruct the story "Little Red Hen." Display *Big Book* page 61 and call attention to the pictures as you ask these questions.

Picture 1: **What was Little Red Hen looking for in the barnyard?** (seeds to eat) **Why was she so happy to find the wheat seeds?** (She knew she could grow wheat to grind into flour and that she could bake bread from the flour.)

Picture 2: **Why do you think Little Red Hen wanted her friends to help her?** (She had a lot of work to do. Work is easier when you have help.)

Picture 3: **How do you think Little Red Hen feels?** (Possible answers include: tired because she has to work so hard; angry because her friends won't help her.)

Picture 4: **What did Little Red Hen's friends offer to help her do?** (eat the bread) **Why didn't Little Red Hen share the bread?** (She did all the work herself, so she wanted to eat the bread herself.)

SAY Sometimes the characters in a story learn a lesson. **What do you think the dog, the duck, and the pig learned in the story of the Little Red Hen?** (Possible answers include: You should help your friends.) **How do you think the story would have been different if the dog, the duck, and the pig had helped Little Red Hen?** (Possible answers include: Little Red Hen would have shared the bread.)

❋ Practicing and Extending

The activities that follow provide practice and extension of skills developed in this lesson. Not every pupil needs to complete these activities. Choose only the activities that are needed to provide for the individual differences in your classroom.

Extending Selection Concepts

LANGUAGE ARTS

SPEAKING: ROLE PLAYING   Select four pupils to portray the characters in "The Little Red Hen." Set the scene by asking where the characters were and what they were doing when the story began. Then ask "Little Red Hen" to tell what she is doing and what she finds. The rest of the class can help the actors by suggesting the next actions and dialog. If needed, ask, "What happened next?" to keep the action going.

SCIENCE

SPEAKING: TELLING ABOUT OBSERVATIONS   Provide bean–planting materials. (See page T215.) Suggest that pupils plant their own seeds and watch them grow. Have pupils water the seeds daily, making sure not to overwater. Have pupils check their plants at the same time each day and discuss the growth they observe. Print pupils' observations on chart paper and display the chart near the plants.

ACTIVITY 2 Recognizing Sequence
page 62 (T220–T222)

Skill Strands

COMPREHENSION/THINKING

R, T Literal: sequence

Materials

Sundrops, Level 1: page 62
Practice Masters: page 41
Resource Box: Picture Cards "Little Red Hen"
Pocket Chart
Teacher's Idea Book

Special Populations

See *Teacher's Idea Book* for additional suggestions to help pupils with limited English proficiency.

Key to Symbols
I Introduced in this lesson
R Reinforced from an earlier lesson in this level
M Maintained from previous levels
T Tested in this level

1 Preparing for the page

R, T Literal: sequence

Display the *Picture Cards* for "Little Red Hen" in random order in the *Pocket Chart.* Ask pupils to think about the pictures and decide what happened first, what happened next, and what happened last in the story. Have pupils select the picture that shows what happened first in the story and place it on the left side of the *Pocket Chart.* (Little Red Hen found a wheat seed.) Have the picture that shows what happened next identified and placed next to the first picture. (Little Red Hen did all the work; her friends did not help her.) Then have the last picture placed after the other pictures. (Little Red Hen ate the bread.) Point to the first picture.

SAY **First, Little Red Hen found some seeds.** (Point to the second picture.) **Next, she did all the work.** (Point to the last picture.) **Then, she baked bread to eat.**

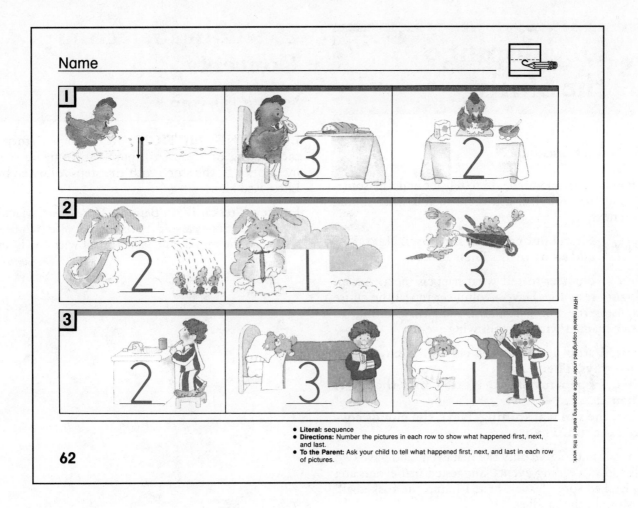

Name _____

- **Literal:** sequence
- **Directions:** Number the pictures in each row to show what happened first, next, and last.
- **To the Parent:** Ask your child to tell what happened first, next, and last in each row of pictures.

62

2 Using the page

R, T Literal: sequence

Have pupils find page 62 in their books and call attention to the three pictures at the top of the page. Explain that these pictures show things that happened in the story "Little Red Hen" but that they are not in the right order. Tell pupils to decide what happened first, next, and last in the story.

SAY You can put these pictures in the right order by printing the numbers 1, 2, and 3 under the pictures.

Call on volunteers to tell which picture shows what happened first. (the first picture) Tell pupils to trace number 1 under the first picture. Ask which picture shows what happened next. (the last picture) Tell pupils to print number 2 under the last picture. Then ask which picture shows what happened then. (the middle picture) Tell pupils to print number 3 under the middle picture. Have pupils complete the page by numbering the pictures in each row 1, 2, and 3 to show what would happen first, next, and last. When the page is completed, have pupils tell about the events in each row, using the words *first, next,* and *then.*

3 Developing the Skills

R, T Literal: sequence

Tell pupils that you will begin to tell about doing something and that you will ask them to tell what should happen next.

SAY | **First, I put cereal in my bowl. Next, I add some milk. Then _____.**

Call on a volunteer to tell what happens next. Accept any logical response. Have a volunteer repeat the entire series, using the words *first, next,* and *then.* Continue in the same manner with the following events:

1. **First, I stop at the street corner. Next, I look both ways. Then _____.**
2. **First, I open my book. Next, I find the page. Then _____.**
3. **First, the sun was shining. Next, the clouds covered the sun. Then _____.**

You may want to give only the first event and have two pupils add succeeding events. Suggested first events are: First, I raked some leaves; first, I found the basketball; first, Mom lit the candles.

✳ Practicing and Extending

The activities that follow provide practice and extension of skills developed in this lesson. Not every pupil needs to complete these activities. Choose only the activities that are needed to provide for the individual differences in your classroom.

Practicing Skills

R, T Literal: sequence

PM 41 ADDITIONAL PRACTICE *Practice Masters* page 41 may be used as optional practice for sequencing events.

Extending Selection Concepts

LITERATURE

LISTENING: FICTION Read aloud a story about the making of bread. Ask pupils to compare the steps mentioned in the story with the steps followed by The Little Red Hen.

Lindsey, Treska. *When Batistine Made Bread.* Macmillan, 1985. Six-year-old Batistine harvests wheat, takes it to the miller, and bakes bread with the flour.

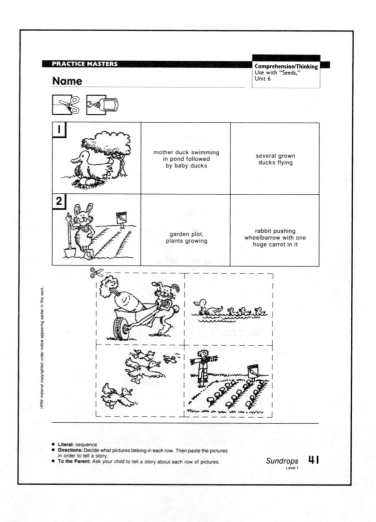

ACTIVITY 3 Relating /ē/ to *ee* and *ea*
page 63 (T223–T225)

Skill Strands

DECODING/VOCABULARY

I, T Sound/symbol correspondence: vowel /ē/*ea, ee*

Materials

Sundrops, Level 1: page 63
Practice Masters: page 42
Resource Box: Letter Cards *d, s, t,*
            Pattern Cards *ea, ee*
Pocket Chart
Teacher's Idea Book

Special Populations

See *Teacher's Idea Book* for additional suggestions to help pupils with limited English proficiency.

1 Preparing for the page

I, T Sound/symbol correspondence: vowel /ē/*ea, ee*

Remind pupils that Little Red Hen found a seed in the barnyard. Use *Letter Cards* and *Pattern Cards* to make the word *seed* in the *Pocket Chart*.

SAY **Here is the word *seed*. Say *seed* with me: *seed*.** (Remove the *s* and the *d*.) **When you see two *e*'s together, they stand for the /ē/ sound. Watch my finger and say the /ē/ sound whenever I touch the letters *ee*.**

Make a game of pointing to the letters, sometimes quickly, sometimes holding your finger on the letters for several seconds.

SAY **I'll say some words that have the /ē/ sound. You say each word after me.**

Use the following words: *tree, bee, feet.*

Remove the *ee* card from the *Pocket Chart* and use *Letter Cards* and *Pattern Cards* to make the word *eat.*

SAY **At the end of the story, Little Red Hen was ready to eat the bread.** (Point to the word in the chart.) **This is the word *eat*. Say *eat* with me: *eat*.** (Remove *Letter Card t*.) **When you see the letters *ea* together, they also stand for the /ē/ sound. Make the /ē/ sound whenever I touch the letters *ea*.**

Repeat the touching game. Then replace the *ee* card in the *Pocket Chart* and have pupils make the /ē/ sound whenever you point to either letter pair.

SAY **I will ask one of you to come to the *Pocket Chart*. I will say a word. If the word has the /ē/ sound, you will point to the letters *ea* and *ee*. If the word does not have the /ē/ sound, put your hands behind your back. Then I will have another pupil come to the *Pocket Chart*.**

Use these words: *eagle, motor, cheese, tree, bug, dream, animal, each.*

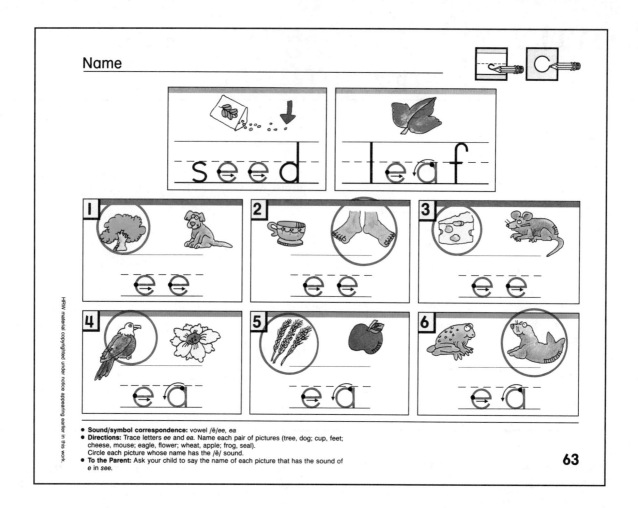

Name _____

- **Sound/symbol correspondence:** vowel /ē/ee, ea
- **Directions:** Trace letters *ee* and *ea*. Name each pair of pictures (tree, dog; cup, feet; cheese, mouse; eagle, flower; wheat, apple; frog, seal). Circle each picture whose name has the /ē/ sound.
- **To the Parent:** Ask your child to say the name of each picture that has the sound of *e* in *see*.

63

---

2 Using the page

I, T Sound/symbol correspondence: vowel /ē/ea, ee

Help pupils find page 63 in their books. Point to the first picture.

SAY This is a seed. The letters *ee* stand for the /ē/ sound in *seed*. Trace the letters *ee* on the writing line by the picture of a *seed*. (Allow time for pupils to trace the letters. Then point to the leaf.) This is a leaf. The letters *ea* stand for the /ē/ sound in *leaf*. Trace the letters *ea* on the writing line by the leaf.

Direct attention to the boxes at the bottom of the page. Have pupils identify the two pictures in the first box. (tree, dog) Ask which picture has the /ē/ sound in its name. (tree) Tell pupils to draw a circle around the tree to show that *tree* has the /ē/ sound. Then have pupils trace the letters *ee* on the writing line. Pupils should complete the page by circling each picture that has the /ē/ sound in its name and by tracing the letters that stand for the /ē/ sound in each box.

3 Developing the Skills

I, T Sound/symbol correspondence: vowel /ē/ea, ee

Tell pupils that you will read several riddles. The answer to each riddle is a word that has the /ē/ sound. Read each of the following riddles and call on a volunteer to answer the riddle.

1. I am something that grows.
   I can be very tall.
   I have leaves on my branches.
   What am I? (a tree)

2. I am made from milk.
   You can eat me on sandwiches.
   Mice like to eat me, too.
   What am I? (cheese)

3. I am a color.
   I am the color of grass.
   What am I? (green)

4. You can stand on me.
   I have toes.
   What am I? (feet)

✳ Practicing and Extending

The activities that follow provide practice and extension of skills developed in this lesson. Not every pupil needs to complete these activities. Choose only the activities that are needed to provide for the individual differences in your classroom.

Practicing Skills

I, T Sound/symbol correspondence: vowel /ē/ea, ee

PM 42 ADDITIONAL PRACTICE *Practice Masters* page 42 may be used to practice associating the letters *ee* and *ea* with the /ē/ sound in words.

ADDITIONAL PRACTICE

SAY Once upon a time, there was a boy named Zeke. Every time Zeke heard a word that had the /ē/ sound in it, he would say, "Eek." Pretend that you are Zeke. Every time you hear me say a word that has the /ē/ sound, say *"Eek."*

Use the following words: *feed, squeak, bottom, please, sneak, butter, leak, sleep, bundle, ant, freeze, snow.*

Extending Selection Concepts

LITERATURE

LISTENING: FICTION Choose a story about seeds and read it aloud to the class. Discuss with pupils how the character in the story cared for the seeds.

Krauss, Ruth. *The Carrot Seed.* Harper & Row, 1982. This is a classic tale of a boy's determination. He knows the carrot seed he planted will grow—and it does.

LeTord, Bijou. *Rabbit Seeds.* Four Winds Press, 1984. The rabbit begins work in his garden in the spring. He plants, tends, and harvests until the leaves turn yellow in autumn.

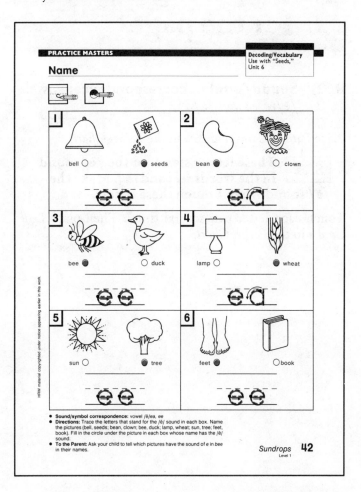

ACTIVITY 4   Discriminating Medial /ē/*ea, ee* and /a/*a* page 64 (T226–T228)

Skill Strands

DECODING/VOCABULARY

R, T   **Sound/symbol correspondence:** vowels /ē/*ee, ea* and /a/*a*

Materials

Sundrops, Level 1: page 64
Practice Masters: page 43
Resource Box: Letter Card a
                    Pattern Cards ea, ee
Pocket Chart
Teacher's Idea Book

Special Populations

See *Teacher's Idea Book* for additional suggestions to help pupils with limited English proficiency.

Key to Symbols
I   Introduced in this lesson
R   Reinforced from an earlier lesson in this level
M   Maintained from previous levels
T   Tested in this level

---

1 Preparing for the page

R, T   **Sound/symbol correspondence:** vowels /ē/*ee, ea* and /a/*a*

Place *Pattern Cards ee* and *ea* in the *Pocket Chart.*

SAY   **These letters stand for the /ē/ sound in the words *seed* and *leaf.* Make the /ē/ sound when I touch these letters.**

Touch each letter pair several times. Then place *Letter Card a* in the *Pocket Chart.*

SAY   **This letter stands for the /a/ sound in the word *cat.* Say the /a/ sound when I touch this letter.** (Touch the letter several times.) **I am going to say some words that have /ē/ in the middle and some words that have /a/ in the middle. I will ask one of you to come to the *Pocket Chart,* to repeat the word I say, and to point to the card or cards that have the letter or letters that stand for the sound in the middle of the word.**

Use the following words: *beak, teach, dad, can, dream, fat, screen, map, meet, pan.*

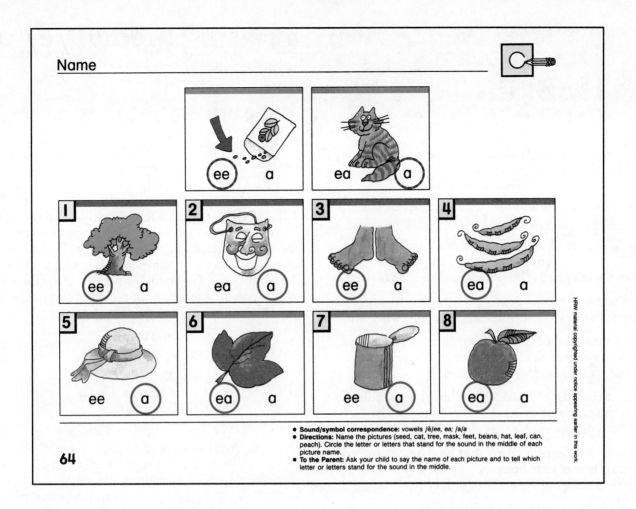

Name _____

64

• **Sound/symbol correspondence:** vowels /ē/ee, ea; /a/a
• **Directions:** Name the pictures (seed, cat, tree, mask, feet, beans, hat, leaf, can, peach). Circle the letter or letters that stand for the sound in the middle of each picture name.
• **To the Parent:** Ask your child to say the name of each picture and to tell which letter or letters stand for the sound in the middle.

2 Using the page

R, T Sound/symbol correspondence: vowels /ē/*ee, ea* and /a/*a*

Have pupils find page 64 in their books and call on a volunteer to name the first picture. (seed)

ASK **What sound do you hear in the middle of *seed*?** (/ē/) **Look at the letters at the bottom of the box. Which letter or letters stand for the /ē/ sound in *seed*?** (*ee*) **Trace the circle around the letters *ee* to show that *seed* has the /ē/ sound in the middle.**

Have the next picture identified. Tell pupils to circle the letter *a* to show that *cat* has the /a/ sound in the middle.

Help pupils identify the remaining pictures. Tell pupils to circle the letter or letters in each box that stand for the sound they hear in the middle of the picture name.

3 Developing the Skills

R, T **Sound/symbol correspondence:** vowels /ē/*ee, ea* and /a/*a*

Tell pupils that you will play a guessing game that uses words that have the /ē/ sound or the /a/ sound.

SAY I am thinking of a word that has the /ē/ sound. It is something you do with your eyes. Is the word *touch, see,* or *look?* (*see*)

Continue in the same manner with the following hints:

1. **I am thinking of a word that has the /a/ sound. It is an animal that says "meow." Is the word *fish, dog,* or *cat?*** (*cat*)

2. **I am thinking of a word that has the /ē/ sound. It is the color of grass. Is the word *green, blue,* or *orange?*** (*green*)

3. **I am thinking of a word that has the /ē/ sound. It is an insect that buzzes. Is the word *grasshopper, ant,* or *bee?*** (*bee*)

4. **I am thinking of a word that has the /a/ sound. It is a part of your body that has fingers on it. Is the word *toes, hand,* or *head?*** (*hand*)

✳ Practicing and Extending

The activities that follow provide practice and extension of skills developed in this lesson. Not every pupil needs to complete these activities. Choose only the activities that are needed to provide for the individual differences in your classroom.

Practicing Skills

R, T **Sound/symbol correspondence:** vowels /ē/*ee, ea* and /a/*a*

PM 43 **ADDITIONAL PRACTICE** *Practice Masters* page 43 may be used as optional practice for identifying /ē/ and /a/.

Extending Selection Concepts

> ### LITERATURE

LISTENING: POETRY Tell pupils that you are going to read a poem that tells about something a boy did. Explain that the boy is named Tommy and that "Tommy" is the name of the poem. Then read "Tommy" by Gwendolyn Brooks. Explain that the word *consulting* means *asking.* Read the poem a second time and ask what Tommy did.

Tommy

I put a seed into the ground
And said, "I'll watch it grow."
I watered it and cared for it
As well as I could know.

One day I walked in my back yard,
And oh, what did I see!
My seed had popped itself right out,
Without consulting me.

Gwendolyn Brooks

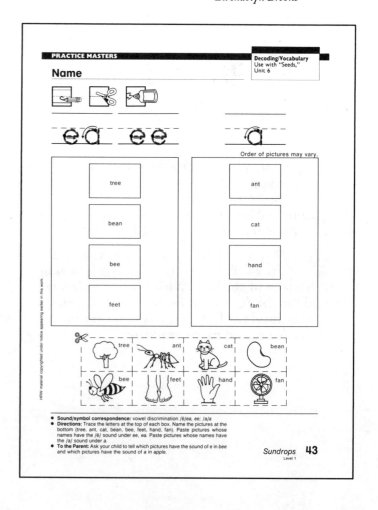

ACTIVITY 5 Building Words
page 65 (T229–T232)

Skill Strands

DECODING/VOCABULARY

I **Vocabulary:** word building
I **Word structure:** inflectional ending -s

COMPREHENSION/THINKING

R, T **Literal:** cause and effect

Materials

Sundrops, Level 1: page 65
Practice Masters: page 44
Resource Box: Letter Cards *d, m, s (2), t,*
                    Pattern Cards *ea, ee*
Pocket Chart
Teacher's Idea Book

Special Populations

See *Teacher's Idea Book* for additional suggestions to help pupils with limited English proficiency.

Key to Symbols
I Introduced in this lesson
R Reinforced from an earlier lesson in this level
M Maintained from previous levels
T Tested in this level

1 Preparing for the page

I **Word structure:** inflectional ending -s

Place *Pattern Cards ee* and *ea* in the *Pocket Chart* and ask what sound these letter pairs stand for. (/ē/) Then place *Letter Cards m, s, t,* and *d* in random order in the *Pocket Chart.* Point to each letter and have pupils say the sound the letter stands for.

Remove the *Letter Cards* and tell pupils that you will place some of the letters together to make a word that tells what Little Red Hen found. Place the word *seed* in the *Pocket Chart.* Ask pupils to read the word with you as you move your hand under the letters. (*seed*) Call on volunteers to read the word.

Now place the second *Letter Card s* after the word *seed* to make the word *seeds.*

SAY Little Red Hen wanted to eat more than one seed. She wanted some seeds. This is the word *seeds.* I added the letter *s* to the end of *seed* to make the word *seeds.* If I talk about just one, I use the word *seed.* If I talk about more than one, I use the word *seeds.* (Point to the word *seeds.*) **Read this word with me: *seeds.* The letter *s* at the end of the word *seeds* has a /z/ sound. Sometimes the letter *s* makes a /z/ sound when it is at the end of a word.**

I will say a sentence that talks about one person or thing. Then I will say part of a sentence that tells about more than one. Finish the sentence for me. I see one boy. I see three _____. (boys) **I have one mitten. I need to have two _____.** (mittens) **I read one book. I like to read lots of _____.** (books)

Remove *Letter Cards d* and *s* from the end of *seeds,* leaving the word *see.* Ask pupils to blend the sounds of the letters together to read this word with you. Move your hand under the letters as you blend the sounds. Call on volunteers to read the word. (*see*) Point to the word *see.*

HRW material copyrighted under notice appearing earlier in this work.

- **Vocabulary:** word building
- **Directions:** Print the missing letters to make the words *seeds, see, meat,* and *eat.*
- **To the Parent:** Ask your child to tell what is happening in each picture and to read the word at the bottom of the picture.

65

SAY I see you and you see me. (Place *Letter Card s* at the end to make the word *sees.*) **Now the word is *sees.* Little Red Hen sees a seed.**

Place *Letter Cards ea* and *t* in the *Pocket Chart* to make the word *eat.* Run your hand under the letters as you say the sounds to help pupils blend the sounds of the letters. Call on volunteers to read the word. (*eat*)

SAY The dog, the duck, and the pig wanted to eat the bread. (Place *s* at the end of *eat.*) **Now the word says *eats.* Little Red Hen eats the bread.**

2 Using the page

I Vocabulary: word building

SAY We can use the letters we know to make words. (Make the word *eat* in the *Pocket Chart* and have the word read.) **Who can**

put letter *m* in front of the word *eat?* (Call on a volunteer.) **What word did you make?** (*meat*) **Meat is something we eat.**

Take out the *m* and replace it with *s.* Ask pupils to read the new word. (*seat*) Explain that you sit on a seat.

Remove the letters *eat* and replace them with *eed.* Have the new word read. (*seed*)

SAY Now you can make some words in your books.

Help pupils find page 65 in their books. Have pupils tell what is happening in the first picture. (A boy is planting seeds in a garden.)

SAY The word under this picture is supposed to be *seeds* because the boy is planting more than one seed. I see the word *seed.* What do we need to add to the end of this word to make the word mean more than one seed? (*s*) Trace letter *s* at the end to make the word *seeds.* Call on volunteers to read the completed word.

Have pupils tell what is happening in the second picture. (The boy is showing off the beans he grew.)

| SAY | The boy wants us to see the beans. He is saying "See." I see the letters that stand for the /ē/ sound in *see*. What sound is missing from the beginning of the word *see*? (/s/) What letter stands for the /s/ sound? (*s*) Print letter *s* in front of *ee* to make the word *see*. |

Have pupils tell what is happening in the third picture. (Meat is cooking on the grill.)

| SAY | The word under the picture is supposed to be *meat*. What sound do you hear at the beginning of *meat*? (/m/) Print the letter that stands for the /m/ sound at the beginning to make the word *meat*. (*m*) |

Have pupils tell what is happening in the last picture. (The boy is eating the meat and his beans.)

| SAY | The word under the picture is supposed to be *eat*. What sound is missing from the word *eat*? (the /t/ sound at the end) Print the letter that stands for the /t/ sound at the end of the word *eat*. (*t*) |

Call on pupils to read all the words on the page.

3 Developing the Skills

R, T   Literal: cause and effect

Remind pupils that in a story one thing sometimes causes, or makes, another thing happen. In the story "The Little Red Hen," the hen planted the seeds and that caused the wheat to grow.

Tell pupils to look at the pictures on page 65 of their books. Explain that you will begin a sentence by telling something that happened, such as "Chris planted seeds in his garden because . . ." Then you will ask them to make up an ending for the sentence by giving a reason for what happens.

| SAY | Let's try it. Chris planted seeds in the garden because _____. |

Call on volunteers to complete the sentence and then to repeat the whole sentence. You may wish to let several pupils give different responses for each sentence. Use the following sentence beginnings for each picture:

1. **I planted bean seeds because _____.**
2. **The beans grew fast because _____.**
3. **We cooked the meat on the grill because _____.**
4. **I ate green beans for dinner because _____.**

✳ Practicing and Extending

The activities that follow provide practice and extension of skills developed in this lesson. Not every pupil needs to complete these activities. Choose only the activities that are needed to provide for the individual differences in your classroom.

Practicing Skills

I   Vocabulary: word building

PM 44   **ADDITIONAL PRACTICE**   *Practice Masters* Page 44 may be used as optional practice for building words.

HOW AM I DOING?

Many pupils need encouragement to participate in group activities. Ask yourself the following questions to check your effectiveness in getting pupils involved.

	Yes	No	Some-times
1. Do I ask pupils questions to focus their attention on key lesson concepts?	☐	☐	☐
2. Do I systematically select pupils for reading or answering questions to insure that all pupils participate?	☐	☐	☐
3. Do I allow enough "wait time" for a pupil to think about the answer before I ask someone else?	☐	☐	☐
4. Do I monitor individual pupils by giving immediate feedback on their answers to my questions?	☐	☐	☐

Extending Selection Concepts

SCIENCE

LISTENING: INFORMATION   Choose a book about plants or gardening to read to the class. Have pupils tell what they learned from the book.

Kuchalla, Susan. *All About Seeds.* Troll Associates, 1982. The brief text and pictures in this book explain how different seeds grow into plants.

Rockwell, Anne, and Harlow Rockwell. *How My Garden Grows.* Macmillan, 1982. Simple words and pictures reveal a child's pride in her garden.

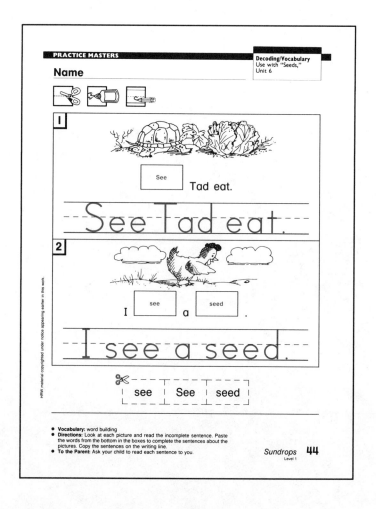

ACTIVITY 6 Reading the Word *said*

page 66 (T233–T235)

Skill Strands

| DECODING/VOCABULARY |

I, T   Vocabulary: word meaning

| LANGUAGE |

I   Conventions of language: quotation marks (with comma and *said*)

Materials

Sundrops, Level 1: page 66
Practice Masters: page 45
Resource Box: Word Cards: Dad, eat, I, sad, said, Sam, See, see, seed, Tad
Punctuation Cards: comma, period, quotation marks
Pocket Chart
Teacher's Idea Book

Special Populations

See *Teacher's Idea Book* for additional suggestions to help pupils with limited English proficiency.

Key to Symbols
I   Introduced in this lesson
R   Reinforced from an earlier lesson in this level
M   Maintained from previous levels
T   Tested in this level

---

1 Preparing for the page

I   Conventions of language: quotation marks (with comma and *said*)

Ask pupils to think about the story of the Little Red Hen.

ASK   **Who said, "Who will help me?"** (Little Red Hen) **Who said, "Not I?"** (the dog, the duck, and the pig) **We use the word *said* when we want to tell who was talking.**

Place *Word Cards Dad said, "See Sam eat."* in the *Pocket Chart.* Point to each word as you read it. Then point to the word *said.*

SAY   **This is the word *said.* Read the word with me: *said.* Now read the sentence with me.** (Point to the words *See Sam eat.*) ***See Sam eat* are the words Dad said. We put special marks around the words someone says. These**

marks are called quotation marks. (Point to the left quotation marks.) **One set of marks goes in front of the words someone said.** (Point to the end quotation marks.) **One set of marks goes after the words someone said. Since the last word that was said is the end of the sentence, we put the marks after the period.** (Point to the comma.) **This is a comma. We use the comma to separate the words that tell who is speaking from the words that were spoken.**

Read the sentence again. Have volunteers point to the words as they read the sentence.

Place the sentence *"I see Sam," said Tad.* in the *Pocket Chart.* Have pupils read the sentence with you. Call on a volunteer to point out the word *said.* Ask who was talking in this sentence. (Tad) Point out the quotation marks and remind pupils that these marks show the words that were spoken. Have pupils point to the words that were spoken and read them to the class.

SAY   **Sometimes the words that tell who was speaking come first in the sentence, and sometimes they come last.**

Then ask pupils to tell what word may be used to tell when someone is speaking. (*said*)

- **Vocabulary:** word meaning
- **Directions:** Trace the word *said* and read each sentence. Fill in the circle under the picture that goes with the sentence.
- **To the Parent:** Ask your child to read each sentence to you.

66

2 Using the page

I, T   Vocabulary: word meaning

Help pupils find page 66 in their books and call attention to the sentence at the top of the page. Tell pupils to trace the word *said*. Then have pupils read the sentence. (*Tam said, "Meet Tad."*)

ASK **Who is talking in this sentence?** (Tam) **What are the words Tam said?** ("*Meet Tad.*")

Then have pupils tell what is happening in the first picture under the sentence. Have pupils tell what is happening in the second picture. (Tam is holding up Tad for her mother to see.) Have pupils fill in the circle under the picture that goes with the sentence *Tam said, "Meet Tad."* (the second picture)

Tell pupils to trace the word *said* in the second sentence. Have pupils read the sentence. ("*Sam eats meat," said Dad.*) Ask pupils to tell who is talking. (Dad) Then have pupils tell what Dad said. ("*Sam eats.*") Tell pupils to fill in the circle under the picture that goes with the sentence. (the first picture.)

3 Developing the Skills

I, T Vocabulary: word meaning

Display *Word Cards said, seed,* and *sad.* Tell pupils that you will play a game with animal noises.

| SAY | I will make an animal noise. Then I will ask you what animal said that sound. I will call on one of you to pick out the word *said* as you tell us the answer. |

Ask the following questions. After each question, mix up the *Word Cards* and have a pupil point to the word *said* as he or she says the answer.

1. **Who said, "Meow?"** (The cat said, "Meow.")
2. **Who said, "Oink-oink?"** (The pig said, "Oink-oink.")
3. **Who said, "Buzz?"** (The bee said, "Buzz.")

Encourage volunteers to suggest other animal noises and to ask who said them.

✳ Practicing and Extending

The activities that follow provide practice and extension of skills developed in this lesson. Not every pupil needs to complete these activities. Choose only the activities that are needed to provide for the individual differences in your classroom.

Practicing Skills

I, T Vocabulary: word meaning

PM 45 **ADDITIONAL PRACTICE** *Practice Masters* page 45 may be used as optional practice for reading the word *said.*

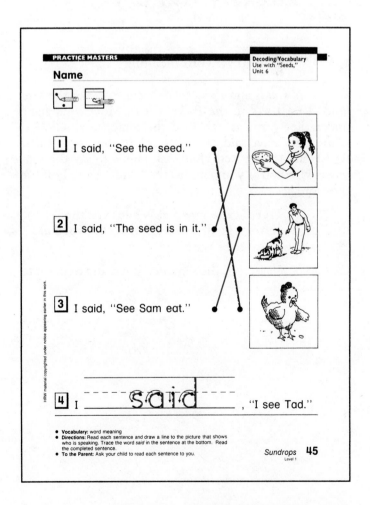

ACTIVITY 7 Reading the word *a*
page 67 (T236–T238)

Skill Strands

DECODING/VOCABULARY

I, T **Vocabulary:** word meaning

Materials

Sundrops, Level 1: page 67

Resource Box: Word Cards *a, am, I, mat, see, seed*
Punctuation Card *period*
Pocket Chart
Teacher's Idea Book

Special Populations

See *Teacher's Idea Book* for additional suggestions to help pupils with limited English proficiency.

Key to Symbols
I Introduced in this lesson
R Reinforced from an earlier lesson in this level
M Maintained from previous levels
T Tested in this level

1 Preparing for the page

I, T **Vocabulary:** word meaning

Use *Word Cards* and *Punctuation Card* to make the sentence *I see a seed* in the *Pocket Chart.* Move your hand under the words as you read the sentence aloud. Ask who might have said "I see a seed" in the story "Little Red Hen" (Little Red Hen) Ask pupils to say the sentence with you as you point to the words again. Point to the word *a.*

| SAY | **Here is the word *a*. Whenever the letter *a* is all by itself, it is the word *a*. Read the sentence with me.** |

Call on pupils to read the sentence aloud and to point to the word *a.*

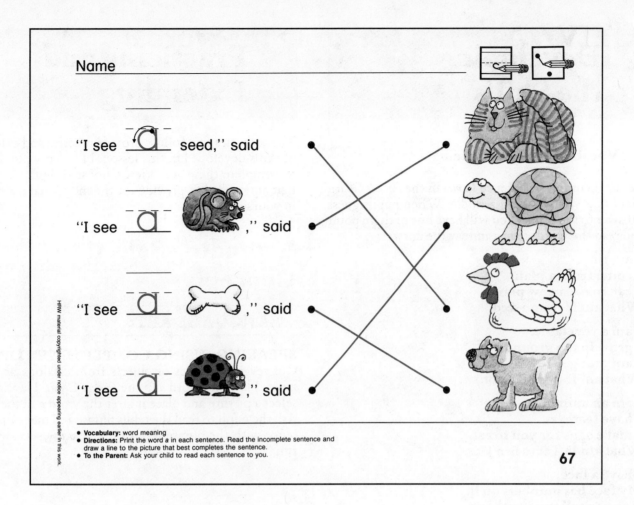

Name _____

"I see __a__ seed," said

"I see __a__ 🐭 ," said

"I see __a__ 🦴 ," said

"I see __a__ 🐞 ," said

• **Vocabulary:** word meaning
• **Directions:** Print the word *a* in each sentence. Read the incomplete sentence and draw a line to the picture that best completes the sentence.
• **To the Parent:** Ask your child to read each sentence to you.

67

2 Using the page

Have pupils draw a line from the dot at the end of the sentence to the dot in front of the picture of the hen. Then ask them to read the completed sentence. ("I see a seed," said the hen.) Explain that pupils are to print the word *a* on the line in each sentence. Then they should complete each sentence by drawing a line to the picture of the animal that might be talking in each sentence.

I, T Vocabulary: word meaning

Help pupils find page 67 in their books. Explain that the sentences on the left side of the page tell what some animals might like to see. The pictures on the right show the animals. Ask pupils to find the word that needs to be traced in the first sentence. Have pupils trace the word and read it. (*a*) Then call on volunteers to read the incomplete sentence.

SAY **Look at the pictures on the right side of the page. Which picture shows an animal that might want a seed?** (the third picture)

Unit 6 "Seeds" (pages 61–70)

3 Developing the Skills

I, T Vocabulary: word meaning

Place the incomplete sentence *I am a* in the *Pocket Chart.* Explain that you will read a riddle. When pupils guess the answer to the riddle, you will have one of them point to and read the words *I am a* and say the answer.

1. **I am tiny.**
   I come from a plant.
   I can make a new plant.
   What am I? (I am a seed.)

2. **I am a vegetable.**
   I grow in the ground.
   I am orange.
   What am I? (I am a carrot.)

3. **I am an animal.**
   I have feathers.
   I make eggs for you to eat.
   What am I? (I am a hen.)

4. **I have a face.**
   My face has numbers on it.
   You can tell time with me.
   What am I? (I am a clock.)

✳ Practicing and Extending

The activities that follow provide practice and extension of skills developed in this lesson. Not every pupil needs to complete these activities. Choose only the activities that are needed to provide for the individual differences in your classroom.

Extending Selection Concepts

LANGUAGE ARTS

SPEAKING: USING COMPLETE SENTENCES
Cut several pictures of objects from catalogs or magazines. Place the word *a* in the *Pocket Chart.* Have a pupil select a picture and place it after the word *a* in the chart. Ask the pupil to read the rebus phrase and make up a sentence with the phrase. For example: *a dog;* "I saw a dog run."

ACTIVITY 8 Reading a Story
page 68 (T239–T241)

Skill Strands

DECODING/VOCABULARY

R **Vocabulary:** words in context
R **Word structure:** inflectional ending -s

Materials

Sundrops, Level 1: page 68
Resource Box: Word Cards *a, Dee, eat, eats, Matt, Meet, said, Sam, See, see, seeds, Tam, the*
    Punctuation Cards comma, period, quotation marks
Pocket Chart
Teacher's Idea Book

Special Populations

See *Teacher's Idea Book* for additional suggestions to help pupils with limited English proficiency.

Key to Symbols
I   Introduced in this lesson
R   Reinforced from an earlier lesson in this level
M   Maintained from previous levels
T   Tested in this level

1 Preparing for the page

R **Word structure:** inflectional ending -s

Tell pupils that they are going to read a story about a day when some children brought their pets to school. Ask if any pupils have pets at home. Encourage pupils who have pets to tell how they care for their pets. Point out that in order to keep a pet, it is important to know what the pet eats.

SAY **One of the pets in the story we will read is named Dee. Here is what Dee eats.**

Place the sentence *Dee eats seeds.* in the *Pocket Chart.* Have pupils read the sentence aloud. Ask what Dee eats. (seeds) Point to the *s* at the end of the word *seeds.*

SAY **The *s* at the end of this word means that Dee eats more than one seed. Sometimes we put an *s* on the end of a word to show that we mean more than one. Now let's read our story to find out what kind of pet Dee is.**

Name _____

1 Tam said, "Meet Dee."

2 "Dee eats seeds," said Tam.

3 "I see the seeds," said Matt.

4 "See Dee eat a seed," said Tam.

● **Vocabulary:** words in context
● **Directions:** Read the story.
● **To the Parent:** Read and discuss the story with your child.

68

2 Using the page

R Vocabulary: words in context

Help pupils find page 68. Explain that you will read part of the story about Pet Day and that pupils will read the parts of the story that are printed in their books. Have pupils look at the first picture as you read the following story part:

> **READ** The boys and girls had been looking forward to Pet Day for a long time. Each of them could bring their pet to show the class. There were dogs, cats, and even turtles. At last it was Tam's turn to introduce her pet. Tam took the cover off the cage she had carried so carefully to school and held up her pet gerbil.

> **SAY** The sentence at the bottom of the first picture tells what Tam said to the class. Read it to yourself.

Then have pupils read the sentence aloud. (*Tam said, "Meet Dee."*)

> **SAY** Look at the second picture as I read part of the story.

> **READ** The boys and girls liked Dee. They wanted to know how to take care of a gerbil. They asked Tam what Dee liked to eat.

> **SAY** Read the sentence at the bottom of the second picture to yourself to see what Dee eats.

Then have pupils read the sentence aloud. (*"Dee eats seeds," said Tam.*)

> **SAY** Look at the third picture as I read more of the story.

> **READ** Matt was a friend of Tam's. Matt was close enough to Dee's cage to look inside.

> **SAY** Read the sentence at the bottom of the third picture to yourself to find out what Matt saw in Dee's cage.

Then have pupils read the sentence aloud. (*"I see the seeds," said Matt.*)

SAY	Look at the last picture as I read more of the story.
READ	All the excitement of coming to school with Tam made Dee hungry. As Dee started to eat her seeds, she threw the shells all over.

Read the sentence at the bottom of the picture to yourself to see what Tam said. Then have pupils read the sentence aloud. (*"See Dee eat a seed," said Tam.*)

Invite any pupils who have gerbils or other pets that eat seeds to tell about their pets.

3 Developing the Skills

R Vocabulary: words in context

Display *Word Cards Matt, Dee, Sam,* and *Tam* and have pupils read the words. Explain that these words name all of the people and animals in the story they read.

Display *Word Cards See, see, said, eat, eats,* and *Meet* in a second group and have the words read. Explain that these words are for the actions that take place in the story.

Display *Word Cards the, a* and *seeds* in a third group and have them read. Explain that these words are needed to tell about what someone ate.

Then display the *Punctuation Cards* and explain that these marks help us to write sentences.

Tell pupils that you will ask them to use the cards from each group to make sentences from the story. Call on a pupil to make the first sentence, using the book as a model. Then have the pupil read the sentence. Encourage pupils to compare the sentence with the one in the book. Have pupils tell if the words and punctuation marks have been placed correctly.

✳ Practicing and Extending

The activities that follow provide practice and extension of skills developed in this lesson. Not every pupil needs to complete these activities. Choose only the activities that are needed to provide for the individual differences in your classroom.

Extending Selection Concepts

LANGUAGE ARTS

SPEAKING: TELLING A STORY Ask pupils to pretend that they had a pet day in their class. Then suggest that on their pet day, someone brought a very unusual pet to school. Invite pupils to suggest animals that would make very unusual pets. (Possible answers include: a gorilla, a giraffe, a penguin.) Select one of the animals and have pupils tell a story about what might happen if that animal came to school. Use a tape recorder to record the pupils' story. Place the tape recorder where pupils can listen to the story on their own.

LITERATURE

LISTENING: FICTION Read aloud a book about an unusual pet. Ask pupils to explain why some animals do not make good pets.

Hamsa, Bobbie. *Your Pet Giraffe.* Childrens Press, 1982. This is one of a series of books that humorously point out the reasons why wild animals do not make good pets.

Skill Strands

DECODING/VOCABULARY

I Vocabulary: words in context

LANGUAGE

R Conventions of language: end punctuation (period, question mark)

R Conventions of language: quotation marks (with comma and *said*)

Materials

Sundrops, Level 1: page 69

Resource Box: Word Cards *Dee, eat, eats, Is, is, mad, Matt, meat, Meet, on, sad, Sam, said, See, sees, seeds, Tam, the*
Punctuation Cards *comma, period, question mark, quotation marks*

Pocket Chart
Teacher's Idea Book

Special Populations

See *Teacher's Idea Book* for additional suggestions to help pupils with limited English proficiency.

Key to Symbols
I Introduced in this lesson
R Reinforced from an earlier lesson in this level
M Maintained from previous levels
T Tested in this level

1 Preparing for the page

R Conventions of language: end punctuation (period, question mark)

R Conventions of language: quotation marks (with comma and *said*)

Display the *Word Cards Dee, eats, Is, Matt, sad, said, seeds, Tam* and *Punctuation Cards period, comma, question mark, quotation marks.*

SAY You read a story about Tam and her pet, Dee. What kind of pet is Dee? (a gerbil) **What does Dee eat?** (seeds) **Let's see if we remember how to make sentences. Who will make the sentence *Dee eats seeds.* in the *Pocket Chart?***

Call on a volunteer. Point to the period and remind pupils that a period is found at the end of a sentence. Ask how you can show that these are the words someone said. (Place quotation marks around the words.)

ASK Who said, "Dee eats seeds," in the story? (Tam)

Have a pupil place the words *said Tam* after the word *seeds.* Replace the period with a comma and remind pupils that a comma goes between the words someone said and the part that tells who said them. Place the period at the end of the sentence. Call on pupils to read the sentence aloud. (*"Dee eats seeds," said Tam.*)

Remove the cards from the *Pocket Chart* and place the question *Is Dee sad* in the chart. Call on pupils to read the words.

SAY These words ask something. What do we call a sentence that asks something? (a question) **What mark should be at the end of a question?** (a question mark)

Have a pupil place the question mark at the end of the question. Then call on pupils to read the question.

SAY We are going to read about another pet at school. (Place *Word Card Matt* in the *Pocket Chart.*) **This is the name of the boy who has a pet to show. Who can read the boy's name?** (*Matt*) **Let's read about Matt's pet.**

Name _____

1	"Meet Sam," said Matt.
2	"Sam eats meat," said Matt.
3	Tam said, "Sam sees Dee eat. Is Sam mad?"
4	"See the seeds on Sam," said Matt.

- **Vocabulary:** words in context
- **Directions:** Read the story.
- **To the Parent:** Read and discuss the story with your child.

69

2 Using the page

I Vocabulary: words in context

Help pupils find page 69 in their books and explain that you are going to read part of the story and that the pupils will read the parts of the story that are printed in their books.

SAY Look at the first picture as I read the beginning of the story.

READ Tam sat down with her pet gerbil. Dee was still busy eating her seeds. Now it was Matt's turn to show his pet. Matt's pet was Sam, who was sitting quietly beside Matt. Matt introduced Sam to the class.

SAY Read the sentence at the bottom of the first picture to yourselves to find out what Matt said.

Call on a volunteer to read the sentence aloud. (*"Meet Sam," said Matt.*)

SAY Now look at the second picture as I read the next story part.

READ Sam liked being at school. There were so many boys and girls to pet him. The boys and girls wanted to know all about Sam. They wanted to know what Sam ate.

SAY Read the sentence at the bottom of the picture to yourself to find out what Matt told the class.

Have pupils read the sentence aloud. (*"Sam eats meat," said Matt.*)

SAY Look at the third picture as I read more of the story.

READ Sam saw Dee's cage. Sam had never seen a gerbil before. He put his nose right up to the cage to take a good look at Dee.

SAY Read the sentences at the bottom of the third picture to yourself to find out what Tam said about Sam.

Have pupils read the sentences aloud. (*Tam said, "Sam sees Dee eat. Is Sam mad?"*) Ask pupils to tell if they think Sam might be mad and why. (Possible answers include: yes, because Dee is eating and Sam has no food; or, no, because Sam just wants to look at Dee.)

| SAY | **Look at the last picture as I read more of the story.** |

| READ | **Sam didn't know what messy eaters gerbils are. Sam soon found out he was standing too close to Dee.** |

| SAY | **Read the sentence at the bottom of the last picture to yourself to see what happened to Sam.** |

Have pupils read the sentence to the class. (*"See the seeds on Sam," said Matt.*)

| ASK | **What happened to Sam?** (He got Dee's seeds in his fur.) |

Ask pupils to tell how Sam and Dee are alike. (Both are pets. Both came to school for pet day.) Ask pupils to tell how Sam and Dee are different. (Sam is big and Dee is little. Sam can walk around while Dee has to stay in a cage. Sam eats meat and Dee eats seeds.)

3 Developing the Skills

R Conventions of language: end punctuation (period, question mark)

R Conventions of language: quotation marks

Display *Word Cards Sam, Matt, Dee,* and *Tam.* Have the words read and explain that these words are the names of the people and animals in the story. Then display *Word Cards Meet, said, eats, See, is, sees,* and *eat* in a second group and have them read. Tell pupils that these words tell the actions that take place in the story. Display *Word Cards meat, mad, the, seeds,* and *on* in a third group and have pupils read the words. Then tell pupils that these are words that help tell about what happened in the story. Have pupils use the cards to make the sentences from page 69. Pupils may use page 69 as a model. Use the *Punctuation Cards* to punctuate the sentences. Ask pupils to explain why each punctuation mark goes where it does.

✳ Practicing and Extending

The activities that follow provide practice and extension of skills developed in this lesson. Not every pupil needs to complete these activities. Choose only the activities that are needed to provide for the individual differences in your classroom.

Practicing Skills

R   Conventions of language: end punctuation

ADDITIONAL PRACTICE Remind pupils that sentences that tell something end with a period and sentences that ask something end with a question mark. Hold up *Punctuation Cards period* and *question mark.* Tell pupils that you will say some sentences. Then you will ask pupils to repeat the sentence and to select the punctuation mark that should be at the end. Use these sentences:

1. **It rained all day.** (period)
2. **What is your name?** (question mark)
3. **Can you run fast?** (question mark)
4. **School is fun.** (period)

Extending Selection Concepts

> ### LANGUAGE ARTS

SPEAKING: TELLING ABOUT A PICTURE
Tell pupils that you will have an imaginary pet day. Have pupils draw an imaginary pet on their paper. Tell pupils to think up a name for their imaginary pet and to think up something for the pet to eat. When pupils are finished, invite volunteers to display their pictures and to say "Meet (pet's name). (Pet's name) eats _____."

ACTIVITY 10 Reviewing /ē/ *ea, ee*
page 70 (T246–T248)

Skill Strands

DECODING/VOCABULARY

R, T   Sound/symbol correspondence: vowel /ē/*ea, ee*

LANGUAGE

R   Writing: language–experience stories

Materials

Sundrops, Level 1: page 70
Big Book: page 70
Practice Masters: page 46
Resource Box: Pattern Cards ea, ee
Teacher's Idea Book

Special Populations

See *Teacher's Idea Book* for additional suggestions to help pupils with limited English proficiency.

Key to Symbols
I   Introduced in this lesson
R   Reinforced from an earlier lesson in this level
M   Maintained from previous levels
T   Tested in this level

1 Preparing for the page

R, T   Sound/symbol correspondence: vowel /ē/*ea, ee*

Display *Pattern Cards ee* and *ea* and ask what sound these letter pairs stand for. (/ē/)

| SAY | I will say three words. Tell me which words have the /ē/ sound. |

Use the following groups of words.

1. **seed, eat, bone** (seed, eat)
2. **laugh, sleep, sneak** (sleep, sneak)
3. **geese, sneeze, feed** (sneeze, feed)
4. **peek, coat, need** (peek, need)

Call on volunteers to name other words that contain the /ē/ sound.

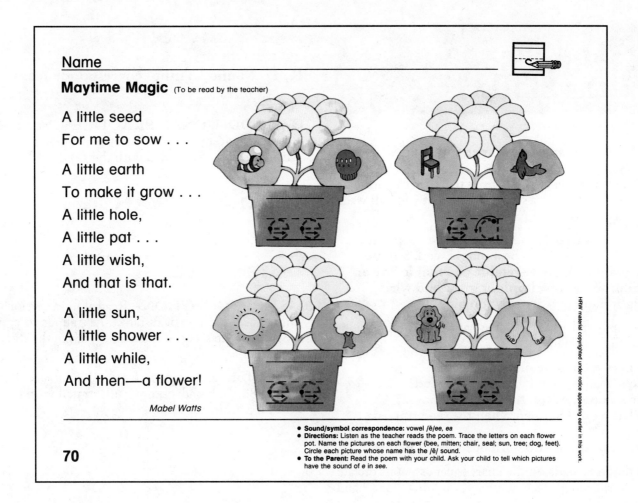

Name _____

Maytime Magic (To be read by the teacher)

A little seed
For me to sow . . .

A little earth
To make it grow . . .

A little hole,
A little pat . . .

A little wish,
And that is that.

A little sun,
A little shower . . .

A little while,
And then—a flower!

Mabel Watts

70

- **Sound/symbol correspondence:** vowel /ē/ee, ea
- **Directions:** Listen as the teacher reads the poem. Trace the letters on each flower pot. Name the pictures on each flower (bee, mitten; chair, seal; sun, tree; dog, feet). Circle each picture whose name has the /ē/ sound.
- **To the Parent:** Read the poem with your child. Ask your child to tell which pictures have the sound of *e* in *see*.

2 Using the page

R, T Sound/symbol correspondence: vowel /ē/ea, ee

Display *Big Book* page 70. Point to the poem and tell pupils that this poem is called "Maytime Magic." Ask them to listen to the poem to find out what magic happens. Run your hand under the lines as you read the poem aloud. Ask pupils to explain what is magic. (A seed turns into a flower.) Read the poem again and ask what a seed needs to grow. (earth, sun, showers or rain) Remind pupils that the word *seed* has the /ē/ sound.

Help pupils find page 70 in their books. Ask what is on the page beside the poem. (some flowers)

SAY **On each flower pot you see the letters *ee* or *ea* that stand for the /ē/ sound. There is a picture on each leaf of the flower. One of the pictures has the /ē/ sound in its name. Look at the first flower pot. Trace the letters *ee*. What are the pictures on each leaf of this flower?** (bee, mitten) **Which picture has the /ē/ sound in its name?** (bee) **Circle the picture of a bee to show that the /ē/ sound is heard in *bee*.**

Help pupils identify the pictures on the remaining leaves as chair, seal; sun, tree; dog, feet. Tell pupils to trace the letters on each flower pot and to circle each picture that has the /ē/ sound in its name.

3 Developing the Skills

M Writing: language–experience stories

Display chart paper and tell pupils that they can make up a story about planting a seed. Explain that you will write their story on the chart paper.

SAY **Let's pretend that the seed we plant turns out to be a magic seed. Should we plant a magic vegetable or a magic flower? Think about how it might grow and what might happen if it grew too big.**

Help pupils tell parts of the story by asking questions such as the following:

1. **Where would we plant the seed?**
2. **How would we take care of the seed?**
3. **How could we tell the seed was magic?**
4. **What would happen when the seed started to grow?**
5. **What would we do with our special plant?**

Print the story parts on the chart paper as pupils dictate them. Read aloud each sentence, running your hand under the words. Have pupils read each sentence after you. Read aloud the completed story. Place the chart paper where pupils can read the story on their own. Encourage pupils to draw pictures to display near the story.

✳ Practicing and Extending

The activities that follow provide practice and extension of skills developed in this lesson. Not every pupil needs to complete these activities. Choose only the activities that are needed to provide for the individual differences in your classroom.

Practicing Skills

R, T **Sound/symbol correspondence:** vowel /ē/*ea, ee*

PM 46 **ADDITIONAL PRACTICE** *Practice Masters* page 46 may be used as optional practice for associating the letters *ee* and *ea* with the /ē/ sound.

Extending Selection Concepts

> ### LITERATURE

LISTENING: FICTION Read aloud a version of the story "Jack and the Beanstalk." Ask pupils to compare the magic bean seeds to the magic seeds in the story they composed.

Cauley, Lorinda Bryan. *Jack and the Beanstalk.* Putnam, 1983. Jack's adventure is illustrated with beautiful oil paintings.

End-of-Book Review
pages 71–74 (T249–T253)

Note: Your own daily observations provide the best information about each pupil's understanding and mastery of skills. The program provides materials to assist in your ongoing evaluation. Pages 71–74 of *Sundrops* are designed to assess pupils' progress. You may tear out these pages after they are completed and send them home to inform parents of their child's progress.

Skill Strands

DECODING/VOCABULARY DEVELOPMENT

R, T **Sound/symbol correspondence:** consonants /d/*d*, /t/*t* (initial)

R, T **Sound/symbol correspondence:** consonants /d/*d*, /t/*t* (final)

R, T **Sound/symbol correspondence:** vowel /ē/*ee, ea*

R, T **Vocabulary:** word meaning

COMPREHENSION/THINKING

R, T **Inferential:** main idea

Materials

Sundrops, Level 1: pages 71–74
Reteach Masters, pages 5–8
Teacher's Idea Book

Special Populations

See *Teacher's Idea Book* for additional suggestions to help pupils with limited English proficiency.

Key to Symbols
I Introduced in this lesson
R Reinforced from an earlier lesson in this level
M Maintained from previous levels
T Tested in this level

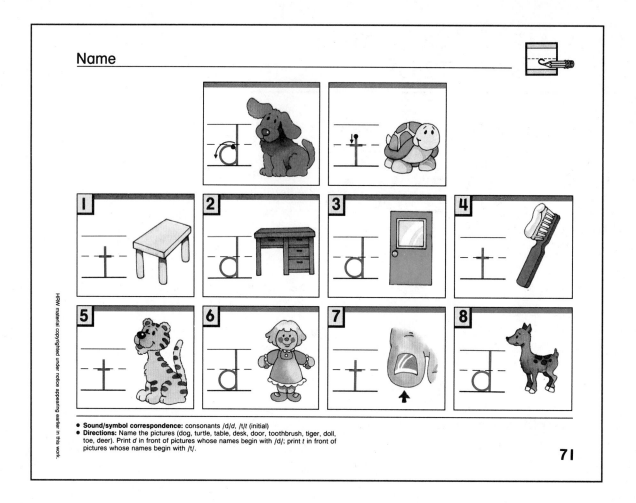

- **Sound/symbol correspondence:** consonants /d/d, /t/t (initial)
- **Directions:** Name the pictures (dog, turtle, table, desk, door, toothbrush, tiger, doll, toe, deer). Print *d* in front of pictures whose names begin with /d/; print *t* in front of pictures whose names begin with /t/.

71

Using Page 71

R, T Sound/symbol correspondence: consonants /d/d, /t/t (initial)

GUIDED PRACTICE Print letters *d* and *t* on the chalkboard. Point to each letter and have pupils say the sound the letter stands for. Then have pupils find page 71 in their books. Ask what letter stands for the beginning sound in *dog*. (*d*) Have pupils trace the *d* on the writing line. Ask what letter stands for the beginning sound in *turtle*. (*t*) Have pupils trace the *t* on the writing line. Explain that they are to print the letter that stands for the beginning sound of each picture name. Identify the pictures as table, desk, door, toothbrush, tiger, doll, toe, and deer.

 Distribute *Reteach Masters* page 5 for further practice of this skill.

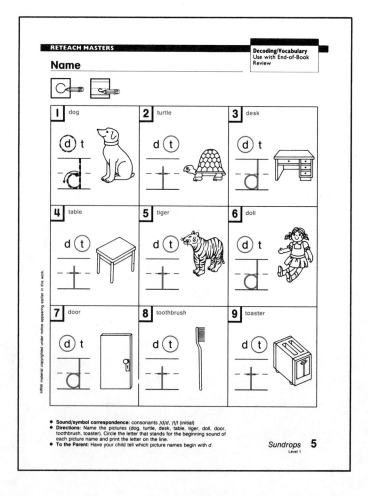

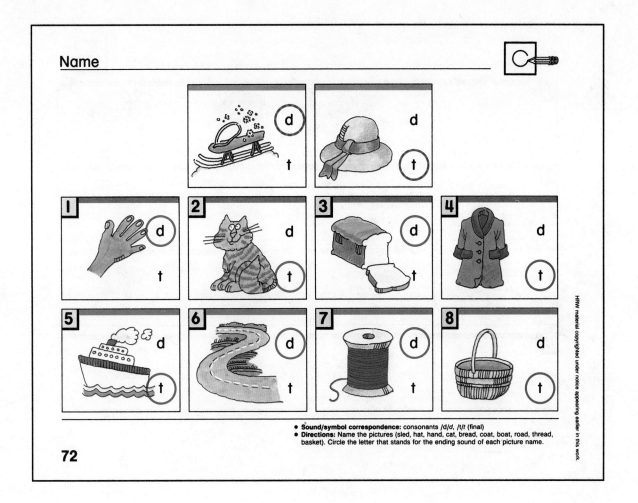

• **Sound/symbol correspondence:** consonants /d/d, /t/t (final)
• **Directions:** Name the pictures (sled, hat, hand, cat, bread, coat, boat, road, thread, basket). Circle the letter that stands for the ending sound of each picture name.

72

Using Page 72

R, T Sound/symbol correspondence: consonants /d/d, t/t (final)

GUIDED PRACTICE Say the word *read* and ask pupils to tell where they hear the /d/ sound. (at the end) Then say *sit* and ask where they hear the /t/ sound. (at the end) Have pupils find page 72 in their books and ask what letter stands for the sound at the end of *sled*. (d) Have pupils trace the circle around the letter *d*. Ask what letter stands for the sound at the end of *hat*. (t) Have pupils trace the circle around the letter *t*. Explain that they are to circle letter *d* or letter *t* in each box to show what sound they hear at the end of each picture name. Identify the pictures as hand, cat, bread, coat, boat, road, thread, and basket.

RM 6 Distribute *Reteach Masters* page 6 for further practice of this skill.

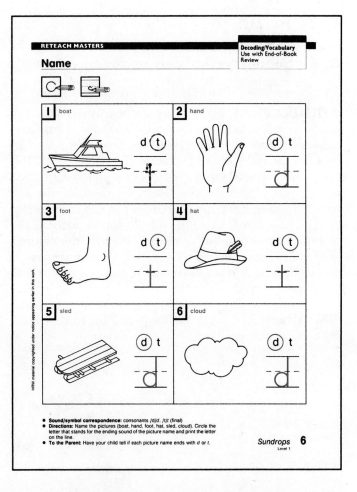

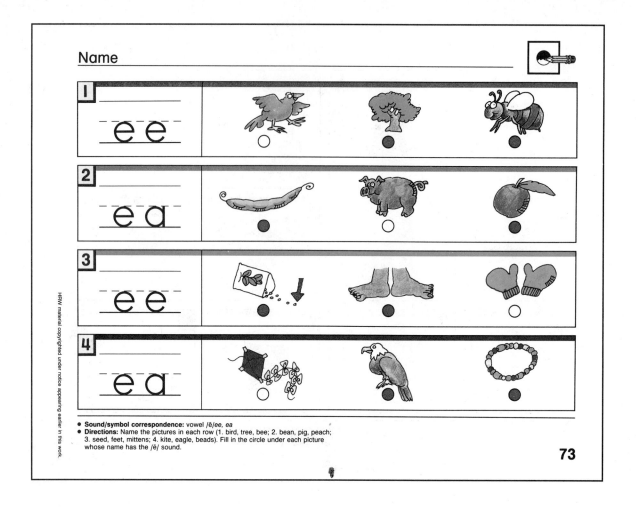

- **Sound/symbol correspondence:** vowel /ē/ee, ea
- **Directions:** Name the pictures in each row (1. bird, tree, bee; 2. bean, pig, peach; 3. seed, feet, mittens; 4. kite, eagle, beads). Fill in the circle under each picture whose name has the /ē/ sound.

73

Using page 73

R, T   Sound/symbol correspondence: vowel /ē/ea, ee

GUIDED PRACTICE   Say the words *bee, goat*. Ask pupils to tell which word has the /ē/ sound. (*bee*) Continue in the same manner with the word pairs *fly, tree; bean, orange*. Have pupils find page 73 in their books. Explain that sometimes the letters *ee* stand for the /ē/ sound, and sometimes the letters *ea* stand for the /ē/ sound. In each row, pupils are to fill in the circle under each picture whose name has the /ē/ sound. Identify the pictures in row 1 as bird, tree, bee. Identify the pictures in row 2 as bean, pig, peach. Identify the pictures in row 3 as seed, feet, mittens. Identify the pictures in row 4 as kite, eagle, beads.

RM 7   Distribute *Reteach Masters* page 7 for further practice of this skill.

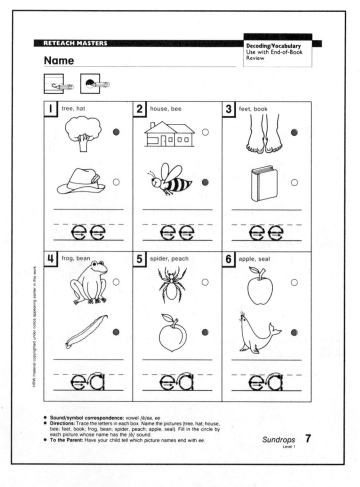

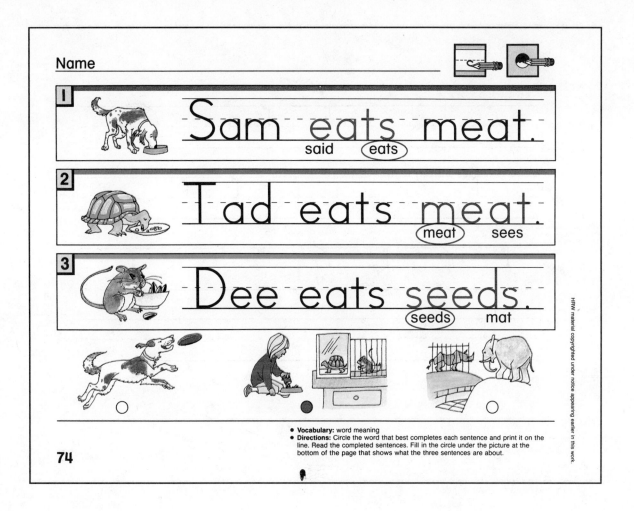

1 Sam eats meat.
said (eats)

2 Tad eats meat.
(meat) sees

3 Dee eats seeds.
(seeds) mat

• **Vocabulary:** word meaning
• **Directions:** Circle the word that best completes each sentence and print it on the line. Read the completed sentences. Fill in the circle under the picture at the bottom of the page that shows what the three sentences are about.

74

Using Page 74

R, T   Inferential: main idea
R, T   Vocabulary: word meaning

GUIDED PRACTICE   Have pupils turn to page 74 in their books and look at the picture in row 1. Then have them read the incomplete sentence that goes with the picture. Explain that one of the words under the sentence will complete the sentence. Tell pupils to circle the word that belongs in the sentence and to print the word on the writing line. Have pupils continue in the same manner with the remaining sentences.

Have pupils read the three completed sentences to themselves. Then ask them to look at the four pictures across the bottom of the page. Explain that one of the four pictures shows what the three sentences are about. Ask pupils to fill in the circle under the picture that best shows what the sentences are about.

RM 8   Distribute *Reteach Masters* page 8 for further practice of this skill.

RETEACH MASTERS

Comprehension/Thinking
Use with End-of-Book Review

Name

1 (mat) sad
Matt is on a mat.

2 seeds (sees)
Sam sees Matt.

3 (on) at
Sam is on Matt.

• **Inferential:** main idea
• **Directions:** TOP — Circle the word that completes each sentence and print the word on the line. BOTTOM — Fill in the circle under the picture that shows what the story of Matt and Sam is about.
• **To the Parent:** Have your child read the completed sentences to you.

Sundrops **8**
Level 1

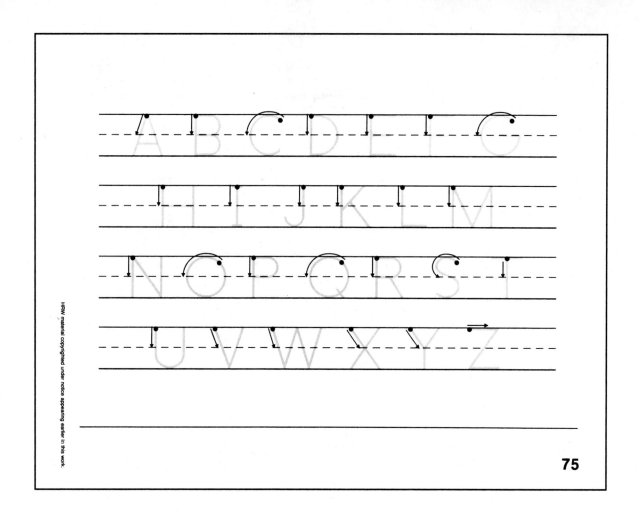

75

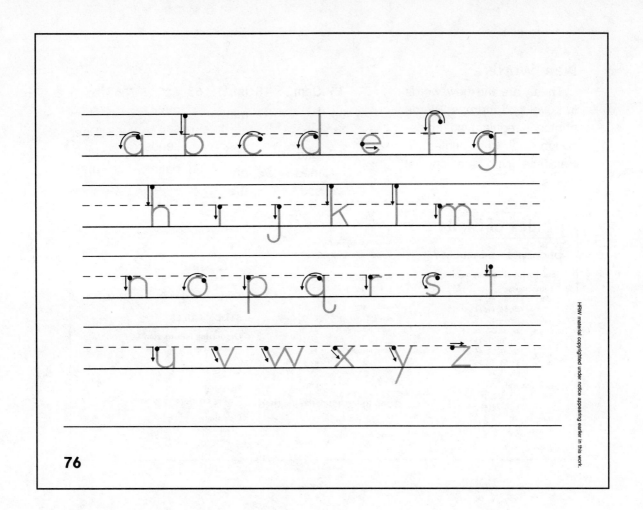

New Words

These are the new words in Level 1, *Sundrops.* Words printed in regular type are decodable. Words printed in **boldface** type are special words.

33 Sam	48 **is**	65 eat	67 **a**
34 **I**	57 mat	meat	seed
am	sat	see	68 Dee
47 Dad	Tad	seeds	Matt
mad	58 **on**	66 eats	meet
sad	**the**	**said**	69 sees
		Tam	

Index of Skills

DECODING/VOCABULARY

Sound/symbol correspondence

consonants

/d/d	43, 44, 45, 46
	50, 54, 71, 72
/m/m	13, 14, 15, 18
	22, 30, 37, 38, 54
/s/s	29, 30, 31, 32
	36, 37, 38, 44, 54
/t/t	53, 54, 55, 56
	60, 71, 72

short vowel

/a/a	21, 22, 23, 24, 26
	30, 37, 39, 44, 64

long vowel

/ē/ea,ee	63, 70, 73

vowel discrimination

/a/, /ē/   64

visual discrimination

3, 4, 5, 6, 7, 8, 10

Vocabulary

concept	2
word building	33, 47
	57, 65
word meaning	34, 48, 58
	66, 67, 74
words in context	38, 49, 59
	68, 69

COMPREHENSION/THINKING

Inferential

main idea   28, 52

Literal

cause and effect	20, 42
sequence	12, 40, 62

Story comprehension   11, 19, 41, 51, 61

STUDY SKILLS

Organizing information

classification   16

LANGUAGE

Speaking

telling a story from pictures   9

Listening

information	27, 51
poetry	1, 17, 25

Level 1 Word List

The list that follows includes the words that are introduced in Level 1, *Sundrops*. The number following each word indicates the page on which the word first appears in the pupil's edition.

a	67	on	58
am	34	sad	47
Dad	47	said	66
Dee	68	Sam	33
eat	65	sat	57
eats	66	see	65
I	34	seed	67
is	48	seeds	65
mad	47	sees	69
mat	57	Tad	57
Matt	68	Tam	66
meat	65	the	58
meet	68		

Index of Skills

Auditory discrimination, (beginning sounds)
/a/, /b/, /k/, T18, T19, T20
/d/, /e/, /f/, /g/, T21, T22, T23
/h/, /i/, /j/, T24, T25, T26
/l/, /m/, /n/, /o/, T27, T28, T29
/p/, /r/, /s/, /t/, T30, T31, T32
/u/, /v/, /w/, /y/, T33, T34, T35

Book features. See **Table of contents, Title page.**

Cause and effect, T78, T79, T80, T96, T148, T149, T150, T231

Classification, T63, T64, T65, T176

Comprehension/Thinking. See **Cause and effect, Main idea, Sequence, Using prior knowledge.**

Concept vocabulary
direction words, T14
left-to-right progression, T16
position words, T15, T16, T17, T77
sentences, T38

Consonants
/d/*d* (initial, final), T151–152, T153, T154, T155, T156, T157, T158, T159, T160, T161, T162, T174, T175, T177, T191, T192, T193, T250–251
/m/*m* (initial, final), T53–54, T54–55, T55–56, T57, T58, T60, T61, T62, T69, T70, T71, T84, T85, T87, T97, T138, T139, T191, T192, T193
/s/*s* (initial, final), T111, T112, T113, T114, T115, T116, T117, T118, T119, T120, T121, T122, T134, T135, T136, T138, T139, T154, T155, T156, T191, T192, T193
/t/*t* (initial, final), T188, T189–190, T191, T192, T193, T194, T195, T196, T197, T198, T199, T210, T211, T213, T250, T251
/z/*s* (final), T229

Conventions of language. See **End punctuation, Quotation marks.**

Decoding/Vocabulary. See **Consonants, Inflectional ending, Long vowel, Short vowel, Word building, Word meaning, Words in context.**

End punctuation
period, T133, T242, T244, T245
question mark, T170, T242, T244, T245

Extending selection concepts
art, T159
language, T87, T126, T187, T219, T238, T241, T245
literature, T14, T17, T20, T23, T26, T29, T32, T35, T41, T48, T52, T56, T59, T62, T68, T77, T80, T83, T93, T97, T101, T107, T110, T116, T122, T126, T133, T147, T150, T156, T162,

T173, T177, T187, T190, T193, T196, T202, T206, T213, T222, T225, T228, T241, T248
music, T119
science, T71, T101, T107, T136, T169, T199, T219, T232
See also **Listening, Singing, Speaking, Writing.**

Graphic aids. See **Illustrations.**

Illustrations, T107, T184

Inflectional ending
-*s* (plural, verb), T229–230, T239

Language. See **End punctuation, Language-experience stories, Poetry, Quotation marks, Retelling stories, Rhyming words, Specific information, Story comprehension, Telling stories from pictures.**

Language-experience stories, T68, T135, T248

Listening
fiction, T17, T20, T23, T26, T29, T32, T35, T41, T52, T56, T62, T68, T77, T80, T83, T87, T101, T110, T122, T126, T133, T147, T162, T173, T190, T206, T213, T222, T225, T241, T248
information, T71, T101, T136, T169, T199, T232
poetry, T12, T13, T14, T48, T66, T67, T86, T87, T93, T94, T95, T97, T107, T129, T150, T156, T177, T196, T202, T228
rhymes, T59
rhyming words, T58–59, T70
specific information, T105–106, T181–183
story comprehension, T45–47, T75–76, T145–146, T217, T218

Long vowel
/ē/*ea, ee*, T223, T224, T225, T226, T227, T228, T246, T247, T248, T252

Main idea, T108, T109, T110, T185, T186, T187, T253

Organizing information. See **Classification.**

Phonics
auditory discrimination (beginning sounds)
/a/, /b/, /k/, T18, T19, T20
/d/, /e/, /f/, /g/, T21, T22, T23
/h/, /i/, /j/, T24, T25, T26
/l/, /m/, /n/, /o/, T27, T28, T29
/p/, /r/, /s/, /t/, T30, T31, T32
/u/, /v/, /w/, /y/, T33, T34, T35
consonants
/d/*d* (initial, final), T151–152, T153, T154, T155, T156, T157, T158, T159, T160, T161, T162, T174, T175, T177, T191, T192, T193, T250–251
/m/*m* (initial, final), T53–54, T54–55, T55–56,

Teacher's Notes

Teacher's Notes

Teacher's Notes

Teacher's Notes

Teacher's Notes

Teacher's Notes

Teacher's Notes

Teacher's Notes

Teacher's Notes

Teacher's Notes

Teacher's Notes

Teacher's Notes

Acknowledgments

For permission to reprint copyrighted material, grateful acknowledgment is made to the following sources:

Laura Arlon: "Slow Pokes" by Laura Arlon.

Atheneum Publishers, Inc.: "Hey, Bug!" from *I feel the Same Way* by Lilian Moore. Copyright (c) 1967 by Lilian Moore.

Marchette Chute: "My Dog" from *Around and About* by Marchette Chute. Copyright (c) 1957 by E. P. Dutton; renewed 1985.

Doubleday & Company, Inc.: Text from *Angus and the Ducks* by Marjorie Flack. Copyright (c) 1930 by Doubleday & Company, Inc.

Doubleday & Company, Inc. and The Society of Authors as literary representative of the Estate of Rose Fyleman: "Mice" from *Fifty-One Nursery Rhymes* by Rose Fyleman. Copyright (c) 1931, 1932 by Doubleday & Company, Inc.

E. P. Dutton, a division of New American Library: Text from *Henry's Awful Mistake* by Robert Quackenbush. Copyright (c) 1980 by Robert Quackenbush.

Greenwillow Books, a division of William Morrow & Company, Inc.: "Play" and accompanying illustration from *Country Pie* by Frank Asch. Copyright (c) 1979 by Frank Asch.

Grosset & Dunlap, Publishers: "The Pancake" by Christina Rossetti.

Harcourt Brace Jovanovich, Inc.: Adaptation of *Sun Up, Sun Down* by Gail Gibbons. Copyright (c) 1983 by Gail Gibbons.

Harper & Row, Publishers, Inc.: "Tommy" from *Bronzeville Boys and Girls* by Gwendolyn Brooks. Copyright (c) 1956 by Gwendolyn Brooks Blakely. "I do not understand" from *ANY ME I WANT TO BE* by Karla Kuskin. Copyright (c) 1972 by Karla Kuskin.

Lothrop Lee Shepard Books: "The People on the Bus" from *Singing Bee* by Jane Hart. Copyright (c) 1982 by Jane Hart.

Houghton Mifflin Company: "The Sun" from *All About Me* by John Drinkwater.

Macmillan Publishing Company: Untitled poem (Titled: "Ant") from *Inside Turtle's Shell and Other Poems of the Field* by Joanne Ryder. Text copyright (c) 1985 by Joanne Ryder. "The Little Turtle" from *Collected Poems* by Vachel Lindsay. Copyright (c) 1920 by Macmillan Publishing Company; renewed 1948 by Elizabeth C. Lindsay.

Random House, Inc.: Text from *Moon Mouse* by Adelaide Holl; illustrated by Cyndy Szekeres Prozzo. Copyright (c) 1969 by Adelaide Holl; illustration copyright (c) 1969 by Cyndy Szekeres Prozzo.

Charles Scribner's Sons: Adapted from *Turtle Pond* by Berniece Freschet. Copyright (c) 1971 by Berniece Freschet; illustrations copyright (c) 1971 by Donald Carrick.

Mabel Watts: "Maytime Magic" by Mabel Watts from *Humpty Dumpty Magazine;* 1954.